D1707044

The Politics of Neurodiversity

Disability in Society

Ronald J. Berger, series editor

The Politics of
Neurodiversity

Why Public Policy Matters

Dana Lee Baker

LYNNE
RIENNER
PUBLISHERS

BOULDER
LONDON

Published in the United States of America in 2011 by
Lynne Rienner Publishers, Inc.
1800 30th Street, Boulder, Colorado 80301
www.rienner.com

and in the United Kingdom by
Lynne Rienner Publishers, Inc.
3 Henrietta Street, Covent Garden, London WC2E 8LU

Library of Congress Cataloging-in-Publication Data
Baker, Dana Lee, 1973–
 The politics of neurodiversity : why public policy matters / Dana Lee Baker.
    p. cm.
 Includes bibliographical references and index.
 ISBN 978-1-58826-754-2 (hc : alk. paper)
 1. People with mental disabilities—Government policy—United States.
2. People with mental disabilities—Civil rights—United States.
3. Discrimination against people with disabilities—United States.
4. Discrimination against the mentally ill—United States. I. Title.
 HV3006.A4B253 2011
 323.3—dc22
                                                    2010027704

British Cataloguing in Publication Data
A Cataloguing in Publication record for this book
is available from the British Library.

Printed and bound in the United States of America

 The paper used in this publication meets the requirements
of the American National Standard for Permanence of
Paper for Printed Library Materials Z39.48-1992.

 5 4 3 2 1

For Alan, Kal, and Maggie,
much adored and admired representatives
of the shining future of neurological difference

Contents

Preface

The Politics of Neurodiversity presents a taxonomy of agendas shaping modern disability policy: cause, care, cure, and celebration. These distinct agendas create tensions that both help and hinder the development of effective disability policy in modern democracies. By taking the reader through the implications of each of these tensions, the book conveys a comprehensive framework from which to study the politics and policy of neurodiversity and neurological differences.

Neurodiversity is an emerging area of disability studies. More important, however, awareness of neurodiversity and neurological differences is an increasingly prevalent characteristic of modern societies. The concept emerged in autism-related activism during the 1990s and has been a developing topic of academic scholarship since 2003. Although some still reserve the term "neurodiversity" exclusively for autism and related differences, in recent years its use has expanded to include the full spectrum of neurological differences. I employ this inclusive approach to the concept and draw from several projects focused on questions surrounding social and political implications that I conducted in recent years.

Writing from the perspective of political and policy analysis, I employ theories of issue definition and agenda setting to explore how the efforts of policy entrepreneurs dedicated to these agenda types interact with one another. I also seek to lay the groundwork for improved relations between stakeholders representing different agenda types. Ideally, such consideration results in increased potential for collaboration and improved understanding of the necessity of variation in political philosophy and policy goals within modern disability policy subsystems.

The Politics of Neurodiversity begins with two introductory chapters detailing the politics of neurodiversity and neurological differences. The first chapter focuses on the concept of neurodiversity using the foundation of a constructivist understanding of disability. The chapter also discusses the distinctions between difference, impairment, disability, and handicap employed in the development of modern public policy. The second chapter describes the four primary goals of political activists and policy entrepreneurs working in the disability policy arena (cause, care, cure, and celebration). The next six chapters of the book examine the nature and implications in all possible pairings of agenda types. The concluding chapter revisits the concept of neurodiversity and its implications for disability scholarship and society.

Acknowledgments

First and foremost I thank my family, spread vibrantly across Canada and the United States. I feel privileged to be part of it. My grandparents, aunts, uncles, and cousins have each helped in their own way to make this book a reality. In my immediate family, I thank my son, Kal, not only for being the bravest person I know, but also for teaching me a great deal about recognizing the possibilities and limitations of social constructions. He has also patiently served as private barista, making me countless, nearly flawless mochas. Kal's sister, Dawn, was the baby in my baby vs. book race, thereby providing necessary constraint on the time it could take her mother to complete this book. Her lovely spirit motivated me from before her birth and has continued to help keep things on track as she and this book now toddle off into the world. My mother, Mary Ellen Baker, gave daily support and encouragement, as well as great insight into living neurodiversity. My father, Don Baker, not only inspired my interest in health care policy but is the best source I have found for insight into interpreting organizational and political realities. As a physician, my sister, Catherine Baker, has often served as a reasoned sounding board for assertions about the roles of health care providers in the politics of neurodiversity. As a best friend, she has provided more support, encouragement, and laughter than one person can possibly deserve. Her husband, Jim Howard, has also given me helpful insight into the world of medicine, as well as ongoing good humor. Caring for my niece, Madeline Howard, provided balance in the earliest days of writing this book, and her evolving personality has given me great joy throughout the writing process. My brother Alan Baker served as my introduction to neurological difference. The effects of his companionship and reflections are deeply woven into this text. Last, but never least, I thank my brother Brian Baker, whose desire to work for justice always inspires my own.

My enthusiastic thanks go out to professional contacts and colleagues who have generously supported me in the creation of this book. Andrew Berzanskis's assistance as editor has been consistent, reassuring, and often inspiring—really all that anyone could ever wish for in an editor of one's first book. Ronald Berger, as editor of the Disability in Society series, provided encouragement and valuable suggestions from proposal right through to final draft, for which I am eternally grateful. Allison Smith, who is also the best of friends, gave generously of her time by reading and providing terrific feedback on an early draft of the book. I owe a great debt of gratitude to the anonymous reviewers whose comments enriched both the experience of writing and the book itself. My much missed friend and sometimes coauthor Trudy Steuernagel and her son Sky deserve my ongoing gratitude for early encouragement of my academic interest in autism policy, which will be ever manifest in remembering that their story of neurodiversity amounts to much, much more than how it ended. My friend and fellow academic Sara Maurer blessed me with unfailing moral support. Finally, I thank Guy Adams at the University of Missouri–Columbia for taking the time to mentor me in the research process as a young academic.

Working for the Department of Political Science and Criminal Justice at Washington State University (WSU) is an honor and a privilege, particularly because of the people with whom I have the pleasure of working. In particular I recognize the "hard core" faculty in the Program of Public Affairs, who are all both dear friends and wonderful colleagues—Laurie Drapela, Carolyn Long, Adam Luedtke, Mark Stephan, Paul Thiers, and Darryl Wood. I also thank Clay Mosher of WSU's Sociology Department for bringing the series to my attention and for his advice about authoring books. Amy Wharton has served as a fabulous mentor and professional exemplar. Furthermore, the program simply would not function without the dedicated assistance of our professional staff, which at the time of this writing included Marie Loudermilk, Ginny Taylor, Linda Campbell, Annette Bradstreet, and Shari Clevenger.

I have had the great fortune to come to know practitioners whose sincerity and hard work have allowed me to glimpse just how beneficial wellconceived and expertly implemented policies surrounding neurological difference and neurodiversity can be. Diane Wiscarson brilliantly negotiates the fine line between representation and alienation, thereby making manifest conditions in which students who might otherwise be cast out can learn and thrive. Susan Cone, one of the best educational administrators in the business, creates an environment of open communication and committed inclusion in one of the toughest of locations (a public junior high school). Kathryn Murdock daily achieves what conventional wisdom often discerns impossible, by providing superb legal representation to a public school district while never losing sight of the individual rights and needs of children who are different. Tom Adams, as vice principal of Columbia River High School, exhibits the patience of a saint and a commitment to creative solutions, which I enthusiastically admire and have sought to reflect. Dan Delepine's talent for working with neurodiversity in teenagers provides a stunning example for anyone lucky enough to come into contact with him. Finally, the Connections Team in the Clark County Juvenile Justice system—especially Terri Chapman, Michelle Karnath, Rick Mason, and Dawn Young—continually demonstrate that unfailing belief in even the most momentarily challenging of youth creates both a world of difference and, ultimately, a different world.

1

Why Public Policy Matters for Neurodiversity (and Vice Versa)

In early 2010, President Barack Obama nominated Ari Ne'eman to the National Council on Disability (NCD), along with seven other people. Unlike the other nominees (and all others who have served on the NCD since its inception), Ari Ne'eman has autism. The seven other nominees were relatively quickly confirmed. Ari Ne'eman was not. In the US Senate, an anonymous hold was put on the motion to allow the vote on his confirmation.

The National Council on Disability was created as part of Title IV of the Rehabilitation Act of 1973. According to the agency's website:

> NCD is an independent federal agency and is composed of 15 members appointed by the President, by and with the advice and consent of the Senate. It provides advice to the President, Congress, and executive branch agencies to promote policies, programs, practices, and procedures that guarantee equal opportunity for all individuals with disabilities, regardless of the nature or severity of the disability and to empower individuals with disabilities to achieve economic self-sufficiency, independent living, and inclusion and integration into all aspects of society. (National Council on Disability 2010)

Given this mission and Ne'eman's status as the founder of the nationally recognized Autistic Self-Advocacy Network (ASAN), this hold appears surprising at first glance. After all, one of the key reasons for ASAN's existence is to promote independence among a rapidly growing group of people recognized as having a disability.

However, as described by Amy Harmon in the *New York Times* in March 2010: "Mr. Ne'eman is at the forefront of a growing movement that

1

describes autism as a form of 'neurodiversity' that should be embraced and accommodated, just as physical disabilities have led to the construction of ramps and stalls in public restrooms for people with disability. Autism, he and others say, is part of their identity" (Harmon 2010). Ne'eman, like many modern disability activists, sees challenges relating to disability as resulting primarily from discrimination and from a failure to effectively support celebration of different ways of being human.

As much as issue stakeholders who are focused on the interests and experiences of individuals with autism might otherwise be thrilled at the prospect of having the voice of an individual with autism serve in such a high-profile, national-level capacity, when it came to the question of Ne'eman's service, many hesitated or even publicly balked at the proposition. In an online newspaper titled *The Age of Autism,* Kim Stagliano (2010) wrote:

> I know of no one opposed to self-advocacy for those who are able, despite the cries within the Neurodiversity community that we in the treatment community are "anti-autism." The reality is that many of our loved ones cannot self-advocate due to the severity of their autism. We use treatments in order to elevate our children's functioning to a place where they too can self-advocate. We bristle when we're told that our children do not deserve treatments and research that could move them "up" the spectrum.

Stagliano went on to argue that when it comes to disability policy, limited resources should be focused on those whose disabilities appear to be most severe from the perspective of the general population. According to Stagliano, the most important challenges relating to disability are tied to an absence of a cure for distressing conditions.

Others, such as the director of Autism Society of America, Lee Grossman, described those who are working to create better policies and programs for autism as "battle-hardened" (Harmon 2010) and sometimes turning on one another rather than working together in their pursuit of different agenda types. Grossman believes that this hardening has come about because "we have this community out there frustrated and bewildered and reaching out for any assistance" (Harmon 2010). The struggle between the various agendas gets in the way of otherwise positive efforts to reframe conversations about disability, such as Ne'eman's nomination.

The Senate ultimately and unanimously approved Ne'eman's nomination in late June 2010. At the time of this writing, though, the identity of the responsible senator or senators, the exact reason for the hold on Ne'eman's nomination, and the reason the hold was ultimately removed remain unknown. What is clear from this event is that the politics surrounding neurological difference are far from simple.

Connecting Policy and Neurodiversity

Diversity means strength. From our basic biology to international relations, a narrow attraction to sameness weakens the human experience. Nevertheless, even our thinking about diversity tends toward homogeny (Gregory 2006; Spinner-Halev, Bowman, and Sanders 2005). At the beginning of the twenty-first century, consideration of diversity in industrialized nations habitually involves organized celebration of the coexistence of individuals with differences conceived in terms of relatively observable characteristics such as race, ethnicity, gender, or sexual orientation. Often, consideration of diversity is limited to racial or ethnic differences.

Diversity is more than skin deep, however. In recent years, human understanding of neurology has progressed beyond its infancy. Part of this expansion in basic knowledge has involved development of increasingly sophisticated taxonomies of neurological differences. Our evolving understanding of the human brain, combined with the engagement of a greater proportion of the population of industrialized nations in knowledge- or service-based work, has stimulated increasing public notice of neurological differences.

Effects of this new awareness extend to both systemic and formal government agendas, making an understanding of the politics of neurological difference important for anyone interested in policy, politics, and public administration, as well as for those interested in neuroscience and neurology. One aspect of this political conversation is the consideration of differences in brains as an element of diversity within societies—this is the realm of neurodiversity. Furthermore, studying the politics of neurological difference, including neurodiversity, can create "renewed interest in the question of how to promote diversity in all its manifestations and to further a more inclusive society" (Bumiller 2008, 967) for those interested in sociology and other social sciences. Furthermore, since conscious engagement in diversity is a cornerstone of the twenty-first-century experience, the politics of neurological difference and neurodiversity should be intriguing to those interested in social justice in general. Finally, as with much that will be explored in this book, these principles, while being exceptionally well-illustrated in the politics surrounding neurological difference and neurodiversity, hold for all disabilities. As Marta Russell put it in *Beyond Ramps: Disabil-*

ity at the End of the Social Contract over a decade ago, "disability and disability policy—past, present and future—is a tool for all to rate our present socio/economic order" (1998, 9).

Defining Politics:
Political Discourse and Public Discourse

For many people, polite conversation excludes politics. Also, declaring one's hatred of or distaste for politics is often considered a reasonable position for a person to take, even in a democratic setting supposedly dependent on the political participation of (at least) citizens. Despite this, all human beings engage in political behavior to some degree or another. The political behavior most people engage in may be on a smaller scale than the governance of even the tiniest of formal political entities. However, from the time a child begins to formulate strategies other than utter loss of self-control to achieve his or her interests, political behavior becomes a part of the day-to-day human experience. Because the experience of human neurological differences involves many unknowns and unsettled questions, and thus creates potential for differing interpretations of norms and situations, this experience necessarily becomes politicized in modern societies.

In essence, politics is conflict management, which ideally turns into collaboration and cooperation. As Oliver Woshinsky describes, "while we may detest politics, the alternative can be worse . . . If conflict cannot be resolved politically, it often denigrates into violence . . . In the ordinary, workaday mode, *'politics is damage control,'* says Peter Berkowitz in one of the best aphorisms I know on the subject . . . Politics provides an arena where people can vent their hostilities without actually killing each other" (2008, 22; emphasis in original). Within the politics of neurodiversity and neurological difference, it may at first glance be difficult to conceive of a potential for outright violence surrounding political debates on the subject of human difference. After all, no known society has ever reached the point of violent revolution over management of functional differences in human beings per se. Nevertheless, an extensive history of depriving individuals of both liberty and life as a response to observed differences in their minds, bodies, or spirits exists (Shapiro 1994). There have also been countless acts of interpersonal violence resulting from the clash between the infrastructures of society and society itself, perpetrated by both those considered normal and those considered atypical. Finally, there exist long traditions of objectification of individuals on the basis of functionality.[1] Such objectification itself constitutes a form of violent oppression.

Politics involves substantial self-expression in a variety of forms by a plethora of stakeholders. Arguments in this book make a distinction between political and public discourse. As used here, the term "political discourse" refers to any statements and expressions made with formal political intent—in other words, statements made by those who deliberately engage the disability policy subsystem with the intent of promoting and supporting specific public policy and programs. Most often, political discourse comes from politicians, government officials, bureaucrats, policy entrepreneurs, and activists. In fact, some scholars of democracy have argued that policy entrepreneurs (or other policy experts) exclusively define policy options for the general public in most cases. As Roger Pielke explained about the writings of E. E. Schattschneider in the late 1970s: "democracy is a competitive system in which the public is allowed to participate by voicing its views on alternatives presented to it in the political process . . . such alternatives do not come up from the grassroots any more than you or me telling an auto mechanic what the options are for fixing a broken car . . . policy alternatives come from experts" (2007, 12). Although such thinking naturally raises questions about what constitutes expertise (including grassroots expertise), it resonates in practice in that, for the most part, innovative issue framing and policy proposals come from political actors directly engaging the policy subsystem, usually through formal roles. Though such arguments limit interpretation of the practice of democracy, they do emphasize the need to distinguish between political and public discourse.

The term "public discourse," on the other hand, comprises a more general category including statements and expressions made by individuals or groups who are contributing to the politicized discussion surrounding neurological difference and neurodiversity, but not necessarily consciously seeking a specific change in policy. Public discourse can come from anyone in a given society, so long as the statement is intentionally made in public (rather than in private conversation or in contemplation).

Why Are Neurological Differences Public Issues?

Taxonomies of neurological difference remain somewhat theoretical because they commonly rely on behavior-based diagnoses. In other words, most definitions of neurological differences are circular—a person becomes described as having a neurological difference as a result of engaging in a set of behaviors observed as characteristics of having a neurological difference that is in turn defined by those behaviors.

While substantial progress has been made in identification of morphological or mechanical factors underlying neurological differences, for the most part unambiguous and fully reliable explanations of relationships between actual differences in brains and assignment of particular diagnoses remain tenuous if not absent. Furthermore, it is important to understand how our limited understanding of brain function invokes the question of voluntariness into the public and political discourse surrounding neurological differences. For example, as David Smukler points out, "although individuals are identified as autistic on the basis of their behavior, it has long been assumed that autistic behavior has its origin in mental function . . . people do not simply 'act autistic' . . . they '*are* autistic'" (2005, 13). This assumption, combined with the remaining ambiguity surrounding neurological explanations, creates tension between different disability policy stakeholders as well as among the rest of the general public. Even so, progress continues in locating pharmaceutical and therapeutic interventions that alleviate the unwanted atypicalities attributed to neurological differences. As a result of perceived and realized potential of this progress, demand for public policy focused on neurological differences has risen dramatically across industrialized nations over the past several decades.

Another factor better understood over time is that neurological differences are not categorically the same as disease. This tends to complicate the development of policy addressing neurological differences, even to the point of opening up basic questions about the necessity of such policy. Furthermore, this realization comes as part of a larger shift in prevalence of the disability paradigms that introduced the concept of cultural relativity into disability. In recent years, conceptions of disability have come to be understood as highly variable across cultures and time (Longmore 2003). Conditions treated as completely disabling in some cultural settings go unnoticed or even create advantages in others (Grinker 2007). Understanding disability as influenced by sociocultural context clarifies the role that development of politics within the disability policy subsystem[2] plays in public efforts to support and encourage social justice. This means that disability becomes an unavoidably public issue, arguably especially in the case of the so-called invisible disabilities, such as many of those believed to be associated with neurological differences.

A Continuum of Understandings of Disability

Conception of disability is socially relative and, therefore, at least somewhat unique to time and place. However, understandings of disability can be classified for the purposes of empirical analysis or more global discussion of politics found in disability policy subsystems. For the purposes of this book, understandings of disability are described as existing along a continuum from purely essentialist to purely constructivist. In going forward with such a discussion, it is of course vital to understand that these two defining conceptions of disability frame a wide variety of possible understandings of disability rather than creating a simplistic binary of two opposing philosophical camps.

A continuum is by definition a spectrum where little—if anything—in the real world is purely black or white. One should hardly expect that most people involved in the political and public discourse surrounding neurological difference and neurodiversity would consciously or explicitly self-identify as either purely constructivist or purely essentialist. This classification scheme is employed not only because it can most fully describe recent innovations in understandings of disability as compared to more traditional interpretations, but also because of the emphasis placed on the social and political aspects of constructions of understandings of disability. Employing this continuum makes the most sense for a sustained examination of the politics of neurodiversity and neurological difference, but not, for the most part, for the classification of individuals involved in the discourse.

Essentialist Understandings of Disability

Essentialist understandings consider disability to be entirely located within an individual who has a culturally relevant functional difference.[3] In such mind-sets, making up for disadvantages resulting from a human functionality considered atypical becomes the responsibility of the individual or his or her family. Assignment of responsibility takes place in this way because the person's mind, body, or spirit is understood to be the cause of the difficulties.[4] Whether articulated as a curse, punishment of ancestors, irresponsibility, stupidity, immorality, or laziness, explanation for the presence of disability more often than not becomes attributed to actions of the individual with the functional difference or to those of his or her family. In addition, as frequently noted in disability studies literature, essentialist understandings of disability usually blame the so-called victim of disability for associated social, economic, political, occupational, or legal disadvantages.

Under a purely essentialist understanding of disability, society incurs no fundamental moral responsibility to mediate effects of disability. Compassionate societies might intervene on behalf of families including individuals with disabilities using charitable or medical strategies. However, such measures represent normative choices about social preferences as opposed to the fundamentals of justice expected of healthy governance, particularly in a democracy. One commonly referenced piece of evidence of historical dominance of essentialist understandings of disability is the rumored etiology of the word "handicapped," which supposedly describes a person with a functional difference holding their cap in their hand and begging more upstanding citizens for money. Another is the extent to which US president Franklin Delano Roosevelt and those surrounding him worked to hide his use of a wheelchair (Fleischer and Fleischer 2000).

Essentialist understandings of disability sometimes are described as "medical" models of disability. This description does not originate with and is rarely used by health care professionals. Instead, this nomenclature is predominantly employed by disability studies scholars, progressive program managers, and disability rights activists. The nomenclature invokes medical practices involving systematic removal of individuals with specified differences from interaction with the rest of the general population to institutional facilities. It also raises the specter of adverse medical procedures such as forced sterilizations performed in the name of eugenics throughout much of the Western world well into the twentieth century.[5] Institutional facilities and adverse medical practices developed prolifically during the late nineteenth and early twentieth centuries, with the supposed purposes of protecting public health and providing prolonged medical care to a historically neglected population. Though at least initially well intentioned, in practice institutional conditions were all too often conducive to abuse. The medical model terminology also highlights a pronounced expectation of professionals engaged in medical treatment to assume full control over their patients, whether strictly medically necessary or not.

Constructivist Understandings of Disability

At the other end of the continuum lie constructivist understandings of disability. Most scholarship considers such conceptions of disability to be the result of recent historical innovation of progressive democracies as tied to a larger history of expansion of human and civil rights (Gross and Hahn 2004; Ishay 2008). A purely constructivist understanding of disability locates the source of disability entirely in the social and political infrastructures surrounding the individual who has the functional difference. Constructivist understandings of disability begin with the axiom that all human beings have differences in functionalities affecting their ability to interact absolutely successfully with any society's infrastructures. Generally speaking, infrastructures include enough flexibility to allow individuals to participate in society without extraordinary or individualized assistance.

In disabling circumstances, however, a public infrastructure becomes too rigid to include all people living in the society. As a result of this created rigidity, individuals with levels of functionality outside the limits of the established norm become disabled (or even handicapped). Constructivist understandings of disability are sometimes referred to as "social" models of disability, particularly when referenced in opposition to understandings described as the medical model or when referring to disability policy in industrialized nations other than the United States.[6] In such discussions, social models describe inclusion whereas medical models connote exclusion. As Gillian MacIntyre explained, "broadly speaking, in many spheres there is a growing rhetoric of commitment to the social model of disability and this is echoed in policies of inclusion for people with disabilities" (2008, 13).

A key observation of constructivist understandings of disability recognizes society's infrastructures as including more than physical infrastructures. This distinction's importance to the politics of neurodiversity and neurological difference arises because disability is stereotypically perceived as physical disability in the industrialized world. After all, an image of an individual in a wheelchair commonly symbolizes all disability in these societies. As a result, social and political infrastructures can become reflexively and exclusively understood as physical infrastructures such as buildings and roads. However, constructivist disability theory highlights historical patterns of disabling limitations incorporated into a variety of basic elements of a society, such as legal, political, ethical, attitudinal, fiscal, health, occupational, and educational infrastructures.

In the extreme, constructivist understandings of disability envision society as uniquely responsible for the creation of disability. Disability results from "what people decide matters" (Smukler 2005, 12). If a society deliberately includes and carefully plans supports for all individual differences, then no one, so the reasoning goes, would become disabled, re-

gardless of how much they might differ from the human norm in any functionality. These theoretical premises support the conclusion that public
policies addressing challenges relating to human functional differences
should seek to change infrastructures and not directly target individuals
perceived as having a disability. As a result, constructivist understandings
of disability can lead to (over)simplification of disability policy subsystems. As Tom Shakespeare (2006) explained, social models of disability
provide a unified goal for disability policy activism in the form of barrier
removal. This simplification helped tremendously during earlier days of
the self-conscious disability rights movement because it established a joint
call to action for an otherwise diffuse and frequently disempowered group.
However, as the policy subsystem matured, this simplification became
more limiting, particularly with regard to issues related to neurological
differences.

The Continuum of Understandings
of Disability in the Real World

Continuums tend to be bounded by archetypes that are approached but never
actually manifest, in even the most extreme of cultural or political circumstances. The continuum of disability paradigms involves no exception to
this general rule. The existence of charitable interventions as well as studies demonstrating traditional societies that are more inclusive of individuals with disabilities suggest at least tacit acceptance of disability predating
the innovation of constructivist understandings. In fact, research conducted
over the past several decades has demonstrated improved outcomes for individuals who have some functional differences in traditional environments.
For example:

> World Health Organization (WHO) studies on schizophrenia conducted
> in the 1970s . . . showed that even though schizophrenia occurred with
> similar frequency all over the world, people with schizophrenia in devel-
> oping countries did better over time than those in the industrialized coun-
> tries . . . they needed less care and fewer medicines, and they have fewer
> traumatic, psychotic episodes. (Grinker 2007, 10–11)

Furthermore, as Tom Shakespeare (2006) pointed out, proponents of medical models of disability are virtually impossible to locate and certainly not
consciously active as such in mainstream policy debates of most nations.
While understandings of disability, perhaps particularly in some of the more
traditional health care settings, may at times approach the essentialist end of

the continuum, prevailing public and political discourses lack real world examples of pure essentialism.

Similarly, most disability theorists, activists, and progressive program managers include some essentialism in their thinking about disability. First, even constructivist understandings of disability recognize agency on the part of individuals with functional differences in their choice to identify as an individual with a disability. In *Make Them Go Away: Clint Eastwood, Christopher Reeve, and the Case Against Disability Rights,* Mary Johnson (2003) describes reasoning drawn from David Pfeiffer to explain this choice as follows:

> To name a person as "disabled" is to give them an inferior position. In our society people identified as disabled are second-class, third-class, or even worse-class citizens . . . We live in a constant state of discrimination . . . Identifying oneself or another person as a "person with a disability" is an ideological act . . . There is no other way to describe it . . . Which is why not everyone with a functional difference will identify as disabled. (198)

Of course, the degree to which this choice exists depends on the specific functional difference and on how this affects the individual's interaction with the surrounding society. Under most modern circumstances, it would be more difficult for a person with Down syndrome than for a person with attention-deficit disorder not to identify as having a disability, due to the general belief that disability is visually obvious. Nevertheless, in the end, such deliberative decisionmaking can only take place at the essential core of the individual, rather than happening entirely in surrounding social contexts.

Furthermore, particularly in more recent constructivist thinking, some human differences are recognized as different ways of being human. As such, specific differences in functionality become core components of select individuals' identity and essential to their unique understanding of self. The deaf community can be understood as an example of this aspect of essentialism found in more constructivist understandings of disability.[7] Often, writings about this essentialist element of largely constructivist understandings of disability point to the origins of the disability rights movement, in more or less exclusively physical functional differences, as contributing to the neglect of disability as a potentially desirable component of individual or community identity by early disability theorists and the efforts of activists. The fact that many of the most famous and persuasive early activists were people who acquired their disabilities as teenagers or young adults (Pelka 1997) might also have contributed to this impression. As is discussed later in this book, this essential component of disability sometimes involves using disability-first (or disability-alone) language wherein people with disabilities refer to themselves as, for example, "autistic individuals" or "autistics" as opposed to employing people-first language.

A Taxonomy of Atypical Functionalities Based on Outcome of Interactions

Modern conceptions of disability fall somewhere toward the middle of the continuum, with some tendency to favor the constructivist end. Conceptions of disability employed in modern public arenas depend on events and circumstances, not diagnosis. Depending on responses to a given functional difference at a particular point in time, interactions between levels of functionality and social and political infrastructures result in four possible outcomes: difference, impairment, disability, or handicap. Literature about disability inconsistently employs distinctions between these categories, particularly outside of mainstream disability studies literature.

This book employs the taxonomy as follows, with distinctions between categories depending on the degree to which a society considers varying levels of particular functionalities as being relevant to participation in society at a given moment in time. It is important to note that the taxonomy describes events and experiences as opposed to static descriptions of particular conditions or functional differences. An individual experiencing an atypical level of a human functionality may find him- or herself in any of the four categories over the course of a day depending on the specifics of the interactions between the individual's functional differences and social and political infrastructures. For the most part, however, because of the consistency of influence of a given sociocultural context, ongoing interaction of an atypical functionality and surrounding infrastructures will produce a stable categorical outcome. In other words, while it is inappropriate to state in this taxonomy that a person with schizophrenia will always be considered to have a disability in modern society, because of a failure to consider the immediate effect of flexibility limitations of the surrounding society's infrastructures, this can nevertheless be reasonably assumed likely, given the observed tendency of modern society's infrastructures to be insufficiently flexible to incorporate the functional atypicalities associated with schizophrenia. Furthermore, in considering interactions between functional atypicalities and society's infrastructures, it is important to remember that only the most extreme of constructivist interpretations would require society's infrastructures to become infinitely flexible and accommodate any and all needs or behaviors associated with functional atypicalities. The general call for increased flexibility responds to a long history of exclusion, not an effort in pursuit of anarchy.

Difference

Of the four categories, difference is the most innocuous and generic. Every human being embodies and experiences functional atypicalities. This book employs *difference* as the generic category to reference individuals, in the absence of connection to a relevant event. In the absence of context, nothing beyond difference exists. Also, types of functionalities considered differences may go completely unnoticed in the society in question. For example, the functional atypicality currently called dyslexia presumably went mostly unnoticed in preliterate societies and even in societies where there was no expectation that the general population read or write with any kind of regularity (Armstrong 2010).

When remarked upon by a society, differences invoke no change in social standing or individual potential. Differences also include variations in human form not known to involve any functional atypicality. For example, in Western societies, interaction between eye color and surrounding social and political infrastructures rarely (if ever) produces anything but passing curiosity. Eye color, therefore, almost always falls into the category of difference.

Impairment

Impairment occurs in situations in which the difference is noted by surrounding society and deemed potentially inconvenient enough, for either the individual or the society, to be worthy of possible correction or assistance. Left-handedness, for example, was in the past often associated with impairment when residual superstition considered this difference to be unseemly (if not evil) and even a possible threat to the health of the individual. Under these circumstances, teachers routinely sought to teach left-handed children to write with their nondominant hand. In contrast, in modern societies under most circumstances, near- and farsightedness have come to be considered impairments given the importance attributed to "perfect" or "corrected" vision. As used in this book, the term "impairment" does not automatically imply reduced social status or ability to become included in society other than at the level of minor inconvenience reflexively accommodated by infrastructures and the general population.

Disability

Disability happens with impairment of major life functions. This definition commonly appears in modern political discourse on atypical functionalities and is written into policies in disability policy subsystems, particularly in North America. Most public and political discourse surrounding atypical functionalities focuses on disability and disabling circumstances. Accordingly, disability represents the major focus of this book.

Major life functions include those activities considered fundamental to full-fledged membership in a given society. Societies completely define major life functions, which tend to change over the course of history and can vary dramatically in different cultures. In modern democracies, for example, ability to become gainfully employed outside the home is routinely perceived as a major life function for adults who have no other prevailing responsibilities, at least between the ages of eighteen and sixty-five. A century ago, however, such a capacity was considered crucial only for men lacking independent wealth. In fact, at some points in history, paid employment implied an impairment, which more fortunate members of society, particularly women, assiduously avoided as a point of pride. Although diagnosis incompletely defines disability, it is disability, of all the categories of atypical functionality, that tends to depend on formal, public definition. It is most exclusively experienced by those given a diagnosis explicitly established as legitimate within a given society. Goals of most progressive disability policies include reduction of conditions that unnecessarily turn impairments into disability.

Handicap

Finally, handicap refers to interactions between human differences and society that inevitably produce lowered social status. In the past, a variety of conditions equated disability inherently and irrevocably with poverty, thereby creating handicap. For example, as James Trent explained in *Inventing the Feeble Mind: A History of Mental Retardation in the United States:* "Between 1880 and 1950 mental retardation had largely been seen as a problem of lower-class teenagers and adults. Not infrequently, that group was regarded as a threat to the social order. During the heyday of the eugenics scare (1908–1920), Americans began to see poor, immigrant and working-class retarded teenagers and adults as the nation's primary 'menace'" (1994, 265–266). Often such attitudes resulted from an essentialist belief in fault or failure on the part of the handicapped individual as a root cause of the individual's difficulties.

Modern societies generally consider handicapping circumstances universally inappropriate. Handicapping infrastructures, such as the condition of most public transport systems, continue to exist, but are not generally considered a desirable part of civilization and are not deliberately endorsed by the general public or promoted by policymakers.

Movement Between Categories of Atypical Functionality

Examining political discourse surrounding neurodiversity requires distinguishing between difference, impairment, disability, and handicap as employed in the development of modern public policy. Furthermore, it is useful to consider which basic policy tools best facilitate movement between categories in the desired direction. Table 1.1 shows this basic schema.

Table 1.1   Categories of Atypical Functionality

Basic Social Construction	Category	Basic Policy Tool
	Difference	
If relevant in society		With mitigation (medicine, therapy, or device)
	Impairment	
If a major life function		With reasonable accommodations
	Disability	
If lower status is presumed		With protection of equal rights
	Handicap	

Understandings of Disability in
Political Discourse Diversify Policy Agendas

The general philosophical trend in popular understandings of disability as reflected in culture and policy is typically understood as moving away from the essentialist dominance culminating in the Western world toward the beginning of the twentieth century. Current sensibilities dictate employing a flexible understanding of atypical functionality as a fundamental component of supporting social diversity. Nevertheless, since effects and implications of interpretations of functional atypicalities in political discourse are as much successively added as replaced over time, an overarching effect of this change involves diversification of types of policy agendas found in disability policy subsystems.

Interactions between these agenda types shape development of policies and programs addressing all aspects of functional differences. Furthermore, ongoing dynamics between policy agendas have amplified influence on neurological disabilities. First, as already mentioned, understanding of the brain has developed considerably in recent years, creating increasingly sophisticated neurological taxonomies. Second, existence of neurological difference often requires a sustained and pervasive degree of belief in the absence of fully objective proof, particularly for those who are not intimately related to the individual with the difference. Third, children are much more frequently diagnosed with neurological differences than ever before. As a result, policy agendas focused on neurological differences may become conflated with modern parenting goals. Also, public representations of individuals with neurological differences most often focus on children, complicating creation of policy that addresses neurological differences across the lifespan. Furthermore, explicit acceptance of multiple agendas helps in the necessary escape from technocratic tendencies involving the expectation that scientific discovery alone will solve political challenges. As Roger Pielke explained, "We often expect science—the systematic pursuit of knowledge—to provide insight into the nature of problems, decision alternatives, and their consequences with respect to desired outcomes . . . with respect to decisions, this technocratic impulse suggests that the reduction of scientific uncertainty necessarily leads to a reduction of political uncertainty" (2007, 35).

Finally, neurological differences include a plethora of distinct conditions, many of which manifest quite differently in different people. This diversity means that individuals with neurological differences, even those who share diagnoses, may have radically divergent public goals, policy preferences, and programmatic needs.

What Is Neurodiversity?

Neurodiversity describes a relatively novel concept. Whereas neurological difference involves individual experiences, which may or may not meaningfully interact with the infrastructures in which the person resides, neurodiversity comprises questions of political and communal identity (Baker 2006). Neurological difference can, given the opportunity and individual choice, remain a private matter. However, neurodiversity—like any kind of politicized diversity—is inherently public (Chambers 2003). After all, regardless of the degree of uniqueness or atypicality of an individual's functionality, no one person or homogeneous group can be diverse alone. Even so, according to Andrew Fenton and Tim Krahn, "neurological diversity is the norm in the natural world" (2007, 3) because it is observed as present (and tolerated) in animals, including the great apes.

The concept of neurodiversity primarily originated in the thinking of adult members of self-aware autistic communities founded during the final decades of the twentieth century (Fenton and Krahn 2007). The term relatively quickly expanded to include all those with neurological differences (Ward and Meyer 1999; Nadesan 2005; Fenton and Krahn 2007; Armstrong 2010). As Fenton and Krahn explain, "the current scope of the term includes not only lower functioning autistics (LFAs) but also those diagnosed with such neurological or neurodevelopmental disorders as attention deficit-hyperactivity disorder, bipolar disorder, developmental dyspraxia, dyslexia, epilepsy, and Tourette's syndrome" (2007, 1). This list of examples is of course designed to illustrate the expansive umbrella of modern neurodiversity rather than a catalog of all possible neurological differences. Some examples of neurological differences, with their clinical descriptions and selected population characteristics, are shown in Table 1.2. Currently, the concept is widely used to include all differences of the human brain that are not considered typical (see, for example, Antonetta 2005).

Some argue for limiting the conception of neurodiversity to include only those individuals who have autism spectrum differences, particularly because of the specific policy agendas of some of the early activists. While such restriction of the conception of neurodiversity is undoubtedly

Table 1.2 Examples of Neurological Differences

Neurological Difference	Clinical Description (based on DSM-IV TR and Draft DSM-V)	Key Population Characteristics
Attention-deficit hyperactivity disorder (ADHD)	Involves recognized and marked inattention, impulsivity, and hyperactivity generally noted as present before age seven, manifesting in two or more locations and including clear evidence of clinically significant impairment in social, school, or work functioning for at least six months.	Roughly 3–5 percent of school-aged children are expected to have ADHD. An estimated 4 percent of adults have ADHD. Observed as being more common in males than females.
Autism and Asperger syndrome	Involves a combination of qualitative impairment in social interaction and communication; restricted repetitive and stereotyped patterns of behavior, interests, and activities; and delays or abnormal functioning in social interaction, language as used in social communication, and/or symbolic or imaginative play with onset prior to age three. Though it appears in the DSM-IV, Asperger syndrome will likely be eliminated from the DSM-V.	Much more prevalent in current generation of young people (approximately 1 in 166). About four times more common in males than females.
Bipolar disorder	Involves experiencing a combination of at least one manic or mixed manic episode, depression, and times of typical mood. The defining characteristics of mania include heightened mood (either euphoric or irritable); flight of ideas and urgency of speech; and increased energy, decreased need for sleep, and hyperactivity.	Approximately 1.5 percent of the general population is expected to experience bipolar disorder over the course of their lives. Bipolar disorder is believed to be equally common among males and females.

(continues)

Table 1.2 continued

Neurological Difference	Clinical Description (based on DSM-IV TR and Draft DSM-V)	Key Population Characteristics
Mental retardation	Involves significantly sub-average intellectual functioning as demonstrated by an IQ of approximately 70 or below on an individually administered IQ test, and concurrent deficits or impairments in present adaptive functioning.	Believed to be the most common developmental disorder, though exact prevalence is unclear. In the United States, it has been found to be more common in males than females.
Posttraumatic stress disorder (PTSD)	Involves development of characteristic symptoms following an extreme traumatic event directly involving death, injury, or threat to oneself or others. Characteristic symptoms include intense fear, helplessness, or horror (or in children, the response must involve disorganized or agitated behavior); persistent reexperiencing of the traumatic event; persistent avoidance of stimuli associated with the trauma and numbing of general responsiveness; and persistent symptoms of increased arousal.	Prevalence naturally depends on the proportion of the population exposed to extremely traumatic events. Recorded rates among high-risk populations (such as military veterans) have been as high as 58 percent.
Schizophrenia	Involves a combination of delusions; hallucinations; disorganized speech manifesting a formal thought disorder; grossly disorganized or catatonic behavior; blunted affect; lack or decline in speech or motivation; and marked social and occupational dysfunction.	About 1 percent of the general population is expected to experience some kind of schizophrenia during the course of their lives. Males are more likely to have early onset schizophrenia than are females.

politically useful in certain contemporary circumstances, philosophically isolating individuals with autism while simultaneously implying that other neurological conditions are not worthy of inclusion makes less sense in academic and philosophical considerations of this concept.

Nevertheless, it is important to understand that the roots of neurodiversity lie in the discourse and activism surrounding autism. Neurodiversity rose to the top of some systemic agendas in response to largely negative publicity and public discourse surrounding perceived growth in autism incidence at the end of the twentieth century. Most of this discussion tended to describe autism as an epidemic and therefore focused almost exclusively on finding a cure for autism. Although the incidence of autism is currently estimated at 1 in 150 children, this kind of alarmist thinking led to statements such as the following, which appeared in the Market Wire on August 4, 2004, in an article titled "GEM Media, Inc. & Spectrum Publications Launch NY Spectrum Magazine": "at this rate, no family will be left untouched by autism with statistical estimates reaching 1 in 7 children diagnosed with autism by the year 2012."

Some adults with autism began to fear increased intolerance of their way of being if not outright eradication of their lifestyles and preferences (Fenton and Krahn 2007). Fundamentally, neurodiversity asserts that neurological differences can be understood and experienced as much as a source of community and communal identity as can differences more routinely associated with politicized diversity, such as race, ethnicity, gender, religion, and sexual orientation. Groups dedicated to neurodiversity evolved to help promote this interpretation of living fully with neurological difference in the face of potentially overwhelming messages to the contrary.

In recent years, neurodiversity groups have become increasingly active. To date, these organizations operate predominantly online. Goals of neurodiversity-oriented organizations tend to include promoting positive understandings of autism, redirecting autism research funding away from its primary focus on treatment, countering public rhetoric describing autism as a disease (or as being otherwise fundamentally undesirable), and, to some degree, opposing efforts to find a cure for autism (Bumiller 2008). Neurodiversity advocates also contend that "neurological diversity is the norm in the natural world" (Fenton and Krahn 2007, 3) rather than a pathology or result of a possibly overly liberal acceptance of personal choice in the modern world. Organizations and groups engaged in neurodiversity activism or advocacy consciously employ language, theoretical constructs, and strategies inspired by those used to promote and support other forms of diversity over the course of the twentieth century. They also emphasize the unique contributions to society of individuals with neurological differences, autism especially. Often these discussions mention famous historical figures retroactively diagnosed with autism, at least by activists.

Identification Involves Choice

Just as happens with other characteristics more commonly associated with diversity, not everyone with a neurological difference identifies with neurodiverse communities. Furthermore, questions surrounding identification and outing of individuals with neurological differences parallel those found in, for example, gay and lesbian communities. A fundamental tenet of this book is that neurodiversity includes the right of individuals to choose not to publicly identify as having a neurological difference while simultaneously not supporting any social and political infrastructures that either universally encourage (or force) "passing" as neurologically typical, or incorporate negative consequences for publicly identifying as having a given neurological difference.

In addition, given the complexity of modern individual identity, neurodiversity as discussed in this book also protects the preferences of those who do not consider their neurological identity as a core element of personal identity while still identifying with neurodiverse communities. Public identification as an individual with a neurological difference incurs no extraordinary communal or political obligation. Someone with a neurological difference has the same right as any other person to create an identity more centered on personal characteristics than on neurological differences.

Basic Characteristics of Neurodiverse Conditions

One of the challenges in discussing neurodiversity involves defining who (and in some sense, what) this category should include. As mentioned previously, articulation of neurodiversity originated in thinking about individuals with autism spectrum differences. Limiting neurodiversity only to those with autism and related differences, however, resembles limiting ethnic diversity to discourse about individuals of African American descent. While it may be that this group comes most immediately to the minds of casual thinkers about ethnic diversity, clearly this perception misrepresents the realities of racial and ethnic diversity experienced in today's societies. Diversity is, after all, a condition of a society or community and never of an individual human being or homogeneous group, regardless of how exotic the particular group seems to other members of the general population.

However, expansive definitions of concepts such as neurodiversity run the risk of death by diffusion. No two human brains are identical. To the extent that neurodiversity includes everything, then it might come to mean nothing. Managing this expansion represents an ongoing challenge for neurodiversity advocates and activists. For example, as Fenton and Krahn (2007) point out:

> This defense of the normalcy of cognitive, and so neurological diversity, must respond to worries about over inclusiveness—i.e., by regarding as normal the neurological structures than underlie the behavior of autistic individuals we run the risk of including maladaptive cognitive and neurological traits . . . a partial response can note that what qualifies as maladaptive, or adaptive, is context sensitive. (3)

For the purposes of this book, neurodiversity refers to atypical functionalities found in individuals who have identifiable neurological differences and to their interactions with individuals considered neurologically typical in the context of public infrastructures built around a presumption of neurotypicality. For the most part, this implies that communities referred to as neurodiverse include only those that incorporate individuals who have been formally diagnosed (or could be, given access to professionals) with a disability believed to involve a significant brain-based difference compared to what is currently considered the human norm.

Defining neurodiversity in this way somewhat complicates matters, as most writing about disability, particularly outside disability studies, does not aggregate atypical functionalities in this way. Most discussion of brain-based disabilities considers these conditions to be of at least three primary types: mental illness, developmental disability, and brain injury acquired through either accident or disease. Some people, even those with other neurological differences, dislike being identified in tandem with the other types, for reasons ranging from simple discomfort and outright discrimination against individuals with other types of differences. This is arguably particularly the case for mental illness and psychiatric disorders, since acceptance of these differences as disabilities has historically lagged behind acceptance of the other two types. For example, as pointed out in the entry for the Americans with Disabilities Act in *The ABC-CLIO Companion to the Disability Rights Movement,* "there were various attempts in the House to derail or weaken the bill, including efforts to limit its protections for people with HIV/AIDS and psychiatric disabilities" (Pelka 1997, 20). However, for the purposes of examining public and political discourse surrounding neurological differences, it is important to include and consider all of the ways in which brains (or minds) are understood as differing. Failing to do so would artificially truncate the political conversation and present an incomplete picture of the dynamics of neurodiversity.

The prevailing taxonomy of neurological difference grows out of an importance placed on whether or not the observed difference is attributed to theoretical differences in brain chemistry, to a critical difference in the morphology of the brain itself, or to an identifiable event that (usually irrevocably) changed a once neurologically typical brain. This traditional distinction matters in the contexts of politics and policy. Often, policies and publicly funded programs are made and designed separately to target individuals with differences in these three categories. For example, in state governments in the United States, programs for individuals with mental retardation are often separated from programs for those with mental illness. This policy division echoes the strongly essentialist understandings of disability that dominated political discourse in the past, particularly the associated importance assigned to reasons for differences as a mechanism for assigning blame for the disabling outcome.

Nevertheless, more modern policies and programs have become increasingly generalist in their orientation, particularly as a result of extreme budgetary constraints and recognition of the prevalence of dual diagnoses (individuals falling into two or more of the traditional categories). Furthermore, the politics of neurodiversity in and of itself does not naturally become overly concerned with the mechanism or origin of differences in functionality, only with the unusual implications that result from these differences interacting with infrastructures. Arguments presented in this book, then, make little distinction between mental illness, developmental disability, or traumatic brain injury. This interpretation will be problematic for some readers. As Fred Pelka explains, "critics of cross-disability organizing maintain that no amount of awareness and sensitivity can alter genuine differences in philosophy and agenda between the various constituencies in the disability community" (1997, 82). Such distinctions are especially relevant to issue activists, but less so for more generalist issue stakeholders engaged in the public and political discourse surrounding neurodiversity (especially those directly involved in policy formulation and development, as this inherently involves compromise between different political philosophies). Furthermore, as Simi Linton points out, disability scholars habitually consider disabilities in a cross-disability context because "we may drool, hear voices, speak in staccato syllables, wear catheters to collect our urine, or live with a compromised immune system . . . we are all bound together not by our collective list of symptoms but by the social and political circumstances that have forged us as a group" (1998, 4). The scholarly literature also points to such grouping forces. For example, in an article about the widespread presumption of incompetence of autistic children in US schools, Douglas Biklen and Jamie Burke point out that "the tradition in American education to assume incompetence of students who have severe communication impairments extends beyond autism, and includes those with other developmental disabilities, such as Down's syndrome, Rett Syndrome, Cri-Du-Chat, and others" (2006, 167). In this book, references to and descriptions of experiences of individuals with neurological differences should be read to include individuals falling into all of the traditionally employed categories unless specifically stated otherwise.

Layout of the Book

This book presents the taxonomy of agendas shaping modern disability policy from the perspective of policy analysis, with particular emphasis on theories of issue definition and agenda setting. Although the primary focus of the book is neurological difference and neurodiversity, the chapters focused on agenda types conclude with thoughts for all disabilities. These distinct agenda types create tensions that both help and hinder the development of effective disability policy. Continuing this introduction to neurodiversity, Chapter 2 describes the four primary agenda types of political activists and policy entrepreneurs who work in the disability policy arena (cause, care, cure, and celebration).

Beginning the focus on agenda types, Chapter 3 explores the relationship between public policy agendas focusing on the civil rights and those focusing on public provision of care for individuals requiring (or perceived as requiring) specialized care as a result of manifestations of a neurological difference. The chapter begins by discussing implications over time of the deinstitutionalization of individuals with neurological differences, including the resulting intergenerational tensions. Next, the policy implications of spectrum differences (such as autism) are explored, with particular focus on issues surrounding guardianship and independence.

Chapter 4 discusses tensions between the goals of cause and cure with regard to neurological difference. The chapter begins with a discussion of policy narratives equating the two, sometimes turning the search for or application of a cure into the source of civil rights for those with neurological differences. The chapter concludes by analyzing the attention to and influence of these two organizational archetypes in official government discourse in recent years in both the United States and Canada.

Chapter 5 focuses on the relationship between disability rights and disability culture from the standpoint of neurodiversity. Emphasis on suffering and discrimination common in early rights-based discussion of disability is first explored. The discussion then turns to an examination of efforts to celebrate disability culture as a positive right in the context of disability activism and policy focused on protection of rights of individuals with disabilities, usually constructed using a negative rights basis. The chapter concludes with an analysis of newspaper coverage of individuals with autism, demonstrating the tensions between celebration and cause as reported over time.

Chapter 6 examines policy and programmatic tensions between caring for and seeking a cure for individuals with neurological differences and how these tensions can hinder participation in society. The role of nonprofits in the relationship between these agenda types is also explored, as are the ways that investments in care and cure efforts can exist symbiotically, particularly in the public sector.

Chapter 7 focuses on tensions between caring for individuals with disabilities who are in need of direct assistance with major life functions, and celebrating the existence and accomplishments of individuals with neurodiverse conditions. The chapter discusses three central topics: the vital role of celebrating disability culture and the accomplishments of individuals with disabilities; the concern that celebrating neurodiversity tends to create a false understanding of limitations by focusing on "higher-functioning" individuals; and the parallel concern that celebrating neurodiversity sometimes tends to objectify individuals with disabilities, particularly when organized by professional caregivers. The chapter concludes with a case study of *Autism: The Musical.*

Chapter 8 explores the tensions between cure and celebration. It begins by discussing the distinctions between events designed to raise money for a cure and those designed to celebrate neurodiversity. The chapter considers the philosophical tensions between neurological difference at the individual level, which could by definition embrace individual or family choices to seek a permanent mitigation, and at the levels of community and society, which depend on the continued and public participation of members of the identified minority. The chapter closes with a discussion of the role of public policies, particularly those that rely on binary diagnosis standards, in augmenting these tensions.

Concluding the book, Chapter 9 revisits the primary implications of each of the six tensions for neurodiversity and for public policy. Recommendations for resolving the tensions within public policy in the short and medium terms are discussed. The chapter concludes by revisiting the concept of neurodiversity and its implications for disability scholarship and society.

Notes

1. See, for example, Pelka 1997 for encyclopedic descriptions of such events, including those directed at well-known cultural figures such as Helen Keller.

2. The term "policy subsystem" refers to the totality of policies and programs that address a particular area of public concern in a given society. Subsystems often overlap with regard to their claims on proposed legislation and public actions. Nevertheless, most public policies and programs fall into one or two primary policy subsystems.

3. People-first language is employed in this book unless other phrases are quoted in context or unless the discussion is referring to individuals or communities who deliberately use their disabilities as defining elements of identity.

4. Such separation of mind, body, and spirit represents a Cartesian understanding of the human condition, and has been contested by many modern neurologists. Even so, both diagnostic categories and policy instruments tend to maintain a division between disabilities rooted in a separation of mind, body, and spirit, at least for operational purposes.

5. For example, in the United States, involuntary sterilizations continued until at least 1979. The Supreme Court case that established the practice as constitutional, *Buck v. Bell* (1927), has yet to be overturned.

6. This difference in nomenclature is most likely due to a general discomfort with social(ist) policies in the United States, more than to an actual difference in understandings of disability.

7. Some members of deaf communities would not agree with this characterization because they consider deafness to be completely cultural and not a disability, regardless of the disability paradigm employed. However, as James Charlton asserted in *Nothing About Us Without Us,* "the category 'disability' includes people with socially defined functional limitations . . . for instance, deaf people are considered disabled even though many deaf individuals insist they do not have a disability" (2000, 8).

2

Competing Disability Policy Agendas: Cause, Care, Cure, and Celebration

Since disability affects individuals in every culture, of any age, and from all socioeconomic groups, diversity of issue stakeholders in disability policy subsystems is pronounced. No one person can expect to comprehend—or even know about—the specifics of all policies oriented toward disability (Berkowitz 1987). Furthermore, specific goals of active participants in the disability policy subsystem vary at least as dramatically as do issue stakeholders. As described by John Kingdon (2003) and others, public agendas go beyond the formal agenda of items being actively considered by a particular government entity at a given moment in time. The broader agenda—called the systemic agenda—includes all aspects of public problems actively considered by interested members of society. Public agendas range from the quite broad-based, such as eliminating child abuse, to highly specific changes to details of a particular standard or requirement (Weimar and Vining 2005).

Public agendas thrive on interest. They become meaningless in the absence of passionate engagement of individuals or groups. As a result, public agendas tend to connect to direct goals of political activists and policy entrepreneurs. Political activists seek to define or redefine policy subsystems in accordance with their preferred agenda type. Policy entrepreneurs seek to create advantageous linkages between defined public problems and policy solutions preferred by the policy entrepreneur or, more often, his or her client (Kingdon 2003). Although specific agendas and policy linkages might become quite numerous within any given policy subsystem, socially relevant agendas pertaining to a particular policy subsystem over time tend to fall into an identifiable set of categories. In the disability policy subsystems of modern industrialized nations, four primary agenda types exist: those of cause, care, cure, and celebration.

27

These agenda types evolved individually, with different moments of cultural dominance in industrialized nations. Although each agenda type focuses on disability, the interests and goals of issue stakeholders associated with the different types tend to be quite distinct. The agenda types did not, however, progress completely independently of one another. Furthermore, while understandings of disability have transformed considerably over the past couple of centuries, this basic taxonomy of common public agendas of disability has remained relatively stable. Importantly, issue stakeholders do not necessarily self-identify as being proponents of particular agenda types according to these categories. Stakeholders often assume their preferred agenda type to encompass the whole of their society's disability policy subsystem. The agenda types employed in this book constitute descriptive categories, not slogans, identities, or mantras.

Cause Agenda Types: The Pursuit and Protection of Rights

As is the case with other diversity-related differences, both human and civil rights of individuals with functional differences were habitually ignored and violated in the past (and, all too frequently, in the present). As described in Chapter 1, when atypical functionalities interact with rigid public infrastructures, impairment, disability, or handicap occurs. Assuming individuals with functional differences should be considered as any other member of the general population, the latter two categories involve violation of rights of individuals with disabilities.

Modern societies widely consider handicap intolerable due to the presumption of lower social status. However, this social value represents a marked exception to the historical rule. For most of human history, at least some functional differences became widely associated with handicaps under all social and political circumstances present in that particular place and time. This universality ultimately inspired activist efforts targeting elimination of handicaps as a basic right of all people and a desirable characteristic of societies. Most often, such efforts are described as the pursuit of disability rights.

Implementation of Disability Rights
Can Confound Positive and Negative Rights

Cause-oriented agendas incorporate efforts to establish and protect both human and civil rights. Human rights involve access to the resources, opportunities, and dignity that are fundamental to the human condition.[1] Human rights, to a largely symbolic but nevertheless important degree, enjoy protection at the international level as a result of the Universal Declaration of Human Rights of 1948. Elements composing human rights have been described as lower needs (meaning more basic) by scholars in the tradition of Abraham Maslow (1943). Lower-level needs create the foundation upon which human beings can ultimately pursue self-actualization. Absent an ability to meet lower-level needs, human beings generally cannot even begin to focus on fulfilling higher-order needs. As a result, both the individual and ultimately the society in which they live languish. While it is arguably possible for an individual to have their human rights protected in the absence of protection of their civil rights, the reverse is not generally considered possible.

For the most part, constitution of human rights employs a positive rights basis. Positive rights depend upon action by another in order to become manifest. Accordingly, human dignity requires recognition on the part of the other that the individual is entitled to that dignity and to any efforts required to sufficiently promote their ability to access that positive right. For example, since access to restroom facilities represents a basic element of human dignity as understood in modern society, current understandings of disability rights require society to modify traditionally exclusive public restroom facilities to allow for wheelchair access.

Civil rights, on the other hand, include responsibilities and privileges associated with legal status in a particular nation. Despite legal or constitutional standards adopted by many modern nations, civil rights of individuals with disabilities routinely become violated. Part of this results from the pace of sociocultural change, which marks time in decades and centuries rather than the shorter time frames anticipated by modern ambitions and attention spans. Another part of this challenge involves confusion of positive and negative rights expectations, which clouds implementation of policies designed to protect disability rights. For example, voting is routinely considered a civil right. In modern democracies, legal protection of the right to vote extends to citizens who meet a short list of qualifying characteristics. Generally speaking, construction of voting policy employs a negative rights basis. In the United States at least, most voting policy innovations focus on restricting or punishing efforts to unjustly stop qualified individuals from exercising their right to vote. Typically the state is not required to take positive action to ensure that specific individuals can vote; it is rather just required not to take action designed to prevent individuals from exercising their right to vote.

When it comes to rights of those with atypical functionalities, however, societies become so habituated to deliberately hindering the exercise of civil rights in response to functional differences that the distinctions between positive and negative rights become extraordinarily confounded. Almost all social and political infrastructures have been constructed with, at best, ignorance of universal design and, at worst, with deliberate insertion of elements accessible only to those with typical functionalities. To many people, exclusionary design elements seem natural. Interestingly, these exclusionary design elements often go unquestioned to such a degree that people have been known to respond in anger and frustration at the mere suggestion of other possible approaches or designs.

For example, standard placement of electrical outlets complicates their use for many individuals who have limited mobility, including those using wheelchairs, pregnant women, and a significant proportion of the elderly. Placement at the standard height rather than a few feet off the ground also endangers young children, who have a tendency to stick their fingers or foreign objects into unprotected outlets. Nevertheless, current placement of outlets represents a common aesthetic preference and is a largely unquestioned practice. Movement of outlets from their unnecessarily exclusionary position is fundamentally an action within the purview of negative rights, because it involves stopping a hindrance rather than creating a special condition under which the right can be exercised. However, movement of outlets can also seem to be part of a positive right, since changing physical infrastructures involves direct cost and the associated perception of the creation of enabling conditions. Nevertheless, a key distinction between a negative and positive rights basis revolves around the necessity of sustained expense or effort required in the case of a positive right, as opposed to the onetime expense associated with corrective action in a negative rights context.

Perceptions of an unusual reliance on a positive rights basis in public challenges associated with disability become augmented by routine overestimation of costs associated with accommodations and, to some degree, universal design in general. For instance, in the United States, whereas the majority of accommodations required under the Americans with Disabilities Act require small or no financial outlays, perceived costs associated with accommodations generally run much higher. According to Paul Longmore, "nearly 70 percent of job accommodations cost $500 or less, with almost a fifth incurring no expense at all because they entail merely the rearrangement of work spaces and work patterns" (2003, 27). Nevertheless, in political and public discourse, more expensive accommodations are typically highlighted. As a result, a common perception of prohibitively high cost remains.[2]

Furthermore, in considering cost, it is important to remember that the expense sometimes derives from a failure to consider universal design in the initial construction. Curb cuts, for example, presumably become expensive only because the initial shaping of cement on curbs excluded cuts. Furthermore, inflated prices often become attached to products considered by many to exist only for the more limited market of individuals with disabilities rather than the rest of the general population. The higher price is associated with either opportunism or simply low demand and limited production. When these products become part of expected, general use, the price falls.

Widespread Habitual Discrimination Against Disability Continues to Exist

Cause agendas found within the disability policy subsystem respond to a prolonged and pervasive history of discrimination against individuals with atypical functionalities. No other type of human difference has so consistently been associated with exclusion from society and the polis. Even so, in terms of numbers, organized protests focused on disability rights pale in comparison to those of other traditionally disenfranchised groups. As Sharon Barnartt and Richard Scotch reported in their analysis of protests during the late twentieth century, "we see that the largest disability protest, with 6,000 protestors, does not begin to approach the size of some of the larger protests in the civil rights or feminist movements" (2010, 81). In fact, differences in functionality became so routinely associated with exclusion that language involving disability became a tool of exclusion and also an argument for inclusion of other nonelite groups from the empowered population. For example, as Douglas Baynton points out:

> Supporters of slavery and opponents of female suffrage and immigration policies often used Disability [*sic*] as a tool to maintain social and political hierarchies. Opponents of female suffrage and abolition, for example, often claimed that both women and slaves lacked sufficient intelligence to be equals in society or to participate fully in the political process. (cited in Burch and Sutherland 2006, 138)

This tendency to employ language describing functional differences in the rhetorical arguments supporting (or against) rights claims of other nonelite groups remains a powerful force in many diversity-oriented policy subsystems. This resistance extends even to the point of ongoing objection to becoming associated with disability-related groups and political conversations for fear of implications of unwanted comparisons between the experiences of other nonelite groups and those of individuals with disabilities. In the past, as Susan Burch and Ian Sutherland explain, "by distancing themselves from disability, suffrage advocates tacitly accepted the idea that disability was a legitimate reason for inequality" (2006, 138).

Today's political discourse tends to continue this tradition, though usually in more subtle forms and expressions than has been the case historically. Intriguingly, recent political discourse also includes some examples of the reverse of this argument. In other words, to a limited degree, acceptance of disability is used as an argument for accepting (or at least tolerating) other forms of diversity. For example, in a statement in an editorial titled "Don't Persecute Homosexual Kids" that appeared in Salt Lake City's *Deseret News* on February 15, 1996, the author asked, "regarding all the hullabaloo concerning the formation of a high school club for homosexuals, what's the problem? Would there be this much concern should the schizophrenics, autistics, or any other unfortunate deviant group ban together for mutual understanding and encouragement?" Of course, such expressions of support for inclusion leave much to be desired when examined from the perspective of neurodiversity. They do, however, represent an interesting twist on the more traditional fear of association with disability on the part of issue stakeholders who represent the interests of other minority or marginalized groups.

Although some exclusion undoubtedly came from indifference as opposed to intentional action, restrictions placed on individuals with disabilities often involved conscious choice and sustained effort. Legal restrictions on exercise of rights as basic as reproduction and as fundamental as going out in public were created and remained in force as recently as the late twentieth century (Schweik 2009). For example, the Chicago Municipal Code included until 1974 the provision that "no person who is diseased, maimed, mutilated or in any way deformed so as to be an unsightly or disgusting object or improper person [is] to be allowed in or on the public ways or other public places in this city, or shall therein or thereon expose himself to public view, under a penalty of not less than one dollar nor more than fifty dollars for each offense" (Section 36034). Cause agendas work to remove such legal restrictions on the lives of individuals with functional differences and to force creation of circumstances under which individuals become best equipped to exercise rights.

A Cause Is Not Always a Cause-Oriented Agenda: Disease and Disability

Finally, not all efforts described as taking on the cause of a particular functional difference fall into the category of cause agenda types. When disease and disability are insufficiently differentiated, cure may become interpreted as the cause associated with a particular atypical functionality. Neurological differences are routinely discussed as diseases, often because of similarities of expression and a lack of scientific consensus surrounding the etiology of neurological differences. For example, in *Evidence of Harm,* David Kirby (2005) describes:

> Researchers now know that pink disease arose when infants with a heightened sensitivity to mercury were exposed to products containing the inorganic form, which was used as an antiseptic in teething powers, calamine lotion and Mercurochrome. They reported that 1 in 500 exposed children developed the disease, roughly the same rate as autism in the late 1990s. Acrodynia, by all accounts, was a miserable condition. Descriptions of many systems would be instantly recognizable to parents of an autistic child. (62)

While in later writings Kirby distinguishes from those with autism and children he believes to be misdiagnosed with autism as a result of what some describe as vaccine-induced mercury poisoning, the overall impression left by such arguments involves equating neurological difference with disease.

Of course, individuals with diseases can be, and sometimes are, rightly categorized within the spectrum of disability. Most disability policies (and at times entire subsystems) designate diseases as disabilities if they involve chronic illness or, in some cases, if having the disease itself invokes disability-based discrimination in the given social context. In the United States, for example, policies tend to describe a disease as a disability if resulting impairment lasts longer than a year,[3] or when the perception of impairment brought forth by the diagnosis (most notably AIDS, cancer, or a history of addiction) has an established history of resulting in discrimination due to the associated assumption of disability on the part of the rest of the general public (Riccucci 2006). This does not mean, however, that the terms become interchangeable or that designating a disability as a disease (or vice versa) involves no political implications. From the perspective of some individuals who have neurological differences, as well as some promoters of cause-oriented agendas, a failure to distinguish between issues relating to the experience of disease and issues relating to the experience of disability be-

comes problematic, since the foregone conclusion to the question of disease implies elimination through prevention or cure.

Given deterioration of health, prolonged physical pain, or mental an-
guish not exclusively associated with inflexibility of infrastructures, cure
could encompass the cause agenda because of the absolute impossibility of
effectively exercising any human or civil rights without the needed, and
perhaps as yet unavailable, medical intervention. However, for many types
of functional atypicalities, cause and cure do not so naturally merge, due to
the role of social and political infrastructures in creating threats to health,
safety, or life experience of those with functional differences. For example,
protecting the rights of individuals with Down syndrome tends to require
treatment or cure of life-threatening cardiac problems, access to which could
be part of a cause-oriented agenda. However, cure of associated neurological differences does not fall under the category of a cause agenda to the
extent that handicapping circumstances (and other physical or mental suffering) connected with this functional difference result primarily from infrastructure inflexibilities rather than inherent physiological aspects of the
particular condition.

Care Agenda Types: Old Impulse, New Purpose

Caring for others epitomizes a basic human impulse. In fact, systematically
caring for those with atypical functionalities has been popularly identified
as a defining characteristic of humanity as compared to other sentient beings
(Millan and Peltier 2008). Care involves provision of time, talent, or resources to others without expectation of reciprocity from the individuals or
groups receiving the care. Human capacity to care for others strengthens
bonds between individuals and creates the social capital necessary for a
functional society and polis (Kingdon 2003).

The vast majority of governments formed throughout human history
have involved (if at all) sporadic care policy or publicly funded programs.
Most often, responsibility for care has fallen to family or religious entities.
Furthermore, particularly in an individualistic society, the social contract
includes a basic discomfort with the concept of care. As a result, even
though care agendas have the longest history in the disability policy subsystem, public care agendas signify a modern policy innovation that is
common only in well-established societies with reasonably secure
economies.

Caring About the Question of Need

Much public and political discourse surrounding care, particularly as a public agenda, revolves around the question of need. In fact, the connection between care and publicly identifiable need is embedded so deeply in modern sociocultural frameworks that this connection routinely goes unquestioned. Caring, especially as discussed in the public sphere, implies caring for those in need. Often, public care is deliberately limited only to those in formally legitimated need. In other words, public care policies tend to include specific definitions of what circumstances make a person eligible for care.

Identifying need involves constant political negotiation and redefinition. This dynamic holds particular relevance in societies deemed individualistic, archetypically represented by the United States. In the context of atypical functionalities, historically most care agendas have tended to emphasize disadvantages associated with differences, typically portraying the individual with the difference as a victim. Victim status is still often considered a necessary condition for provision of care, particularly in the context of care provided through public funding for a prolonged period of time.

Rehabilitation: A Progressive Innovation in Care

Modern care-oriented agendas divide into two basic subtypes: maintenance and rehabilitation. Maintenance becomes the focus of care agendas when the expectation of society is that functional difference irrevocably associates with deterioration or, in many cases, when the targeted group includes those with relatively short life expectancies as compared to the rest of the general population. Until the early twentieth century, most care agendas focused on developing separated physical locations for such individuals, ideally medical or quasi-medical establishments, to alleviate their particular suffering. Beginning in the late nineteenth century and especially after World War I, however, perceptions of individuals with disabilities changed as more young men survived injuries sustained in battle for longer periods of time. Individuals with disabilities, particularly young men with disabilities, came to be seen as having the potential to recover as active members of society and the polis. Care policies and programs began to focus on the goal of rehabilitation.

Rehabilitation is defined as restoring individuals to so-called useful life (and ideally good health) through professionally guided therapy and specialized education. The emergence of rehabilitation as a guiding philosophy embedded three core elements into the care agenda types, which remain in force today: a loosening of the link between functional differences and permanent entitlement to care; emergence of disability-specific professional stakeholders; and solidification of the common perception of disability as being physical disability.

Traditionally, selected functional differences automatically invoked handicapped status. Unless defined as a social anathema supposedly necessitating complete social exclusion or more or less preemptive involvement with the judicial system, having a functional difference identified as handicapping defined an individual as member of the deserving poor. As Harold Pollack explained about the United States, "fiscal accounting reveals the latent generosity of an American welfare state that draws stark distinctions among recipients of public help . . . the same society that stigmatizes millions of people deemed unworthy of help proves surprisingly generous toward those, such as intellectually disabled persons, it deems in genuine need of help" (2007, 96). Although the provided care was often deplorable and sometimes outright harmful to the recipient, this characterization afforded individuals with selected functional differences a dependable social status. Rehabilitation philosophy, on the other hand, understands individuals with functional differences as able to adapt toward becoming contributing members of society. Furthermore, the word "rehabilitation" itself suggests existence of a loss of status in society to which the individual is entitled, given a favorable set of circumstances and sustained effort, to return. One consequence of this change in expectations is that individual efforts of people with atypical functionalities become more subject to external judgment with regard to sufficiency of personal investment in recovery. The possibility of deeming an individual's personal effort as insufficient creates potential for loss of status as a deserving recipient of care.

Professional-Issue Stakeholders
Emerge Through Rehabilitation

A second element of care agenda types that developed alongside rehabilitation philosophy was the creation of disability-specific professional stakeholders. As was the case with many efforts that defined the Progressive Era, rehabilitation not only involved making public certain elements of the human experience that were once private, but also emphasized benefits held as uniquely associated with professionalized efforts directed at social problems. Such professionalization legitimizes a class of individuals who, through long-term commitments to particular functional differences, become issue stakeholders in the politics surrounding the functional difference. In fact, professional stakeholder status often involves professional associations to a greater degree than individual practitioners. Furthermore, in some circumstances, credibility of the professional regarding the functional difference is deemed superior to that of the individual experiencing the functional difference or that of the individual's family.

Organizations themselves became stakeholders in care agendas comprising organizational interests that may or may not correspond to those of the individuals experiencing atypical functionalities. Though professional stakeholder organizations are generally well intentioned, their interests at times opposed those of other stakeholders. For example, superintendents of institutions for the mentally retarded became powerful issue stakeholders in care agendas targeting challenges attributed to those with atypical cognitive function. These superintendents fought to maintain the institutionalization model long after other issue stakeholders revealed a preference for community-based care (Trent 1994; Noll 2009). Care-oriented agendas generally invoke questions of control. However, the nature of rehabilitation philosophy, embedded as it was in an era of faith in science as an organizing principle for humanity and social progress, served to embolden tendencies to legitimize external control over those having atypical functionalities determined to be unacceptable (Snyder and Mitchell 2006).

Finally, emergence of rehabilitation philosophy solidified perception of disability as stemming nearly exclusively from atypical physical functionalities. Although rehabilitation techniques and technologies developed well beyond those that only targeted atypical physical functionalities, the stereotypical image of rehabilitation involves efforts to recover physical capacities lost in accident, illness, or injury. Such dominance of physical differences in the construction of understandings of disability affects all disability policy agendas to this day.

Cure Agenda Types:
A Locus of Modern Controversies and Quandaries

Cure agenda types arguably involve the greatest potential to inspire conflict and controversy in modern industrialized nations. Cure-oriented agendas focus on ultimate elimination of atypical functionalities. Cure agenda types also tend to include the goal of complete prevention of functional differences, either through selective termination of pregnancy or through as yet largely hypothetical manipulation of the human genome. In the absence of a capacity to eliminate underlying causes of functional differences, cure agendas also focus on controlling undesired characteristics attributed to identifiable differences, as a secondary goal.

As mentioned, cure agenda types typically equate disability with disease. Distinction between disease and disability can become clouded, but typically depends upon whether a reasonable expectation of relatively rapid decline in functionality or shortening survival horizon associates with the condition. Cure agenda stakeholders habitually employ the same tactics used by issue stakeholders for diseases such as cancer. These tactics tend to be both highly emotional and connected to fascinating scientific research. As a result, issue stakeholders representing cure agendas tend to become exceptionally able to amass interest, sympathy, and resources from the general public.

Cure-oriented agendas tend to be popular among those experiencing newly acquired functional differences, including parents of young children who have functional differences. Such inclinations are both unsurprising and rational, since a return to an experienced level of functioning (or to a habitually expected level, in the case of one's offspring) constitutes the natural preference of most individuals. Changes in functionality away from the human norm, whether ultimately a source of community identity or not, involve loss to which no one might be expected to become easily accustomed.

Disability studies scholars and activists often deride cure-oriented agendas as part of a vilified medical model of disability. Presentation of cure as potentially forced, or at least strongly favored in public discourse to the point that most people will reflexively choose cure before considering other options, is typical in such discussion. Underlying much of the anti-cure rhetoric is fear that development of cure will result in eradication of functional differences, even those unassociated with pain or expectation of unusually rapid decline in functionality. In extreme cases, this could involve forced eradication of a condition regardless of the desires of an individual who has a functional difference, or the desires of his or her family. Reflections upon historical experiences surrounding the eugenics movement prove particularly germane to such arguments.

Celebration: Embracing Disability Creatively

Celebration-oriented agendas can arguably be thought of as creating culture. After all, celebration agendas fundamentally involve nurturing a sense of community identity, one that may have been historically stifled in societies that are intolerant of differences in functionality. Such nurturing involves at least two prongs. It includes integration into mainstream society's cultural activities and, at least in some circumstances, a focus on development of vibrant subcultures of individuals with particular functional differences. However, public policy does not create culture per se. Instead, public policy can support and encourage the ability of select groups to engage in positive community-building efforts. This final agenda is therefore designated "celebration."

A core function of celebration-oriented agendas and efforts focuses on expanded understandings of disability. As Linda Ware (2008) explained about the decision that the annual Disability Studies in Education Conference should include arts produced by individuals with disabilities, this effort

> provided the opportunity to consider educational inclusion against the backdrop of aesthetic, political and cultural concerns conveyed through an interdisciplinary lens shared by artists and scholar activists . . . this lens, uniquely shaped by the shared interests in disability issues interpreted in the twenty-first century, stands in marked contrast to historical interpretations of disability shaped by the reductionist ideology of special education research and practice. (563)

Whereas changes in understandings of disability affected goals and preferred policies associated with each of the agenda types, celebration-oriented agendas also include an explicit focus on deliberate diversification of understandings of disability. For many activists and even policy entrepreneurs directing their energies toward these types of agendas, a primary expected outcome of political discourse and policy efforts comprises voicing, promoting, and ultimately protecting variant understandings of the implications of atypical functionalities. As a result, celebration-oriented policies and programs tend to become the most amorphous component of disability policy subsystems, at times not even recognized as genuine public policy by other disability policy stakeholders and members of the general public.

From Tolerance to Awareness and Beyond

More primitive aspects of celebration policy agendas focused on the concept of tolerance. Though the concept lost currency in recent years as stakeholders began to object to the notion of mere toleration, celebration agenda types cannot take hold without a basic social tolerance for individuals with functional differences.

Especially in recent years, stakeholders pursuing celebration agendas became more inclined to formulate goals on the basis of awareness than tolerance. Awareness in the context of policy takes two primary forms: symbolic and education policy. Symbolic policy constitutes policy without specific programmatic effects. It aims to recast current public efforts and attitudes toward a (typically) newly preferred philosophy or orientation of political discourse, usually with the widespread expectation that more programmatic policy will follow. It can also include innovative policy that its formulators know full well will take decades to implement properly. In recent years, the most common type of symbolic policy employed in North America has involved declaration of periods of time as dedicated to a particular individual or group. For example, governments at both national and subnational levels have declared various days, weeks, and even months as dedicated to autism awareness.

The second major form of awareness-oriented policy involves education and training. In this case, governments create, provide, or require education for professionals or the general public about (usually specific) atypical functionalities. As compared to more cautionary, if not hysterical, public education provided in the past, in modern times these programs tend to emphasize the humanity and potential of those with functional differences. Despite ongoing changes in perception of disability, such programs target very real knowledge gaps typical of members of the general populations of modern societies. As Katherine Owen, Jane Hubert, and Sheila Hollins (2007) put it:

> People with severe intellectual disabilities are seen as being too different, too disabled, and too challenging to lead lives like "us" . . . They are not thought of as people who have pasts, have emotions, who experience feelings of loss, who grieve for all old friends . . . the reasons for these perceived differences lie in their disability, rather than in what they are taught, the opportunities they are given, how they are supported, and the expectations of those around them. (224)

Celebration-oriented agendas focusing on awareness seek to close this gap and focus attention on the humanity of individuals with neurological differences and, to a more limited degree, the concept of neurodiversity.

Language as a Form of Celebration

Celebration-oriented agendas also target culture more directly. One policy tool employed involves deliberate crafting of language. Though hardly a new element of politics, an increased sense of the power of careful planning of language developed over the past couple of decades. Such strategic use of language is often derisively described as "political correctness," suggesting both disingenuousness and ultimately meaninglessness of the word choice. While this may be the case for some proposed language choices, in disability policy subsystems in at least the English-speaking world, disability policy issues stakeholders take questions surrounding people-first language seriously as a necessary element of modern disability policy.

In the disability policy subsystem until very recently, the majority of stakeholders pursuing celebration agendas nearly universally promoted people-first language as a way of encouraging celebration of individuals with functional differences. As part of the politics of disability, the names of several laws, public policies, and programs were changed to include people-first language. For example, the Education for All Handicapped Children's Act of 1975 was renamed the Individuals with Disabilities Education Act as part of its 1990 reauthorization. The intention of people-first language involves drawing attention away from the tendency to define people in terms of their disabilities and forces recognition of the basic humanity of people with functional differences.

Positive Focus of Celebration-Oriented Agendas

Celebration-oriented agendas also focus on support of cultural events and community activities deliberately designed to promote a sense of pride among individuals with disabilities. Although public and third-sector funding distributed to such efforts pales in comparison to that awarded for pursuit of cures or provision of care, funding for such efforts has diversified and increased in recent years.

Celebration-oriented agendas also involve targeting construction of expectations placed upon individuals with disabilities by society at large. Historically, expectations of individuals with disabilities were uniformly adjusted downward as compared to those with no perceived limitations of major life functions. Generally speaking, this resulted from both social realities and good intentions. For example, in the United States, whereas individuals without disabilities are generally expected to attain the age of at least sixty-five with sufficient work history before receiving regular income assistance from the public sector, social security policies include different expectations for those with functional differences classifiable as disabilities, so that those who are unable to engage in paid employment (or who, alternatively, find society unwilling to accept their involvement in the labor force) qualify for long-term public assistance at younger ages.

Such lowered expectations, however, also potentially handicap individuals with functional differences, particularly when broad-based policy instruments are employed. In some cases, help intended by policies and programs limits a society's capacity to recognize value in functional differences. Celebration agendas seek to control negative effects of expectations on the lives and potential of individuals (and communities) with functional differences.

Celebrating the Diversity of Disability

Finally, one challenge extant in the celebration agenda involves potential for presumption of uniformity among individuals with disabilities as a side effect of enthusiastic support of the disability culture. This tendency creates political tension between the necessity of avoiding becoming conquered through division, and remembering that "a common label of Disability [*sic*]—or even Deafness—does not imply a common experience" (Burch and Sutherland 2006, 141). To the extent that promotion of disability culture creates a perception of a singular disability experience, celebration-oriented agendas become more complex to formulate and implement into effective public policy in keeping with the core intentions of celebration-oriented agendas.

Disability Policy Agendas over Time

Agendas in disability policy subsystems continually resist similitude and assimilation. Even in the earliest conscious efforts, conflict between different types of disability policy agendas shaped political outcomes. Furthermore, throughout history, different agenda types have dominated particular societies during given eras, at times virtually eclipsing other agenda types. For example, although self-conscious cause-related efforts have existed in the United States since at least the mid-nineteenth century, the ascendance of care-oriented agendas so completely dominated the disability policy subsystem of the time that scholars routinely consider early rights-based disability policy efforts as originating a century later.

Whereas sophisticated disability policy subsystems represent a modern policy innovation, disability policy did not originate in the twentieth century. Examples of disability policy date back thousands of years. Public discourse about disability began quite early in the history of the US federal government. A search of compiled congressional records from the first century of US federalist government turns up a hundred documents that contain the words "disability," "disabilities," "handicap," or "insane." Early references to disability focused on setting standards for disability pensions for those acquiring disabilities while in public (military or postal) service. This early political discourse included some discussion about neurological differences under the guise of insanity. For example, in December 1819, in the 1st session of the 16th Congress, a bill was introduced "to authorize certain insane persons to be placed on the pension list and for guardians to receive pensions" (H.R. 28). Several of the early references also described more overtly constructed disability in the form of restrictions placed on Southerners after the Civil War. Following this early history, disability policy expanded into its own policy subsystem with considerably more scope and depth than found in early political discourse.

Agenda heterogeneity combined with episodic dominance exists in most policy subsystems. Whereas changes in understandings of disability (if not outright shifts in paradigms) happen, interpreting disability policy history simply as a succession of different policy agendas represents an oversimplification of a complex living history. Furthermore, especially given the goal of understanding and ultimately making positive use of interactions between types of disability policy agendas, it is important to resist a temptation to think of agendas as evolutionary successions or being inherently mutually exclusive.

Broad historical trends were common to the development of the disability policy subsystems in modern democracies. Prevalence in rights-based policy increased over the course of the twentieth century. Nevertheless, most disability policy remained care-oriented. Furthermore, as suggested in the descriptions of the basic agenda types, celebration-oriented policy has a much less established independent history. Formulation of celebration-oriented policy, where present, often occurs at subnational levels of government. Celebration-oriented agendas also tend to be secondary agendas in much of modern disability policy, as opposed to the primary focus of the policy itself. Finally, whereas virtually no federal disability policy existed at the beginning of the twentieth century, by the century's end functional differences had been addressed in virtually all areas of domestic policy. The full effect of this rapid-fire policy innovation remains unknown.

* * *

The next six chapters discuss the relationships and dynamics between the four types of policy agendas. Each chapter considers a pair of agenda types. Of course, in the disability policy subsystems of modern nations, agenda types interact in combinations of threes and sometimes all at once. Nevertheless, examination of the basic binary relationships helps to structure thinking about the complex dynamics between all agenda types in disability policy subsystems.

Notes

1. Human rights are sometimes described as including civil and political rights as well. For the purposes of this text, it is useful to consider human and civil rights separately, as they tend to be most actively pursued and articulated differently in the disability policy subsystem, particularly in policy associated with the cure and care agenda types.

2. In the case of the Americans with Disabilities Act in the United States, this perception involves additional distortion of policy because accommodations required under the act must be "reasonable" in order to be considered necessary. The policy was intentionally developed so as to avoid causing undue financial hardship on those required to make accommodations.

3. The designation of a year as a minimum time period for designation of disability creates some severe challenges in the United States, especially given that the primary policy instrument for employment leave on the basis of disease, the Family and Medical Leave Act, limits such leave to twelve weeks per year.

3

Securing Civil Rights
vs. Providing Care

Dynamics between cause- and care-oriented agendas create opportunities for fascinating public and political discourse, particularly in democracies with market-based economies. Interactions between these agenda types tend to revolve around the relationship between evolving understandings of disability and intricacies of construction of individual identity in the modern world. The individual is the dominant unit of analysis employed in the theories of both neoclassical economics and democracy. As a result, dynamics between cure and care agenda types touch on philosophical underpinnings of modern societies extending well beyond disability policy subsystems. Furthermore, since operation of both market-based economies and democratic governance fundamentally assumes individual-level independence, participants in both are expected to exist willfully without limitations of major life functions.

Despite this, modern societies value collective experience to a degree largely unknown in human history. Community, while rarely understood exactly the same way by two different people, is deliberately treasured and actively engaged as a potentially scarce resource. A growing awareness that societies that more successfully cultivate social capital thrive, while those less successful in this endeavor falter, exists in modern times (Putnam 2001; Gladwell 2008). Despite our frequent despair over human progress and our enthusiastic publicity surrounding implementation mishaps, on the whole we plan and provide constant care to one another to a previously unimagined scope and degree.

This behavior strengthens modern societies. As Andrew Fenton and Tim Krahn put it, "recognition of interdependence motivates the construction and maintenance of social institutions that protect the vulnerable and enhance the opportunities of the dispossessed" (2007, 4). Nevertheless, balancing rights and needs of individuals and communities represents a fundamental challenge in democracies. Examination of public and political discourse focusing on care and cure clarifies our understanding of this reality of modern society in addition to providing a more complete picture of the politics of neurodiversity and neurological difference.

Using Rights to Give and Receive Care in the Public Sector

Care is involvement of another person in an activity that could, under other circumstances, be completed by the individual alone. From the standpoint of public policy and for the purposes of public agendas of disability, care refers to such involvement on the part of the state. As happens in most areas of policy, programmatic mechanisms of publicly provided care vary considerably.

For starters, in modern industrialized nations, publicly provided care habitually involves direct provision of public funds to natural caregivers. For example, in the United States, tax expenditures include deductions on personal income tax to individuals caring for children. Another common form involves tax subsidization of community groups—notably faith-based organizations in the United States—understood as at least partially designed to provide care for community members. These forms of care policy have become so ingrained in modern democracies that they are not consciously considered as part of social welfare policy by the general public.

Of course, direct government provision involving publicly financed programs directly employing individuals to provide specifically defined care also exists. While the rest of the general public tends to ignore specifics of such policies unless and until they need them, the existence and nature of policies creating direct government provision of care inspire widespread concern in most modern democracies. In the United States, nineteenth- and twentieth-century policies generally employed less overt policy mechanisms (such as tax expenditures) when publicly providing care to the general population than when providing care to those considered members of the deserving poor, including individuals with disabilities.

Valuing Individuals

This difference in strategy reflects deference to a fundamental cultural illusion, particularly present in the United States, that the self-sufficient possess higher value because they do not engage care. Capitalist societies encourage thinking about individuals in terms of their estimated cost or benefit to society. Ideally, members of society pass their lives providing net benefit to society. In this way of thinking, people do not necessarily have intrinsic value. Rather they acquire or lose value on the basis of their ability to generate wealth or provide labor to the economy and the state. By extension, population growth tends to be reflexively considered a national liability rather than an asset, despite the fact that such growth is at least potentially helpful both to economies and to the implementation of policies involving intergenerational transfers toward the elderly (such as Social Security in the United States).

A couple of core ironies emerge from this mode of valuation of members of society. First of all, past societies, which generally afforded less sustained concern to rights of individuals, nevertheless tended to consider people as inherently valuable. Even young children and old slaves could be considered evidence of wealth. Part of the difference comes from a tendency to employ household, family, or tribe as the basic political and economic unit of analysis in traditional societies. The modern concept of the individual as distinct and separable from family is a historically recent innovation and foreign to most human experience. In other words, in coming to specifically value individuals, human beings lost intrinsic economic value. Of course, substantial social benefits accompany the disappearance of consideration of human beings as commodities!

Operation of capitalist systems depends entirely on individual needs. At the most basic level, economic theory rests on exchanges between producers and consumers driven by economic (hu)man's opportunity to increase individual utility through acquisition of the specific goods and services that producers supply (Weimar and Vining 2005). Without demand, economic trade falters or even vanishes. Rudimentary economic theory does not fully distinguish between necessities of survival and needs perhaps more proximate to greed. Operation of a capitalist economic system depends on need-based demands. Despite our illusive preference for individuals without need of care, for a market economy to function we need each other's needs because needs create demand. As a result, the simultaneous need for needs and need to be without needs creates tension between cause and cure agenda types.

For most of human history, care became a less urgent policy agenda type because care obligations assigned to the many made formulation and implementation of cause-oriented policy possible for a select few. A general lack of human and civil rights for individuals who were not wealthy males of socially preferred ethnic background existed in the past. Simplification of private decisions surrounding care took place through strict control of social roles and oppression of the vast majority of human beings, either through generally immutable assignment to lower social position or through outright slavery. Such social conventions allowed for a definition of individual freedom that excluded both a (perceived) need for care provided by those entitled to rights and any obligation of the entitled few to directly provide care for others. Care provided by those not free held no relevance to the construction of freedom of other individuals. A final dynamic affecting care and cause agenda types in modern disability policy subsystems results from expansion of rights to ideally include all persons and the associated loosening of class restrictions (Ishay 2008). As a result of this dynamic, public care provision and its associated policy also becomes a locus of tension between rights of different individuals in modern societies.

Rights to Gendering (and Degendering) Care

Care rooted in obligation represents an essential privilege of human life. Forging and maintaining vital and invigorating connections to family and friends involves providing regular care to others on a more or less voluntary basis. Despite this, providing care for loved ones more often than not becomes taxing at some point. Once upon a time, management of this fact took place through irrevocable assignment of primary responsibility for care to women. Girls were taught of a fundamental connection between caregiving and womanhood, thereby rendering less feminine those who chose not to provide care and minimizing complaints raised by overwhelmed care providers.

Women tend to still be the primary caregivers, at least within relationships involving the care of those with higher level needs, such as children and those with atypical functionalities resulting in disability. Nevertheless, ongoing emancipation of women over the past two centuries complicated this ancient solution to challenges found in disability policy subsystems (MacIntyre 2008). As Camilla Stivers explained, "Provision of care becomes complicated in the modern life style. Feminist theory sees the barrier between public and private, erected ostensibly to protect the freedom of all, as supportive of the oppression of many. In a space constructed out of the exclusion of half of the human race, as long as this exclusion remains unexamined no heroism of practice is possible" (Shafritz and Hyde 2007, 477). As a result, the rights of those providing care rest increasingly in tension with the rights of those needing care in the modern world.

One resolution of this tension involves professionalization of care. Paid employment, though certainly not optional for most adults, constitutes a voluntary relationship. One person agreeing to carry out unusual tasks for the sake of another's needs does not violate either person's rights so long as the services exchanged break no laws and involve proper compensation. Debate arises on this principle as a result of a widespread tendency to pay unusually low wages to professional caregivers, and because professionalized caring relationships sometimes become unnecessarily paternalistic, if not exploitive (Pfeiffer 1993; Gornick et al. 2009). These circumstances may become especially likely to occur within institutional settings.

Such settings enjoyed particular popularity during the nineteenth and twentieth centuries. Individuals with disabilities were hardly alone in this experience. For example, as David Rothman (2002) describes, tremendous popularity of institutional settings for a variety of disenfranchised groups took hold in the United States beginning in the early nineteenth century as part of a shift in general attitudes toward the management of (perceived and real) danger in society. A brief overview of the history of institutionalization and deinstitutionalization in Western democracies is included later in this chapter. The historical account provided in this book employs a broad brush, glossing over many fascinating historical details and debates as well as a genuine need for much more historical research into the meaning and implications of deinstitutionalization (Felce 2006). The overview herein is intended to provide just enough historical information to permit comprehension of the deep roots of modern disability policy tensions.

Institutional professionalization of caregiving relationships remains the predominant solution to tensions between the rights of the carer and the rights of the individual receiving care. In some cases, this resolution even involves professionalization of natural caregivers, such as family members of individuals with disabilities, paid by governments to provide care specifically associated with functional differences. As Harold Pollack (2007) explained, public acceptance of such policy provisions tends to exist when it comes to neurological differences even when absent given other circumstances:

> A key political dilemma of traditional AFDC [Aid to Families with Dependent Children] was that voters and policymakers wished to help low-income children but seemed unhappy about the prospect of subsidizing the unmarried mothers with whom most such children lived. No such dilemmas arose in intellectual disability. Drawn from a broad cross section of society, family caregivers have been performing an honored, increasingly public role. (96)

Pollack went on to describe the political capital (in the form of both resources and ability to gain attention at all levels of government) amassed by
such caregivers as "impressive" (2007, 96). Professionalization of care helps
negotiate tensions between cause- and cure-oriented agendas in the disability policy subsystem. However, day-to-day negation of this relationship
can itself create tensions in the articulation of rights of individuals with disabilities and their professional caregivers because of the difficulty in establishing boundaries and of continually implementing practices that honor the
rights of both individuals.

Creating Lifespan and Intergenerational Equity

Another dynamic related to this valuing of individuals involved generational and lifespan differences. Cause and care agenda types have been particularly affected by time and timing because their policies and programs
sometimes become (or are perceived as) mutually exclusive in the context
of constrained public resources. Transition toward increased community inclusion of individuals with disabilities impacted public care infrastructures
that older individuals with disabilities relied upon (or at least became accustomed to) for decades. Those who preferred older policies and programs
experienced either actual loss or fear of loss of public resources.

This aspect of social change exists beyond the disability policy subsystem. For example, in the United States, welfare policy once rested on
the assumed importance of keeping mothers at home. With changing expectations of female participation in the work force (as well as a perceived
change in the behavior preceding participation in public welfare), the social
goal moved toward rapid entry or reentry of mothers into the paid work
force. This change in expectation validated economic emancipation of
women, but nevertheless also involved a feeling of loss on the part of mothers missing the historically protected opportunity to stay at home with their
young children. The fact that some individuals within a target population of
policy change experience loss even with the seemingly most beneficial of
policy changes is routinely ignored in political discourse of disability policy subsystems and beyond.

Children vs. Adult "Children"

One of the most striking sources of intergenerational conflict shaping the relationship between cause- and care-oriented public agendas surrounds grow-

ing distance between the interests of children and so-called adult children brought on in part as a result of deinstitutionalization and other late-twentieth-century disability policy innovations. Though the phrase "adult children" is an oxymoron, it is routinely employed to describe adults with living parents, particularly when the adult in question has a neurological difference or other disability. Part of the intent of the phrase involves acknowledgment of the fact that active parenting extends far beyond an offspring's eighteenth birthday, arguably especially when the offspring in question has a neurological difference that either slows or restricts development of fully matured decisionmaking capacities.[1]

As a result of deinstitutionalization movements, institutionalized populations declined and were perceived by many to have diminished to the point of possible extinction. Many institutions dwindled toward actual or threatened closure. As this happened, parents of adult residents of institutions began to fear the future. Many of these parents, most of whom were by that time well into the age of retirement, could not imagine a world in which their children successfully lived outside of the institution. They had a point, particularly in the case of people with developmental disabilities who had spent the majority (if not all) of their lives in the institutional settings, embodying the only lifestyle that they knew. Destroying this kind of community represented a loss for these individuals.

Parents of these adult "children" with disabilities often became reasonably preoccupied by their own mortality. In meetings with parents of younger children, they would hear of the potential of community inclusion, but also thoroughly understood the work and planning involved in the successful creation of community inclusion. Furthermore, parents began to fear that their "children's" institutions would close sometime after the parent died, leaving their utterly unprepared offspring alone with insufficient planning and support. As a result, elderly parents began to politically mobilize to support continuation of institutions and the disability policy infrastructures that supported their survival. Instances of busloads of senior citizens showing up wearing buttons with pictures of their adult "children" to testify at public meetings were reported. This became especially common in the United States following the Supreme Court's 1999 Olmstead decision, which asserted a broad right to receive community-based care as opposed to institutionalization.

In many cases, such events put these parents in direct opposition with parents of young children or of slightly older children who had been more or less successfully included in public schools. Calls for protection of institutions tended to strike fear into younger parents' hearts (not to mention parents of slightly older children and adolescents with neurological differ-ences who interpreted such calls as being for their own institutionaliza-tion). After all, if the decline of institutionalized populations were interpreted as problematic, one simple answer would be to repopulate them. Furthermore, especially as the deinstitutionalization movement revealed the complexity of planning and funding community-based services, stake-holders primarily focused on younger generations of people with neuro-logical differences became (all too often correctly) concerned that their cause-oriented programs would be placed in direct political opposition to those of the traditional institutional care. Since the political tenacity of sen-ior citizens represents a well-known phenomenon of modern democracies, concern arose that discourse in support of needs of older "children" would drown out consideration of the needs of the young in the name of political expediency.

Aging and Disability

As individuals age, particularly as they become elderly, need for care be-comes increasingly universal. Decline associated with age can become dis-ability, but the attitudes, needs, and positions of the elderly may not be adequately represented by cause-oriented agendas nor fully addressed by care agendas more focused on younger populations. As Tom Shakespeare pointed out, "in western countries approximately half of all people with im-pairments are over the age of 50 . . . yet most activists enter the movement at a much younger age, and older people who have impairments neither make up a significant proportion of the movement, nor are likely to identify with a civil rights perspective" (2006, 74–75). Embracing disability status as a cause appears trickier for those with late onset of disability, especially when the disability connects to a disease likely to ultimately prove fatal. For example, an individual with Alzheimer's, while certainly experiencing neurological differences, likely interprets the relationship between cause and care quite differently than a younger person with a neurological differ-ence. Furthermore, given the (relatively) rapid changes in perception of dis-ability over the past several decades, it is now difficult to tease out which observed differences between the currently young and elderly are associ-ated with transcendent differences in lifespan experiences and which result from divergent generational experiences. Public and political discourses of cause- and cure-oriented agendas tend to present contradictory interpreta-tions of this balance in modern disability policy subsystems.

Language Differences

In public and political discourse surrounding neurological differences and neurodiversity, a nascent intergenerational debate surrounds the issue of language used to discuss disability. Since the 1970s, disability scholars and activists as well as the vast majority of nonmedical professionals who work with people with disabilities have increasingly promoted use of people-first language to describe people with functional differences. The basic argument is that individuals with disabilities cannot be defined primarily by their functional differences. Using disability-based descriptors such as "retarded" or "autistic" became understood as reflective of old discriminatory practices that employed such language to exclude individuals with functional differences from the rest of the general population. In some cases, failure to use people-first language has been interpreted as being stand-alone evidence of discriminatory intent and a reason to dismiss the speaker as an enemy of the cause of people with disabilities. Failing to use people-first language has even been described as a way to ruin people's lives (Snow 2008). The rhetorical question asked in the promotion of people-first language is usually something along the lines of, "Do you want to be known primarily by your psoriasis, gynecological history or warts on your behind?" (Snow 2008). For activists of the baby boom and early generation-X generations, the presumptive answer to the question has been a firm no.

Use of people-first language is unevenly applied in public discourse. For example, in a study of the discussion of people with intellectual disabilities in the British press during the last decades of the twentieth century, Penny Wilkinson and Peter McGill found that "more 'people-first' terminology was now used except in respect to people with autism" (2009, 65). Similarly, B. Haller, B. Dorries, and J. Rahn (2006) found that the use of people-first language in the *New York Times* and *Washington Post* increased during the 1990s.

In recent years, however, some younger activists have sought to reclaim disability-first language as part of their political engagement of neurological difference and neurodiversity. Rejection of people-first language—or at least of the exclusivity of person-first language—is particularly common among individuals with neurological differences connected to neurodiversity movements (see, for example, Smukler 2005). A basic assertion is that the disability composes a fundamental element of personality, similar to gender. The rhetorical question asked tends to be, "Do you think of yourself as a person with femaleness or a woman?" This shift in language indicates different stages in the evolution of cause-oriented public agendas. It also reflects increased experience with care programs involving at least the possibility of allowing for self-actualization rather than the oppressive care environments almost universally experienced by previous generations. The shift in language highlights intergenerational tensions and misunderstandings similar to moves to reclaim racial epithets (though thus far the tension surrounding use of language in the context of disability is nowhere near as divisive).

A Tension of Ethical Foundations

Another ongoing dynamic in the relationship between cause and care agendas results from what Tom Shakespeare describes as a tension of ethics. As he points out, "the ethic of care is based on relationships and responsibilities, while the ethic of rights is based on rights and rules . . . the former emerges from concrete circumstances, rather than formal or abstract situations . . . finally, the ethic of care depends on activity, while the ethic of rights depends on principles" (2006, 144). In other words, difficulties arise in joint consideration of care and cause agendas because they most intimately connect to radically different areas of policy with divergent institutional histories. Despite the fact that both areas of policy involve public and political discussion about the lives of individuals with disabilities, the two agendas do not directly relate to each other and therefore are not subject to easy combination into a single policy.

Target population differs from policy purpose. Considering the two together in discourse bears resemblance to considering policy about child safety seats in cars and elementary school class size in tandem simply because both involve young children as their target population. Of course, in the case of disability policy subsystems, this ethical distinction becomes less clear in the minds of many because of the positive rights basis of some of the policies and the associated changes in habits and infrastructure. These cause-oriented policies can be perceived as providing care to those having to adapt away from exclusionary habits.

One way in which mitigation of conflict between these two agendas takes place involves an openness to (if not insistence upon) active participation on the part of individuals with neurological differences in the development of care plans. For example, in a discussion in the British House of Commons in May 2006 during which the question of ongoing design and implementation of a national service plan for long-term neurological care was raised, the secretary of health officially responded:

> The Department is coordinating a range of activity to support national and local implementation of the national service framework (NSF) for long-term neurological conditions . . . this includes: working with key national health service, social care, voluntary and independent sector stakeholders, as well as service users and carers, to identify and address key issues in neurological services and the stakeholders' role in implementation; ensuring that other key delivery programmes, most especially the White Paper "Our Health, Our Care, Our Say" and the long-term conditions strategy help deliver key NSF objectives; and work to support local delivery, including regional implementation workshops, a web-based getting started pack and self-assessment tool for services through the Care Services Improvement Partnership to provide practical help to local health and social care organizations. (www.publications.parliament .uk/pa/cm200506/cmhansrd/vo060524/text/60524w0023.htm)

Such involvement of individuals with neurological differences in political discourse has proven challenging. However, a healthy motivation and desire to do so exists in most modern democracies.

Instrumental Reactions

The relationship between cause and care agenda types also includes a belief on the part of many activists that most care programs have represented little more than poor substitutes for necessary cause-oriented policy (Charlton 2000). This was especially the case in many Western democracies during the 1970s and early 1980s. As Samuel Bagenstos (2004) explained:

> From the left, many disability rights activists contended that disability welfare programs promoted political quiescence among people with disabilities. They argued that disability welfare programs are essentially symbolic government acts . . . instead of making fundamental changes to social relations or the built environment that would allow people with disabilities to achieve actual integration and equality in society, the nondisabled majority uses relatively small cash benefits as a means of dulling any urge among people with disabilities to protest existing power arrangements . . . from the right, many disability rights activists argued that welfare programs promoted a culture of dependence among people with disabilities. (15)

In other words, care became interpreted as a form of pandering to current economic infrastructures and social preferences that were standing in the way of inclusionary changes to these systems as articulated in cause-oriented political discourse. In the extreme, care-oriented policy became just another barrier to inclusive social infrastructures that could not, therefore, effectively coexist with cause agenda types.

Pondering Place over Time:
Joint Articulation of Cause and Care Agenda Types

Political and public discourse surrounding cause- and care-oriented agendas focused on a broad spectrum of specific policy questions over the past couple of centuries. Of these questions, however, arguably the most illustrative surrounded movements to institutionalize and subsequently deinstitutionalize individuals with neurological differences. A quick look at the development of these movements reveals key dynamics between these two agenda types.

Care-Driven Cause: The Rise of the Institutions

Removal of individuals with functional differences from mainstream society has a long, often tragic history. Plato's *The Republic* includes the recommendation to put away children of inferior people as well as the deformed (Roberts 2009). In Europe, formal removal policies date back to at least the middle ages (Scotch 2001). Later, as Michel Foucault described in *Madness and Civilization* (1973), facilities originally created to quarantine people with leprosy were repurposed to house those with neurological differences. Especially during the seventeenth century, these incarcerations cast a wide net, in some areas confining as much as 1 percent of the general population. According to Foucault, a prime motivator for this effort was the disappearance of leprosy from Europe and an attendant need to keep institutions running for economic purposes.

For the most part, medical and therapeutic care was sparsely provided in these settings, if at all. When provided, procedures were largely based on superstition and misinformation rather than on proven practice rooted in scientific understanding of neurological differences. The primary purpose of these asylums was to remove from the general population (and then often ritualistically display) people with neurological differences. Later, this tradition continued in the New World. For example, as A. Rosen explained about Australia during the early nineteenth century, "people with mental illness were confined in irons on ships (including grounded wrecked ship hulks) and in jails alongside troublesome convicts" (2006, 82).

Care agenda types emerged partially in response to this history, to some extent motivated by the desire to arrest social tendencies to forcefully abandon or actively destroy individuals with functional atypicalities. A change in perception of humanity supported this desire, connected to an emerging understanding of genetics and evolution. Institutions as locations of specifically planned, scientifically based care, formulated in political discourse, were largely an invention of the nineteenth and twentieth centuries. For example, in Great Britain, the Lunacy Commission was first created in 1845. Under the 1913 Lunacy Act, asylums sought to separate out individuals with neurological differences for the explicit purpose of ensuring their exclusion from the human gene pool. In fact, the Mental Deficiency Act of the same year included a provision "for the detention in long-stay hospitals of women with mental deficiencies who bore illegitimate children" (MacIntyre 2008).

Removal of individuals with neurological differences was a fashionable topic in popular culture of the time. Many books and, later, movies addressed the subject of families replete with members with neurological differences reproducing at a rate outpacing the rest of the general population. Among the most famous examples of this genre was *The Kallikak Family: A Study in the Heredity of Feeble-Mindedness* (1912) by Henry Goddard. The book traced the descendants of a soldier in the Revolutionary War dubbed by Goddard "Martin Kallikak." According to Goddard, Kallikak fathered two families—one legitimate and the other with a barmaid described as having a neurological difference. In the book, Goddard compares and contrasts the two resulting family trees, arguing that the legitimate side of the family produced morally upstanding, high-quality citizens, whereas the other side produced generations of offspring prone only to crime and poverty due to what he described as genetic feeblemindedness. *The Kallikak Family* enjoyed wild popularity, making Goddard one of the leading voices in public and political discourse on neurological differences in the United States in the early twentieth century.

Arguments for Institutions
Expressing Care-Oriented Agendas

Formal explanations for existence of institutions for people with neurological differences varied. However, according to Alexandra Hamlin and Peter Oakes (2008, 49–50), general types of arguments characterized most public discourse when it came to developing institutions for people with intellectual disabilities. Hamlin and Oakes's list includes: protecting people with intellectual disabilities; protecting members of the wider community; protecting society as a whole; powerlessness of people with intellectual disabilities; that individuals with neurological disabilities were less than human and therefore required special management or treatment; and that individuals with neurological differences were unable to contribute to society.

Public and political discourse surrounding provision of care developed alongside nature and nurture arguments about the human condition in industrialized countries. For the most part, the nature versus nurture debate rages less forcefully today than it once did. According to Jonah Lehrer: "By demonstrating the limits of genetic determinism, the Human Genome Project ended up becoming an ironic affirmation of our individuality . . . By failing to explain us, the project showed us that humanity is not simply a text . . . it forced molecular biology to focus on how our genes interact with the real world . . . Our nature, it turns out, is endlessly modified by our nurture" (2007, 45). Nowadays, a general understanding of a joint effect dominates (that is, relevance lies in how nature is nurtured). Nevertheless, debate remains as to the degree to which a person's individual experiences become shaped by their genetics or by their environment. In the public and political discourse surrounding care and cause agenda types, popular interpretations of this distinction have often proven especially influential.

During the late nineteenth and early twentieth centuries, care agendas within disability policy subsystems involved proponents of both sides of the nature-nurture debate. This divided political discourse created internal inconsistencies in purposes and practices of institutions. For those who believed deeply in the nature side of the debate, institutions represented a vital component of social protection and improvement of the human race. Proponents argued that individuals with socially undesired atypical functionalities needed to have their rights restricted primarily to halt their reproduction, either through surgical intervention or through social control within institutions that deliberately limited heterosexual interactions. The policy problem was defined as managing propagation of deficiency. This problem definition generally contained a concern about potential contagion or contamination of the gene pool. Whether articulated directly or not, undesired characteristics were routinely publicly discussed as though dominant in the Mendelian genetics sense.

For those who believed in the nature side of the debate, on the other hand, institutions provided an important opportunity to change the environment of individuals with undesired functional differences. Proponents of the nurture side of the debate believed that deliberately planned surroundings could result in a dramatic reduction of differences in functionality (particularly if careful attention was paid to the supposed moral elements of environments). If the difference itself resisted elimination through access to a more beneficial environment given the proper setting, individuals could be coached to effectively "pass" so that their differences might go undetected by the general population. Of course, for the vast majority of individuals entering into the institutional population, a return to the general population was neither genuinely expected nor experienced (Lamb and Bachrach 2001). As a result, institutionalization became, for a remarkable proportion of the population, a fully separate way of life.

Institutionalization also became an alternative way of life in the minds of the rest of the general population, who embraced this exception to the convention of democratic self-sufficiency. Both the nurture and nature philosophical strains assumed necessity of reduction or elimination of contact between the individual with the functional difference and his or her family and community of origin. This confluence of purpose interacted symbiotically with other social changes promoting the professionalization of caring in Western societies. Policy innovations produced as a result of caring-as-cause public discourse included growth of regulatory standards and professional licensure. As a result, public institutions designed to provide care on the basis of disability grew prolifically in much of the industrialized world. As Roy Grinker explained about the United States, "most of these institutions were less than thirty years old, but by 1904, 2 in every 1,000 Americans lived in one . . . by mid-century, more than 500,000 Americans lived in mental institutions, more than 3 in every 1,000" (2007, 37). In the United States, the population of institutionalized individuals peaked at 559,000 people in 1955 (out of a population of 165 million people) (Lamb and Bachrach 2001), with an admission of 178,000 individuals in that year alone (Gros 2005).

During the era of institutionalization, populations of Western countries came to expect that individuals with neurological differences would be systematically (and generally permanently) removed from society. For parents of children with neurological differences, pressure to institutionalize often began early—sometimes as early as birth in the case of visible neurological differences such as Down syndrome (Haslam and Milner 1992). Parents of children with neurological differences were sometimes directly punished if they did not institutionalize them. For example, in the state of Washington, parents were fined if they kept so-called feebleminded children out of institutions (Pelka 1997). Public and political discourse surrounding this removal involved the notion of stewardship of both the individual and the rest of society. The idea was that professional caring constituted the only way to protect individuals with problematic neurological differences, by removing them from the pressures of day-to-day life while at the same time protecting other members of society from harm expected to be perpetrated either directly or incidentally by these individuals. Professional care was also believed to protect families from the presumed overwhelming burden of caring for children and young adults with disabilities. As a result, professionally provided care was believed a more humane approach and more in keeping with the protection of the rights of both individuals with neurological differences and those without. This conclusion held for all individuals with neurological differences, but especially for those with mental illnesses (unless the individual happened to be very wealthy).

Particularly when presented as simultaneously addressing cause-oriented agendas, it is vital to remember that perceived necessity of institutionalization was not limited to those whose individual behavior had been deemed individually problematic as a result of identifiable incidents. According to Mary Johnson, in the United States "as late as the early 1990s, some states still had laws on their books requiring the institutionalization of people with mental disabilities" (2003, 101), which could be uniformly implemented regardless of the specific abilities, circumstances, experiences, or behavior of the particular individual. Furthermore, children with disabilities were barred from many public schools until the 1970s (Armstrong 2010), thereby providing additional incentives for parents and primary caregivers to seek or accept institutionalization of young people with differences. After all, at that time, institutionalization often became the only publicly provided source of services for children with neurological differences. In the context of caring-as-cause in public discourse, rights of individuals with disabilities were primarily discussed as access to specifically planned treatment. Since without institutionalization there was no perceived possibility of access to such rights, institutionalization became a cause agenda in both public and political discourse of the era. This confounding inspired suspicion between those advocating cause and care agenda types, which continues to be present in modern politics of neurodiversity.

During this period, rights of individuals with neurological differences became portrayed as fully encompassed by professionally planned care, generally in an institutional setting. Social responsibility became understood as ensuring the existence of facilities. This conception of social responsibility continued well beyond the end of the period of institutional growth in many countries. Ultimately, this expectation of removal persisted among some members of society even when the perception of rights changed. As H. Richard Lamb and Leona Bachrach explained, "society has a limited tolerance for mentally disordered behavior and the result is pressure to institutionalize persons who need 24-hour care wherever there is room, including jail" (2001, 1042). Under institutionalization, care and cause became co-defined as a (separate) place for individuals with neurological differences. Though planning for care provision would be ideal, it did not precede the question of place. Interestingly, this basic reality of place before planning also framed public discourse on deinstitutionalization.

Cause-Driven Care: Deinstitutionalization

Deinstitutionalization sought to return individuals with neurological (and other) disabilities to the community. Deinstitutionalization involves three primary components: "the release of these individuals from hospitals into the community, their diversion from hospital admission, and the development of alternative community services" (Lamb and Bachrach 2001, 1039). As implemented, deinstitutionalization became a blunt-force policy instrument focused almost exclusively on (ideally rapid) movement of people.

Deinstitutionalization began in earnest in the middle of the twentieth century for those with mental health diagnoses, and a generation or so later for those with developmental disabilities. The process unfolded unevenly. For example, as Marina Morrow and Brenda Jamer explain, "although psychiatric deinstitutionalization is a process which began in Europe and North America in the late 1950s and peaked in the 70s, the process was slowed, in part, because of the abysmal failure on the part of governments to provide community based supports to people leaving institutions, including adequate housing and sources of income" (2008, 2). Looking internationally, as J. Beadle-Brown, J. Mansell, and A. Kozma point out, "the process of deinstitutionalization for intellectual disability services is at different stages across the world, varying from complete closure in Sweden to a vague hope in Taiwan" (2007, 437). In Canada, on the other hand, according to Patricia Sealy and Paul Whitehead, "the deinstitutionalization of psychiatric services has in fact been continuous for the past 40 years" (2004, 249). In another study, Mark Salzer, Katy Kaplan, and Joanne Atay found that in the United States, "state hospital census continues to decline but has slowed significantly during the post-Olmstead period" (2006, 1501). On the whole, modern industrialized nations have demonstrated at least some level of commitment to deinstitutionalization (Emerson 2004b). Persuasive evidence of cost savings at the individual level as a result of deinstitutionalization exists (see, for example, Hayden, Larson, and Lakin 2002, and the annual reports produced by the Research and Training Center on Community Living, available at http://rtc.umn.edu/main). Furthermore, outcomes for individuals with neurological differences who are engaged in community-based services have improved substantially over time (Lakin, Prouty, and Coucouvanis 2006).

However, the politics of deinstitutionalization involved significant debate and, particularly as an ongoing public exercise, becomes subject to much historical revision. Perhaps unsurprisingly, the pace of deinstitutionalization slowed over time (Lakin et al. 2004). Some even question if deinstitutionalization in fact took place. For example, in an article titled "The Last Half-Century of Psychiatric Services as Reflected in *Psychiatric Services*," Jeffrey Geller "uses the term 'dehospitalization' to describe the movement of patients out of state hospitals, reject[ing] the widely used term 'deinstitutionalization' as inappropriate; one reason is that the term implies that the many settings where the patients ended up were not institutional" (Geller 2000, 41). This interpretation reflects the focus on characterization of place as only one of many equally important aspects of cause-oriented agenda types.

Political Motivations for Deinstitutionalization

Explanations of the prime mover for deinstitutionalization vary, but tend to include increasingly effective rights-based disability activism; fiscal concerns; changes in the labor force after World War II; the (at least perceived) success of military professionals in treating soldiers who experienced mental illnesses during the war, thereby allowing them to return to active duty; and pharmaceutical innovations demonstrating preliminary mitigation of undesired elements of neurological difference once considered intractable.

As is the case with most big change taking place in relatively small policy subsystems, it is likely that these factors all played a part, with differing levels of influence across time, space, and the separate perceptions of issue stakeholders. What seems clear is that single-factor explanations—notably either innovations in medications or changes in attitudes—are incomplete. For example, as Enric Novella (2008) points out:

> As many different epidemiological studies have repeatedly shown, the reduction of inmate population and the increase in number of patients discharged from mental hospitals had already begun in many countries before

the generalized introduction of neuroleptic drugs . . . Data from the U.S., for instance, showed that whereas the absolute number of mental hospital residents peaks in 1955—one year after the introduction of drug treatment—the rate of hospital use—i.e., the proportion of the general population treated in mental hospitals—peaked in 1945. (306)

It is worth noting that one explanation less frequently mentioned as a motivating factor for public and political deinstitutionalization discourse is the novel aversion to anything associated with eugenics that emerged alongside growing public awareness of the atrocities of the Holocaust. As the scope of the Nazi efforts with regard to the so-called purification of the human race became more known, willingness of the vast majority of people and organizations to become even remotely associated with eugenics efforts quickly vanished.

A similar argument has been made about motivations for changing attitudes toward the rights of ethnic minorities in the United States during the same time period. For example, in *The Pursuit of Fairness: A History of Affirmative Action,* Terry Anderson (2004) explains:

The war laid the foundation for the future Civil Rights movement. African American military experiences wounded Jim Crow. The "master race" had lost the war, which discredited the idea of racial superiority, especially as allied soldiers liberated German concentration camps, and magazines published photographs of emaciated Jews and other prisoners. The release of film footage of the Holocaust, and the subsequent war crimes trials at Nuremberg had a profound impact on most Americans. (37)

Since eugenics arguments routinely came into play in discourse supporting creation of institutions, conversion of political discourse toward deinstitutionalization philosophy likely connected to a widespread desire to destroy evidence of both individual and communal association with eugenics philosophy.

Movement toward deinstitutionalization came about as a result of change in prevailing public and political discourse rather than empirical evidence of community-based successes in inclusion of individuals with neurological differences in society. Though some evidence of success existed, such as the aforementioned return of some affected soldiers to active duty, acceptance that individuals traditionally confined to institutional settings would do better with appropriate community-based services started out as an article of faith rather than a conviction based on empirical evidence. As Gerald Gros described it with regard to individuals with mental illnesses, deinstitutionalization "represented the triumph of ideology over reality, for it

ignored the context in which persons with severe and persistent mental illnesses received care" (2005, 425).[2]

This is not surprising. Obviously, one fundamental challenge facing
many cause-oriented public agendas is that direct evidence of the benefits
of a just society becomes difficult to locate in the absence of justice. This
represents an ongoing dynamic with care-oriented political discourse, since
evidence of harm created through unsuccessful inclusion is rather easy to
come by. The argument that "this is just the way things (or people) are" all
too often persuades a retreat toward traditions of exclusionary care. For example, in the United States, parents of children with neurological differences are routinely warned during Individualized Education Program
meetings of the likelihood of their child being bullied if included in classrooms with typical peers. This often motivates placement of children in the
care-oriented environment (special education rooms) as opposed to the
cause-oriented environment, with or without community-based supports
(the general education classroom, with or without accommodations). As
John Talbot explained several decades ago, however, being an article of
faith does not automatically imply inaccuracy: "there is sufficient evidence
that deinstitutionalization's failures were not due to ideological or philosophical deficiencies . . . failures were due to implementation of the underlying ideas" (1979, 1114). Over time, much evidence of successful
deinstitutionalization accumulated as policies and programs became more
sophisticated (Emerson 2004a).

Nevertheless, it was an exceedingly compelling article of faith, one that
remains similarly strong today. As Hamlin and Oakes explained, "the arrival of community-based services was expected to give increased choice in
environments that are enriched by opportunities in the field of leisure and
work . . . this in turn was expected to lead to sharp reductions in the extent
to which people with intellectual disabilities express their distress in the
form of what has become known as severe challenging behavior" (2008,
48). Such public and political discourse surrounding deinstitutionalization
still turns on this argument.

Arguments for Deinstitutionalization
Were Primarily Anti-Institution

Deinstitutionalization rests on the assumption that individuals with neurological differences benefit from inclusion in the surrounding community.
Often, the reverse is also assumed, at least as a possibility (Armstrong
2010). Evidence for this argument has consisted primarily of data drawn

from investigation into abusive and inhumane practices sometimes found in institutions. At a minimum, institutions typically severely restricted patients' opportunities to make choices, often including rigid scheduling, limited menu and clothing options, and little variation in organized activities. However, both physical and later chemical restraints were frequently employed to simplify caregiving logistics for large patient populations. In other words, in order to counter arguments of unavoidable harm coming from intractable community-based discrimination, a case for existence of greater harm inside institutions has been largely employed in the place of direct evidence of success in community-based programs. The community has been portrayed as at least the lesser evil (if not the greater good).

Evidence of harm in institutions abounded. Expressions of the extremity of limitations of rights made in the name of care were particularly prolific. Patients were afforded little privacy or access to private property. For example, many institutions housing individuals with neurological differences lined up beds in long rows in large rooms with no curtains or walls between them. As Steven Noll explained, "established to both care for and to control a population of individuals labeled as feeble-minded and deviant, these facilities provided little support and help for patients and quickly devolved into over-crowded, under-funded operations" (2005, 25). Furthermore, individuals living in institutions were often designated "inmates."

Even if given the opportunity to work for pay at the institutions, patients were not initially paid a minimum wage, if at all. As a result, institutions often depended heavily upon the captive labor of patients for their day-to-day operations. In addition to these typical conditions, much more extreme practices (up to and including torture unto death) existed in some institutional settings. Popular movies, such as *One Flew Over the Cuckoo's Nest* (1975), provided starkly memorable images and characters from institutional settings. When exposed to such conditions, individuals in institutions tended to worsen rather than improve over time.

Furthermore, becoming institutionalized was arguably all too easy during the first half of the twentieth century. Unusual or undesired behavior, especially if combined with another characteristic associated with social ostracism such as poverty or membership in minority ethnic groups, could trigger institutionalization. So could too much independence of thought or value preferences on the part of women or minorities. As a result, by mid-century, more people began to question public expenditures on institutions. Although factors such as preliminary successes with pharmaceutical interventions and rights-based activism would become cornerstone arguments in later public and political discourse, populations of institutions began to decline ahead of these changes in political discourse surrounding institutionalization. Furthermore, as the economies of the developed countries expanded after World War II, increased labor demands rendered institutionalization of potential laborers less desirable than it might have been during the decades leading up to the war. Because the pioneering motivations focused on fiscal and economic concerns, initial reductions of populations of institutions largely preceded public deliberation of programs aimed at facilitating the inclusion of individuals with neurological differences in the community at large.

Deinstitutionalization Did Not Include Extensive Planning of Community-Based Services

Most deinstitutionalization initially involved quite minimal planning of community services. Relatively early on, negative implications of deinstitutionalization became obvious. Talbot wrote that as a result of deinstitutionalization, "two new syndromes were described: 'falling between the cracks' and the 'revolving door,' the former indicating a total lack of follow-up and aftercare for discharged patients, and the latter their continued readmissions" (1979, 1113). This came partly from the confounding of cause and care discourses. Since the rhetoric of institutionalization involved a reconception of basic rights into provision of centralized state-run care for individuals with neurological differences, in deinstitutionalization it was somehow expected that the goals of the movement would be accomplished primarily (if not exclusively) through return of individuals with disabilities to communities. The logic applied held that under idealized circumstances, society might become sufficiently inclusive so as to habitually include unusual behavior exhibited by those with neurological differences, without any need for ongoing support provided through care-oriented policy.

However, as Beadle-Brown, Mansell, and Kozma explain, "just moving people out of institutions into community settings does not bring about automatic improvement in quality of life in terms of choice and inclusion as well as self-identity and access to effective healthcare and treatment" (2007, 437). As a result, absence of public and political discourse about community inclusion did not persist. In the United States, planning of community-based services began to take off during the 1970s. Part of the transition to a care-as-cause and cause-as-care discourse involved an expansion of the population theoretically covered by the public policy. Nevertheless, as issue stakeholders proliferated, achieving consensus around specific policy and programmatic goals became more difficult.

Incorporating Discussion of Suffering into Deinstitutionalization Discourse

A rights-based approach to disability policy focused on neurological differences starts with elimination of legal limitations on behavior based solely on (largely learned) preferences of the surrounding society. However, complete recognition of the rights of those with neurological differences as fully functioning members of societies includes a realization that some neurological differences involve suffering on the part of those experiencing them, regardless of social or political infrastructure. Assuming that this suffering lacks internal legitimacy departs from how such feelings are addressed in the rest of the general population. Furthermore, some individuals with neurological differences have underdeveloped or otherwise impaired survival skills, at least compared to the degree expected in other individuals of a similar age. As a result, exercise of the rights of those with neurological differences often falters in the absence of the public provision of targeted care. In order for deinstitutionalization to become something other than another mechanism of social exclusion, it needs to take place in a context of active development of well-planned community-based services.

Unfortunately, most communities struggled with this development. As mentioned, one of the major sources of tensions between cause and care agendas surrounds mechanisms for establishing need for public action in the two agenda types. Particularly in civil rights–oriented traditions, protest of specific discriminatory practices inspires action in cause agendas. It turns on principles and individual choice and behavior, rather than on ongoing collective activities. Once discriminatory actions are stopped, the only needed action on the part of the state is some level of vigilance ensuring that such actions will be punished if repeated.

However, care requires consistent effort. It also naturally recurs in public discourse, because publicly provided care requires public expenditures, which become subject to repeated reconsideration as part of the public budgeting process. Ironically, in the age of institutionalization, sustaining this effort was accomplished through creation of powerful, organized stakeholders. Institutions involved large, publicly funded budgets. Not only were those who owned or operated the institutions natural members of an easily identifiable interest group, but so too were many living in surrounding communities. As has been the case with towns surrounding land-grant universities, prisons, and major factories, institutions became major employers in the towns and areas in which they were located (Levine 2007, 65). Families depending on jobs at institutions developed a vested interest in keeping institutions open. Interests of the local population became intimately connected to those of publicly providing care, thereby simplifying political discourse surrounding neurological differences because locally elected politicians spoke of closing or reducing the size of institutions only at considerable personal political risk.

On the other hand, one of the major challenges of not having large, aggregate, and powerful economic and political interests such as the institutions of the early twentieth century is not having large, aggregate, and powerful economic and political interests. A focus on community-based services necessarily and deliberately involved a preference for small, targeted organizations, each working with relatively small numbers of individuals with neurological differences. Presumably the potential of this model to provide individualized, local, and appropriate care in a community-based setting far exceeded the capacity of any large-scale institution to adapt to a rights-based model rooted in the discourse of rights to individuality. Of course, these smaller organizations involved tiny budgets by comparison to the behemoth organizations found in the old institutional service model. As a result, each individual organization became far less politically and economically powerful. Furthermore, unlike the typical case in the past, organizations providing services for individuals with disabilities engaged in direct competition with one another (Rosen 2006). In fact, since community-based services tended to involve fewer startup and sunken costs, organizations could be set in competition with others willing to provide services to their clients at lower cost (even if such competition was only theoretical). Monopsony conditions developed wherein the government became the major (and sometimes sole) buyer of services from a plethora of real or potential service providers.

Arguments for care agendas become most persuasive given an ability to document a long-term unmet, unavoidable, and ideally desperate need. As mentioned, care agendas in the Western world, particularly the United States, once divorced from the cause discourse, are by and large limited to the provision of needs fundamental to human (and not necessarily civil) rights. Caring is provided to the point of sustenance of life, not in regard to the exercise of citizenship or other social status. Deinstitutionalization argues care through cause, whereas in the period of institutionalization, care preceded cause. As Bagenstos (2004) explained in "The Future of Disability Law":

> Although the disability rights critique of disability welfare programs had
> its roots in the broader welfare rights movement of the late 1960s and early

1970s, disability rights advocates ultimately grew a great deal more am-
bivalent about the very idea of welfare than did welfare rights advocates
more generally. But by the 1970s, many disability rights advocates were
presenting antidiscrimination laws as an alternative to social welfare provisions for people with disabilities—a tool that would obviate welfare programs by giving people with disabilities opportunities to make a living on
their own. (5)

One difficulty present in the deinstitutionalization process involved a
lack of clarity on how to provide community-based services within an economic and political environment likely to drive down the level of public
funds available to organizations. Frequently, a plethora of well-intentioned
individuals and groups from a diverse set of perspectives became involved
in the effort, all too often neglecting sustained consideration of economic
forces until too late in the budgetary process. This resulted in a diversity of
preferences and expectations about community-based services, often confounding efforts to provide for either care or rights. As Gros put it, "the
states' policy decisions to reduce their public mental hospital populations
and to make admission to these hospitals more difficult, along with other
changes in public attitudes, treatment ideologies, and social and economic
factors, supported the development of a confusing array of organized and
unorganized settings for treating persons with mental illness" (2005, 425).

Equity in Deinstitutionalization

Another major challenge involved difficulty in protecting equity in the geographic distribution of publicly provided care. Although many inequities
existed in the quality of public institutions, aggregated institutions were not
inherently geographically selective. Since individuals could be brought from
anywhere in the state to an institution, living in an urban area did not necessarily make an individual more able to access care than living in a more
remote, rural environment. However, the same principle does not necessarily hold for provision of community-based care. Particularly to the degree
of need for specialized care to help an individual manage implications of a
functional difference, rural environments tend to have less access to care
providers. As Tom Shakespeare explained, "the claim that people are disabled by society, not by their bodies, has been effective in highlighting the
human-created obstacles to participation in society . . . yet outside the city
the social model seems harder to implement" (2006, 45).

Entitlement-based social policies initially included provisions to
counter such regional disparities. For example, Medicaid policies in the

United States were originally written to include provisions requiring uniformity of services available across a given state. Such equity represents a fundamental tenet of cause agendas given the principle of equality under the law.

However, over time, demand for exceptions to rules such as the Medicaid waivers increased, often in the name of protecting the individual rights of people able to secure services in their home community should their family be in a position to privately finance the care. For example, Indiana has three waivers for individuals with developmental disabilities. On May 23, 2008, the *Intelligencer Journal* reported in an article titled "Pa. Gets Autism Aid OK" that "in what might be the first in the nation, Pennsylvania received approval to use federal Medicaid money to pay for support programs for autistic adults and their caregivers." The program was expected to include 200 individuals with autism each year, with the goal of moving them toward more independent lives. Dating back to 1990, these waivers fund community-based care for a limited number of individuals as an alternative to institutional care. Although the number of waivers available has increased over time, waiting lists for these waivers are several years long. Similarly, in the United Kingdom, a national review of community-based services for individuals with learning disabilities relating to person-centered planning, direct payments, and other innovative partnerships found that "implementation was patchy . . . and variable by geographical area" (MacIntyre 2008, 7).

Criminalization in Deinstitutionalization

Another result of deinstitutionalization involved reinforcement of the relationship between disability and criminal justice. As mentioned, when members of the general population crave removal of individuals with differences from their communities, often the location to which the individual is removed is not of general concern. Popular thought all too often begins and ends with removal of the individual from one's community. In recent years, neurodiversity-oriented activists have begun to include this reality in political activism. For example, in a 2003 letter to the United Kingdom's Joint Committee on the Draft Disability Discrimination Bill, Andrian Wyatt of the Developmental Neuro-Diversity Association wrote:

> In separate studies done of young offenders institutions (in Edinburgh and Durham) it was found that over 60% of young offenders had dyslexia and related conditions and over 60% had dyspraxia and related conditions. None had been previously diagnosed . . . this means that comprehensive

screening of the entire population, including all age groups, and the comprehensive implementation of equality and diversity training for all members of society is required . . . Long-term Government commitments to mainstreaming equality and diversity can only be achieved through these means . . . it also means that the money spent on this and the billions saved from having the biggest jail population in Europe, will enable comprehensive implementation of the Social Model of Disability for all and still save money and leave room for tax cuts. (www.publications.parliament .uk/pa/jt200304/jtselect/jtdisab/352/352we41.htm)

With the closure of public institutions, jails became, both in de facto practice and in the minds of many, an alternative place to which to systematically remove individuals with neurological differences. Furthermore, either because of the inherent characteristics manifested as a result of a given neurological difference or because of the tendency of members of the general public to engage in often relatively unprovoked negative social interaction with people perceived as unacceptably different, people with neurological differences tend to become subject to law enforcement more often than other members of the general population. Public discourse references this phenomenon. For example, the *Boston Globe* reported on July 5, 2007, that individuals with autism are seven times more likely to become subject to police interaction than are other members of the general population.

In considering such statistics, it is vitally important to remember that such interactions with law enforcement are not part of the experiences of the majority of individuals with neurological differences. Pop culture and historical prejudice lead people toward the impression that most people with neurological differences habitually engage in criminal, if not violent, behavior. People all over the world have been conditioned to fear the worst of all possible outcomes from interactions with individuals with differences.

Often this results from the logical fallacy of attraction to inappropriate denominators. The basic innumeracy rests on the assumption that if all members of a particularly undesirable group of individuals share a characteristic, then all people exhibiting this characteristic are members of the undesired group. While such logic all too often appears in public discourse, it is inherently as flawed as believing that the plural of anecdote is evidence. For example, believing this logic would be akin to thinking that because all rapists arrested in a given community are men, then all men rape. Such faulty logic frequently motivates fear of individuals with neurological differences, especially when supported by a particularly upsetting anecdote.

Modern studies of individuals with neurological differences speak to false conclusions driven by this type of logic. A study of the general population in England published in 2001 reported the prevalence of severe challenging behavior among individuals with intellectual disabilities to be approximately 7.8 percent (Hamlin and Oaks 2008).[3] While this proportion may be higher than the observed prevalence in the overall general population, it appears clear that the argument that neurological differences lead to criminal activity, to the degree that fear of danger is used to promote control-based care agendas, fits for only a small fraction of the target population. Particularly in the context of a modern democratic society, such a low prevalence cannot justify preemptive violation of basic civil rights of the majority of the population of individuals with neurological differences.

Nevertheless, deinstitutionalization (or dehospitalization) in an era of pharmaceutical innovations and experimentation also contributes to the connection between neurological differences and violence. Some, though not all, neurological differences include internal suffering or a tendency toward production of harm through aggression that is most reasonably addressed through pharmaceuticals rather than solely through therapeutic intervention or accommodation.

Although substantial progress has been made in the identification of potentially beneficial medications, the exact way in which medications work remains largely unknown. Prescribing medications for effects of neurological difference tends to involve periods of trial and error. Furthermore, specific medications do not have the same effect on all individuals experiencing the same undesirable aspect of neurological difference. For example, a medication that successfully alleviates depressive symptoms of one person may not have the similar effect on another individual, even if the two people share the same diagnosis. Nevertheless, and counter to what popular culture would lead us to believe, treatment is often successful when undertaken fully. For example, studies of men with schizophrenia who have been released upon completion of recommended treatment (who are, statistically speaking, among the most likely to become involved in violent activities) have "reported favorable outcomes and low criminal recidivism rates" (Hodgins et al. 2007, 64).

Arguably most important for the context of deinstitutionalization, many of the medications used to help individuals with neurological differences include a period of adjustment (typically at least six weeks) during which the effects of the medication remain unclear and side effects can be unusually pronounced. One outcome during this period is that a person who is not normally psychotic, for example, may become temporarily psychotic in response to the medication. As a result, during this period of experimentation and adjustment, individuals with neurological differences (like any other individuals recently put on new medication) may become particularly prone to violence, self-harm, or other criminal behavior. Similarly, many medications in this class, when a person stops taking them, can have adverse affects on, for instance, impulse control and ability to control anger. Even carefully planned and monitored cessation of medications may result in periods of unexpected behavioral changes. Furthermore, especially in the United States, where access to prescription drugs depends on employment or ability to qualify for restrictive public programs, individuals with neurological differences requiring medications may periodically find themselves without prescription drug coverage, resulting in unplanned cessation of medications.

In the past, periods of medication adjustment tended to involve hospitalization and attendant close monitoring of the individual. As a result, negative—and especially criminal—implications of this period of adjustment could be confined to within the institution. One effect of deinstitutionalization, however, particularly in the United States, has been the introduction of firm limits on the period of time individuals may spend in behavioral health hospitals as well as, in many cases, strict quotas with regard to the percentage of affected individuals receiving publicly provided care who are institutionalized at any moment of time in a given geographic location. Public discourse surrounding creation of these limitations focused on the historical tendency to keep people with neurological differences in hospitals much longer than strictly medically necessary. The intent of the policy was to force very deliberative thinking about which individuals to keep in institutions, especially for prolonged periods of time.

As a consequence of such policies, however, individuals tend to increasingly experience periods of medicine adjustment in the community, often with little or no community-based services designed to assist in the management of this volatile time. Family caregivers, particularly mothers, increasingly endure the associated violence resulting from ongoing adjustments in medication. As a result of this limited access to hospitalization in times of crisis, individuals with neurological differences and their families face increased risk of long-term exclusion from society (all too often in the form of jail sentences) resulting from temporary effects of medications. Despite these problems and policy limitations, it is vital to recognize that the circumstances of individuals with neurological differences tend to be much improved over what was typically experienced in the past, and that extreme criminal activity remains rare even in these periods.

Finally, tensions between care- and cause-oriented agendas also revolve around the question of allowances for unconventional behavior. Despite an elevated preference for individual freedoms and self-expression in modern democracy, license to behave outside bounds of conventionally expected behavior is still hard-won. Furthermore, consensus that such allowances should exist is far from complete. Many people, particularly but not exclusively those with more traditional preferences, become quite irate when confronted with planned tolerance of unconventional behavior. For example, use of service animals in public areas has generated this type of concern and outcry among certain individuals who find their presence irritating, allergy-inducing, or simply distracting.

Blurring Lines: Defining Disability

Tensions between the cause and care agenda types also come about as a result of homogeneous perceptions of disability. For example, in a 2008 letter submitted to the United Kingdom's Human Rights Joint Committee on the subject of ratification of the United Nations Convention on the Rights of the Disabled, the London Autistic Rights Movement wrote:

> The UN Treaty on the Rights of Persons with Disabilities and the Optional Protocol must be ratified in full . . . But the specific provisions in the Treaty to cover some types of disabled people (e.g., the deaf sign community) do not meet in full the needs of all disabled people. Most notably those not resourced, despite pleas to the contrary, to be there, such as neurodiverse people (people with uneven neurological profiles whatever the cause, ranging from brain injury to mental health survivors to autism, tourette's, Parkinson's, dyspraxia and dyslexia). The UN was prepared to ensure that poor countries were represented, but was deliberately deaf (pun intended) to demands from those at the wrong end of the hierarchy of impairments in the developed world. (www.publications.parliament.uk /pa/jt200809/jtselect/jtrights/9/09we02.htm)

Such statements reflect a desire for simplicity when it comes to establishing what constitutes impairment. In particular, it suggests a craving for increased clarity with regard to what constitutes disability deserving the attention of policymaking entities attempting to implement inclusionary policy.

However, despite humanity's great love of dichotomies, the universe appears a greater fan of continuums. Of course, many continuums of human characteristics tend to appear bimodal. The physical appearance of most people, for example, can be clearly identified as either male or female. However, a subset of the population embodies phenotypical characteristics of both genders. Ongoing preference for the gender dichotomy had led societies to more or less explicitly identify where the line between the two genders exists, forcing those of more combined characteristics into one category or the other.

So it is with disability. One of the first questions addressed by the majority of disability-oriented policy is a definition of what constitutes disability (and what does not). As a result, judgment of disability becomes a nexus of controversy for the cause and care agendas. This situation arises particularly frequently in policies and programs creating entitlements. In the United States, for example, Medicaid and Social Security Disability Insurance are, generally speaking, entitlement programs. Designation as an entitlement program, particularly in the context of intergovernmental funding structures, involves the expectation that no qualifying individual may be turned down for a program regardless of program capacities. This creates substantial fiscal (and in some cases moral) incentive to make sure everyone allowed into the program embodies the qualifying characteristics.

Entitlement programs tend to create perception of rights on the part of the target population. For example, in the United States, whereas typically functioning children have no explicit right to public education per se, public education's status as an entitlement program creates a widespread impression of such a right. No child of appropriate age living within a school district may be turned away from his or her public school on the explanation that the school lacks room for the child. School districts are required to figure out a way to place each and every child in their district if the parent presents the child for public education. Given this tendency to conceive rights out of entitlements, when eligibility for an entitlement program depends on the official declaration of disability, particularly when said program involves public provision of care, modifying or clarifying standards of identification can become a cause-oriented policy goal.

Neurological differences exist on a continuum with even less clear bimodality than the continuum of human characteristics. First of all, with a few notable exceptions such as Down syndrome, formal diagnosis of neurological difference depends on the professionally judged presence of a defined set of behaviors deemed indicative of a specific neurological difference. Generally speaking, an individual does not have to exhibit all of the defined characteristics. Also, how individuals exhibit a given char-

acteristic varies. Furthermore, neurological differences are frequently described as being spectrum disorders. These factors make neurological differences difficult to fit into policies with eligibility standards rooted in a
standard of simple presence or absence of a given qualifying characteristic.

Substantial power connects to the issue of identification. Within disability policy subsystems, as mentioned, a primary result of this is a tension of ethics between cause- and care-oriented agendas. One outcome of
this tension of ethics involves the potential for the interests of individuals
described as being low-functioning to be set in opposition with the interests
of those described as being higher-functioning. This tension was described
by Joseph Brean on October 7, 2006, in an article in Canada's *National Post*
titled "Redefining Autism":

> It is this variability in autism that poses the main problem for the neuro-
> diversity movement . . . For one child, autism might seem like a gift, the
> clinical name for a sensitive soul turned in upon itself . . . But for another,
> the condition might be so severe as to leave him an anguished mute, un-
> able to make friends or relate to his family, at risk of self-harm, and a phys-
> ical danger to anyone around him.

Given such spectrums, policies rested in bimodal entitlement make for an
inherently awkward fit for public challenges attributed to neurological differences.

Much of the public and political discourse surrounding modern conceptions of deinstitutionalization can be understood as an outcome of this
tension. As Murray Levine put it, "we will never do without some institutions . . . in the field of mental retardation, as most residents were discharged
to the community facilities, the institution itself was left to cope with the
most difficult and most disabled individuals" (2007, 71). As more time
passed, it became clear that deinstitutionalization, particularly into conditions lacking availability of community-based care, could be quite haz-
ardous for those with less-developed life skills. As Lamb and Bachrach
(2001) explain:

> Caring for homeless mentally ill persons has become one of the greatest
> challenges to public mental health and to society in general. This prob-
> lem has taken on greater importance because of evidence that a third to a
> half of all homeless adults in the United States have major mental illness—
> schizophrenia, schizoaffective disorder, bi-polar disorder, or major de-
> pressive disorder . . . evidence has emerged that homeless mentally ill
> persons have a greater severity of illness than do mentally ill persons in
> general. (1041)

For the purposes of intelligent design and effective discussion of disability policy, important issues of cause and effect embed in this observation—that is, whether the severity or the homelessness tends to come first. While a bicausal relationship is arguably most likely (that is, homelessness both causes and is caused by increased severity), policy models surrounding the question of deinstitutionalization may rest on the assumption of one direction of causality. For example, if severity is assumed to be caused by homelessness, arguments for publicly provided housing (even in the form of institutionalization) may become more persuasive.

Since deinstitutionalization involved taking away housing security from many people with neurological differences, concern expressed in political discourse surrounding neurodiversity came to include the assertion that the movement resulted in worse outcomes for lower-functioning individuals in the name of securing the freedom of those able to function at a higher level in modern society.[4] In California, for example, a significant growth in the homeless population was observed immediately following deinstitutionalization. Of course, since early on in the era of deinstitutionalization, this growth has been understood by some stakeholders as not attributable to deinstitutionalization per se, but to deinstitutionalization in the absence of development of effective community-based services (Lamb 1984; Bassuk and Lamb 1986).

Spectrum of Difference, Spectrum of Care

Ideally, a spectrum of care would exist, matching appropriate levels of care to each individual. As Morrow and Jamer explained in the context of deinstitutionalization of individuals with neurological differences categorized as psychiatric disorders: "in the new model of deinstitutionalization people are meant to move through facilities to increasing levels of independence" (2008, 6). In fact, while some locations approximate such a spectrum, it has proven a difficult sell politically. Spectrum of care is expected to prove extraordinarily expensive. Implementation is therefore uneven at best. According to Morrow and Jamer, "despite the intention that people move through facilities the reality is that there are limited housing options for people with mental illness in their communities and so many will remain in institutional forms of care even after they are capable of living independently" (2008, 7). Ironically, this matching constituted the original intent of both the institutionalization and the deinstitutionalization movements. Such matching has almost always also fit with cause-oriented public discourse, even as the fundamental understanding of the nature of the rights of those with neurological differences has completely changed. Nevertheless, dynamics between cause and care agenda types as well as fiscal constraints complicated creation of a spectrum of services in the contexts of both institutionalization and deinstitutionalization.

The spectrum nature of diagnosis also becomes a source of care-cause–oriented discourse with regard to the issue of adult guardianship or conservatorship. As a general rule, people living in industrialized countries attain a right to expanded control over their lives upon reaching the age of majority. Provisions for legal guardianship for individuals with disabilities (and others deemed incompetent) prolong into adulthood the period of legal control by another. The assumption underlying such arrangements holds that protection of the human and civil rights of the individual with the functional difference becomes best accomplished by limiting the participation of the individual in decisions about their personal affairs. This is based on the expectation that otherwise the individual would be prone to making either ill-informed or unusually nonsensical decisions or be vulnerable to exploitation by others (Moye et al. 2007). In some cases, also, the individual is found to be so impaired as to potentially endanger their health or life if left up to their own devices in the same way a small child might be. As Bagenstos explained, "when persons can not make their own way—even for fully understandable reasons—then a society that undertakes to care for them will necessarily also undertake to make their decisions for them" (2004, 17). Such provisions embrace the expectation that under certain circumstances with some kinds of functional differences, care becomes cause even in the context of deinstitutionalization.

Guardianship of adults has a long history. In the past, guardianship provisions were taken as a matter of course for many people, including individuals with neurological differences. Furthermore, during that time, a large proportion of the population, including most women, were legally expected to require some level of external provisions for the exercise of their rights. Adult women remained, therefore, almost always under the legal control of men, especially their husbands. Not too many decades earlier, many people, including such luminaries as Benjamin Franklin, sold themselves temporarily into the care of others through arrangements such as apprenticeships or indentured servant contracts (Wood 2005). So it was hardly a stretch for people with disabilities to presumptively become subject to guardianships. Above and beyond widespread tolerance of external limitations to the decisionmaking of many adults, additional provisions for individuals with neurological differences have deeply established historical roots. For example, since at least the end of the thirteenth century, the right of a monarch to take control of the "land and natural food" of those with mental illnesses existed in England (Roberts 2009).

With the progression of civil rights movements, however, the question of legal guardianship was revisited, setting in direct opposition the management of care and cause in the lives of individuals with neurological differences. After all, as S. L. Reynolds explained, "guardianship is an intrusive intervention that usually removes an adult's basic civil rights" (2002, 109). In particular, those who considered themselves on the higher-functioning side of the spectrum of neurological differences began to resist the notion that others could better protect their rights, even if they had functional differences complicating the exercise and practice of rights.

As a result, individuals with neurological differences are no longer simply assumed to be subject to legal guardianships as a matter of course. Policy changed to make it more difficult for loved ones, including parents, to successfully assert need for control over their adult progeny's choices, such as where they might live, what kinds of jobs they might work at, which medications they might take, or how they might spend their money. In fact, sometimes allowance for independence in making such decisions extended even into the period of life traditionally described as childhood. For example, in the state of Washington, a parent's access to their child's psychiatric records and medication decisions become limited when the child turns thirteen. Some have argued that as a result of these provisions, people with neurological differences, particularly younger people with emerging mental illnesses or developmental delays, are being allowed to "die with their rights on" (Lewis 2007, 94). However, research on guardianship literature has found, as Reynolds explained, that while "it may seem self-evident that evidence of Alzheimer's disease, schizophrenia, or confusion, disorientation, or forgetfulness should be grounds for placing an adult under guardianship . . . we find many adults with legal guardians who do not show such evidence" (2002, 117).

Guardianship decisions are not made on the basis of diagnosis alone. No neurological difference, in and of itself, constitutes proof of a need for external management of an individual's human or civil rights. Only well-defined, evidence-based legal procedures now establish necessity of guardianship. Although the policy is often implemented spottily (Lewis 2007), modern guardianship policy asserts that evidence of incapacity must first be presented and deemed conclusive. As a result, ethical tensions between cause and care agendas become especially relevant to this area of disability policy.

Collision of Rights in Care

A blurring of lines between the rights of those who give and receive care happens in other areas of disability policy as well. Disability studies literature frequently notes an expansive tendency on the part of caregivers to presume agency in life choices and day-to-day activities of individuals with disabilities. As Tom Shakespeare aptly put it, "the lives of disabled and older people are colonised by service providers" (2006, 138). The provision of care almost always includes involvement of others in decisions and activities that are normally considered extremely private. One implication of this intimacy is that some caregivers, particularly those pressed for time or lacking training, find it prudent to substitute their own choices rather than to leave decisions up to the individual with the disability.

The relationship between cause and care becomes complicated by attitudes toward paid employment in industrialized nations. As Gillian MacIntyre (2008) explained:

> The 1944 Disabled Persons (Employment) Act focused on the employment of disabled people and introduced the quota system whereby employers had to employ a certain percentage of disabled people as part of their workforce . . . Although the quote system was not taken seriously by many employers and few prosecutions were made, it was an excellent example of a demand-side measure where the onus was on the employer and the workplace to change their practices and facilitate the employment of disabled people. (41)

This quota system was abolished in 1995 as part of the Disability Discrimination Act.

In the case of neurological difference, this substitution can become especially tempting because of the possibility that additional time and effort may be required to discern an individual's preferences. Furthermore, particularly in the case of neurological differences that profoundly affect cognitive capacity, it may be impossible for the individual with the disability to make the choice at a given moment in time. Often, people providing care for those with neurological differences construct or limit the options in order to allow the individual to weigh in on the choice when otherwise they would lack the capacity to do so. However, preferences and prejudices of the individual providing the care unavoidably affect the list of choices, thereby manifesting a tension between cause and care agendas. Ultimately, the balance of these goals shifts from moment to moment and depends heavily on the perceptions of those involved as well as the point of view of any observers. Since policies for publicly provided programs must be written in a much more general sense in order to be realistic and implementable, this tension is a transcendent aspect of the politics of neurodiversity.

Confounding Cause and Care:
The Case of the Americans with Disabilities Act

Not all politics of neurodiversity emanating from the interaction between the cause and care agenda types exist in the context of publicly funded programs designed to provide care for individuals with neurological differences. In fact, during the late twentieth and early twenty-first centuries, one of the major loci of tensions between these agenda types in the United States involved implementation of the Americans with Disabilities Act (ADA) of 1990. This law, signed by a Republican president and supported by an unusually bipartisan effort led in part by Senators Ted Kennedy and Bob Dole, embraced quite constructivist intent. The law focused on elimination (or at least minimization) of infrastructural barriers to participation in employment of individuals with disability in major life functions. The law was emphatically designed in the tradition of civil rights–based policy. However, because the law became routinely misunderstood as a part of care-oriented agendas of the disability policy subsystem, substantial implementation slippage quickly emerged, causing increased tension between care and cause agendas in the United States.

Implementation Slippage and Gaps

Implementation of public policy—even broadly supported policy—is rarely a simple task (Shafritz and Hyde 2007, 267). More often than not, implementation of particularly innovative public policy involves both substantial implementation slippage and implementation gaps. Gaps in implementation refer to an absence of related programs or enforcement of the policy either in particular geographical locations or with regard to a defined subset of the circumstances that the policy was designed to address. For example, Montana has a reputation for ignoring federal policy with regard to vehicular speed limits. Implementation slippage, on the other hand, refers to circumstances wherein those involved in the implementation of a particular law or policy adjust the interpretation of the policy toward their preferred policy. Implementation slippage can be both volitional and accidental.

From the outset, implementation of the Americans with Disabilities Act involved a high degree of both gaps and slippage. It was, however, the unusually high (and relatively organized) degree of slippage that most force-fully contributed to the politics of neurodiversity during the first ten years of the law's existence. Because many who interpreted the ADA did not appear to comprehend even the possibility of disability policy not being connected to a care-oriented agenda, many of the provisions put in place through the implementation process stood at odds with the original cause orientation of the law (Gross and Hahn 2004).

Furthermore, a history of judicial policymaking undermining the intent of the original ADA emerged in the decade after the law's introduction. Even the Supreme Court began interpreting the ADA as a social welfare, care-oriented policy as opposed to a civil rights policy. As mentioned, historically all disability policy was predominantly health or welfare policy wherein people with disabilities were assumed to be of lower status within society and basically unable to care for themselves. However, a core characteristic of US social welfare policy is an extreme restriction on who qualifies as deserving and not able to care for themselves. As a result, according to Mary Johnson: "The bill now reads less like a truly civil rights law than a strange hybrid based on the understanding US national legislators and their staffs had about disability law, which in general was benefits-based legislation that gave something to a group of people, like Social Security disability benefits or rehabilitation services—services that you only got if you qualified as disabled" (2003, 54). The applications for those programs put the burden of proof on the individual (or their family) to prove disability and, by extension, need for publicly provided services. The Supreme Court spent quite a bit of time and effort on ADA cases focusing on this question of whether a person is actually disabled in the social welfare sense (and therefore deserving) when interpreting issues concerning the act. The question of proof of disability took center stage in questions surrounding the Americans with Disabilities Act, rather than the intended central question of proof of discrimination.

This represents a fundamental error in interpreting the policy, rooted in a limited understanding of modern conceptions of disability. The ADA was designed as a civil rights–based policy, which means that the core question is meant to be "Did discrimination take place that was motivated by disability?" as opposed to "Does this person deserve 'services' under the ADA?" Civil rights policy typically employs this type of reasoning. If a person experiences discrimination because she is a woman or an ethnic minority and goes to court to address the matter, the anticipated focus during court proceedings is the behaviors or events constituting the discrimination, not whether this person was actually a woman or the nature of her pedigree.

With the ADA Amendments Act of 2008, Congress sought to reform the ADA back toward its original intent. According to the website of the Equal Employment Opportunity Commission (EEOC), the ADA Amendments Act

> directs EEOC to revise that portion of its regulations defining the term "substantially limits"; expands the definition of "major life activities" by including two non-exhaustive lists: the first list includes many activities that the EEOC has recognized (e.g., walking) as well as activities that EEOC has not specifically recognized (e.g., reading, bending, and communicating); the second list includes major bodily functions (e.g., "functions of the immune system, normal cell growth, digestive, bowel, bladder, neurological, brain, respiratory, circulatory, endocrine, and reproductive functions"); states that mitigating measures other than "ordinary eyeglasses or contact lenses" shall not be considered in assessing whether an individual has a disability; clarifies that an impairment that is episodic or in remission is a disability if it would substantially limit a major life activity when active; provides that an individual subjected to an action prohibited by the ADA (e.g., failure to hire) because of an actual or perceived impairment will meet the "regarded as" definition of disability, unless the impairment is transitory and minor; provides that individuals covered only under the "regarded as" prong are not entitled to reasonable accommodation; and emphasizes that the definition of "disability" should be interpreted broadly. (www.eeoc.gov)

Fundamentally, the correction sought movement away from the care-oriented interpretation of the ADA and back toward interpretations more focused on cause. This revision bears a resemblance to revisions of affirmative action–oriented policies that occurred a decade or two after the introduction of the major federal policies (Anderson 2004). As implementation of affirmative action–oriented policies progressed, one question that continually arose concerned whether and to what degree specific individuals raising complaints should have to prove that they had been personally affected by discriminatory policies, or whether the focus should be on determining the existence of discriminatory policies or practices. Ultimately, resolution of the question generally favored the latter.

Assuming the correction to the ADA works as intended in coming years, it should hold particular relevance for people with so-called invisible disabilities whose rights became increasingly less well protected given the Supreme Court's misinterpretation of the ADA. After all, proving that someone has a neurological difference beyond a shadow of a doubt becomes especially complicated in the legal arena. The politics of neurodiversity will continue to play heavily into the implementation of the Americans with Disabilities Act for the foreseeable future. In particular, confusion between construction of rights necessitating changes in practices and infrastructures and provision of care will continue to exist in the minds of many as well as in the day-to-day implementation of the law.

Concluding Thoughts for All Disabilities

The line between caring about rights and a right to receive appropriate care is likely to be forever tenuous and all too often variable depending on the eye of the beholder. Although the discussion in this chapter has focused on the politics of neurological difference and neurodiversity, this line is equally variable when it comes to other differences associated with disability. Arguably the line is especially variable in the case of so-called invisible disabilities, including many neurological differences. In moving policy beyond deinstitutionalization, it will be important to move away from physical location as the defining aspect of this distinction.

Drawing the line between articulation of care and cause typically requires insertion of others' opinions (especially professional judgments) into the construction of the person's individuality, regardless of the nature of the disability, so long as both politically articulated rights and public resources are in play. Eliminating others' input is hardly a solution to this challenge. First, it potentially simply reverses the direction of exploitation away from the individual with the disability and toward their caregiver (or possibly toward society at large). Second, and more important given the modern predilection to take the individual as the unit of economic and political analysis, excluding the input of others in this way ultimately isolates individuals with disabilities from the rest of the general population. The time for creation of new blunt-force policy instruments around this aspect of disability discourse has, for the most part, passed into history. In going forward, public and political discourse surrounding the relationship between care and cause agenda types will become more of a conversation involving both those with disabilities and those without, on progressively more equal terms.

Flexibility of interpretation at the level of specific disabling circumstances turns out to be a quite necessary component of sophisticated policy for all disabilities, not just neurological differences. Insufficient flexibility of this kind fails to acknowledge how other diverse characteristics within a population interplay with disability in society. Without such flexibility, policy will not keep pace with the perpetually changing nature of disability in society. Also, any trend toward decreased cultural tendencies for discrimination against individuals with functional differences over time will cease or at least diminish. Remedying less than helpful interactions between cause and cure agenda types begins with the understanding of these orientations as separable components of the disability policy subsystems both in the case of neurological differences and for the larger category of functional differences associated with disability.

Notes

1. The phrase "adult children" also describes situations in which the dependency runs the other direction—that is, when offspring have stepped into caregiving roles for parents as the parents enter into old age (see, for example, Pezzin, Pollak, and Schone 2007). This usage currently holds less relevance for disability policy subsystems.

2. Of course, the same argument might be used for institutionalization, since that too followed primarily belief as opposed to empirical evidence.

3. It is worth noting that this is somewhat higher than the 5.7 percent reported by Qureshi and Alborz (1992).

4. Such explanations of decline in outcomes are not without potentially confounding variables. For example, John Quigley and colleagues present findings that the increased rate of homelessness among those with neurological differences is most attributable to "simple economic principles governing the availability and pricing of housing and the growth in demand for the lowest-quality housing" (2001, 37). They argue for policy solutions focused on modest improvements in the affordability of housing.

4

Securing Civil Rights vs. Finding a Cure

Cause and cure agenda types both involved high levels of political volatility in the late twentieth and early twenty-first centuries. These two agenda types frame central controversies inherent in the transition toward more constructivist understandings of disability. As Kristin Bumiller (2009) described with regard to autism:

> The neurodiversity contingent is committed to affirming quirkiness and countering what its members see as neurotypical people's obsession with normality. From the perspective of the neurodiversity movement, mainstream activism [described by Bumiller as cure-oriented activism] is counterproductive to the cultural acceptance of autism. Both sides engaged in the controversy, however, subscribe to a genetic understanding of autism and downplay the possibility of other complex factors in the etiology of the disorder. While the major advocacy organizations are fully aligned with the medical establishment and the biomedical industry in supporting research to find a cure, the neurodiversity movement is resistant to medicalization in all of its aspects and asserts that autism is a desirable genetic variation. (882)

Cure, at least as understood in modern political discourse, can be seen as archetypically essentialist, since in the modern context cure always takes place inside the person receiving the cure. Cause, on the other hand, aims for the constructivist end of the disability paradigms continuum, since cause agendas imply violation of rights. Such violations require participation of at least one other person. Also, in order for a politically relevant question to become manifest, social complicity allowing for violation of rights of an iden-

87

tified subpopulation must exist. In other words, when it comes to alleviating harm associated with functional differences, cure generally looks inward whereas cause mostly looks outward.

Disciplinary Divisions
Relating to Cause and Cure Agenda Types

Given these separable realms of interest, one might expect these agenda types to coexist relatively unproblematically except when it comes to competition for scarce resources. To some degree, such coexistence occurs in basic research about disability taking place outside ongoing political conversations. Research focusing on discovery and elimination or alleviation of the physiological root of functional differences takes place in different university departments, is usually funded through distinct requests for proposals, and generally gets published in different academic journals than research about disability as a social, cultural, or political phenomenon. Genuinely multidisciplinary studies, while highly desirable in some contexts and possibly on the rise, still constitute an academic rarity. The parallel play going on between these areas of inquiry rarely involves much genuine attention to agenda types other than the ones most naturally connected to their particular research interests.

A certain amount of (sometimes healthy) disciplinary prejudice underlies this seemingly serene division of intellectual efforts. Arguably most vitriolic at times is the tendency of modern disability studies to deride research about disability (and indeed all conversation about disability in some cases) taking place outside of disability studies as being oppressive. As Tom Shakespeare pointed out in *Disability Rights and Wrongs,* "there has been a dangerous political tendency to assume that progressive approaches are impossible in the absence of the social model, or to label any rights-based or humanitarian response as 'social model,' regardless of the definitions adopted: in other words, social model comes to stand for 'good research and practice' and medical model comes to stand for 'bad research and practice'" (2006, 27). When it comes to research outside writings oriented toward cause agenda types in activist or at least action research, a presupposition on the part of some scholars and activists exists of this research being both antiquated and, to some degree at least, against the interests of individuals with disabilities (Linton 1998).

Similarly, there exists a long tendency in the academy for the basic sciences to consider research in the arts, humanities, and social sciences generally less rigorous than that in the natural sciences, such as biomedical research. This assumption tends to be frequently made about younger academic disciplines in particular, such as disability studies, especially those less restricted to only conducting falsifiable studies in the tradition of Karl Popper. A pronounced tendency of some researchers from some of these newer disciplines to forge closer connections to activist or advocacy communities than to traditional ones under conventions of scientific objectivity also enhances this impression. As a result, though little active conflict between academic disciplines may emerge, enough mutual prejudice exists to increase the likelihood of related tension between public discourse engaging cause and cure agenda types.

Furthermore, despite this distance between basic research conventions, political discourse surrounding these two agenda types routinely becomes antagonistic, at least from the perspective of policy entrepreneurs and issue stakeholders interested in cause agenda types. First, difficulties arise because cause and cure become confounded, particularly by those with less experience with the disability policy subsystem. Advocates for cause-oriented policy express frustration when those less attuned to disability policy history assume that their preferences and efforts focus on finding a cure for neurological differences. More than a few politicians (and others involved in the policy process) have unexpectedly found themselves on the receiving end of a certain amount of scorn after proudly announcing funding for the quest for cures when asked questions about rights for individuals with neurological differences.

Cures as Rights: An Examination of
Recent Legislative Discourse in the United States

Substantial concern exists that cause and cure are at times confounded in policy narratives. In order to gain a sense of the extent of this practice, it is helpful to look at statements made in the formulation of public policy within disability policy subsystems. A random sample of fifty documents from the 108th Congress of the United States were examined in order to gain a sense of the degree to how this practice was employed in political discourse in the United States. Sampled documents came from the population of documents returned when the keyword "disability" was used to search the Library of Congress. The population included documents from both the House and the Senate, extensions of remarks, and daily digests. In addition, in order to focus the examination more closely on neurological differences and neurodiversity, the record was searched for use of the word "neurological." This search returned a total of twenty-one documents, each of which was also included in the document sample. The full texts of the documents were read and coded for explicit mention of cure, explicit mention of rights, and references that explicitly confounded the two.

As might be expected given the ongoing dominance of care-oriented agendas in political discourse, the vast majority of the sampled documents focused on modifications to publicly provided care extant in the disability policy subsystem. Generally speaking, the primary focus was on specifics of access, often with the intent of refining or expanding access for veterans returning from the wars in Afghanistan and Iraq. Of the fifty documents examined, only one mentioned disability rights and none included explicit discussion of cure (though many included discussion of general or specific treatments for particular disabilities and the need for access to care). For example, in the extension of remarks for an act introduced by Congressman Bob Filner from California titled the Huntington's Disease Parity Act of 2009, Filner stated: "Many people with HD who apply for Social Security disability benefits experience delays and denials due to the continued use of outdated and insufficient medical criteria. Often, by the time persons affected by HD are 'under review' for [Social Security] disability, many have already lost their employer-provided health insurance benefits."

As this statement demonstrates, although the discussion of health insurance concerns could include cure-related efforts, the argument emphasizes care-oriented policy goals. This finding suggests that overt confounding of the cause and cure agenda goals is less prevalent in legislative discourse than feared by some. Of the twenty-one documents returned when the record was searched for discussion of the term "neurological," none included discussion of rights. However, nine (or almost half) of the documents included discussion of the term "cure." This result suggests that neurological differences are presented as being especially in need of cure in modern political discourse, even by comparison to all disabilities. However, the findings also suggest the simple absence of discussion of cause from the discourse at this time. Part of the reason for this could be that substantial cause-oriented policy development took place in the fall of 2008, including a major clarification of the Americans with Disabilities Act.

Description as a Disease

Part of the reason for the relative prevalence of discussion of cure agenda types in current legislative discourse relates to the less than firm distinction between neurological differences and neurological diseases. In many circumstances, the conditions described were degenerative and ultimately fatal, rendering presentation of the condition as a difference problematic. However, this distinction often becomes difficult to maintain in practice when the period of degeneration constitutes an extended period. Alzheimer's disease, for example, causes a gradual decline, usually over a period of seven to ten years. Especially during the early stages of the disease, the experiences of and implications for the individual likely bear a stronger resemblance to disability than disease. Of course, conditions where the reverse is true also exist. In the case of brain injuries that ultimately stabilize at a given degree of functional atypicality, an individual may experience a short period of disease followed by a prolonged period of disability. Traditional neurodiversity advocates generally prefer to avoid comparison (or confounding) of neurological difference with disease, insisting instead, regardless of the circumstances or experiences, on separation. This separation, however, was not found in the legislative discourse examined.

Instances of political discourse directed at cure agenda types were found in justifications for earmarks for medical facilities. For example, Representative John Culberson, a Republican from Texas, included the following statement in an earmark declaration made on February 25, 2009:

> Scheduled for completion in 2010, the Neurological Research Institute will be a new model of excellence as the first dedicated facility in the United States to use a multidisciplinary research approach to understand the unique issues of a child's brain structure, development patterns and related diseases. The 370,000 square foot building will be home to more than 170 researchers who will bring new promise to those afflicted with neurological diseases as they look for new treatments for common pediatric neurological disorders like autism, epilepsy, Rhett syndrome, cerebral palsy and learning disorders.

Several of the specific conditions mentioned—particularly autism and (some) learning disorders—have contested descriptions as diseases in the politics of neurodiversity. Nevertheless, discourse unequivocally refers to the conditions as diseases. The representative makes this point even more emphatically in a later part of the statement, this time describing autism as degenerative. He recommends a project that

> provides $238,000 for equipment and faculty recruitment, which will advance breakthroughs in the understanding, prevention and treatment of developmental and neurodegenerative diseases including autism, Alzheimer's and brain injury; accelerated exploration and clinical testing

of new pharmacological agents and new neurological and behavioral interventions with a reduced need for animal and human testing; and investment opportunities as technologies are developed and tested.

Including autism as part of this particular list not only reflects the elevated
public profile of autism but also ignores or possibly deliberately rejects any
description of the difference as a so-called different way of being. Whether
intentional or not, such discourse directly opposes cause-oriented agendas
and forcefully demonstrates the ability of cure-related discourse to eclipse
concerns related to cause agendas in modern political discourse.

Another intriguing example of cure-oriented discourse came from Ron
Paul, also a Republican congressman from Texas. Paul, a physician and former flight surgeon for the US Air Force, made a serious run for president in
the 2008 election, campaigning as a third-party candidate largely on issues of
limited government. On March 26, 2009, Paul introduced the Cures Can Be
Found Act, which proposes a $2,000 tax credit to parents who donate umbil-
ical cord stem cells to research. He stated that "cord blood stem cells have
. . . proven useful in treating spinal cord injuries and certain neurological disorders." He went on to point out that, "by encouraging private medical research, the Cures Can Be Found Act enhances a tradition of private medical
research that is responsible for many medical breakthroughs . . . for example,
Jonas Salk, discoverer of the polio vaccine, did not receive one dollar from the
federal government for his efforts" (Statement on Introducing the Cures Can
Be Found Act, March 26, 2009, http://paul.house.gov/index.php).

Although Paul's motivation more likely lies with Libertarian concerns
than with tensions between disability policy agendas (or even the rights of
individuals with disability), removing public sector funding has been used
in the past as a way of avoiding controversy with regard to medical research.
In this case, this strategy could have the largely unintended effect of emphasizing the role of personal choice in the resolution of tensions between
cause and cure disability agenda types. When public funds play little role in
the search for the cure, the decision to participate in cure has increased potential to at least appear private and optional. When this happens, the relative strength of cure- and cause-oriented agendas becomes better reflected
in private sector behaviors rather than in public sector choices.

Coordination of Efforts

Increased and improved collaboration and coordination are commonly invoked as important process goals in disability policy subsystems (Baker
and Stahl 2004). The legislative documents examined included calls for in-

creased coordination, especially in efforts directed at finding cures for neurological diseases and differences. Efforts to increase coordination in disability policy subsystems can include programs connected to different agenda types. Complication of coordination of cause- and cure-oriented agenda types result from their seeming cross-purposes. This does not, however, make coordination impossible.

The coordination called for in the legislative discourse examined generally involved cure-oriented efforts. For example, Senator Patty Murray from Washington made the following statement about an introduced bill on March 12, 2009:

> The Neurotechnology Initiative Act of 2009, which I am introducing today, would coordinate our efforts to support new developments in research, speed up our understanding of the human brain, and help lead to treatments for all victims of neurological disorders . . . The legislation would make needed improvements to the research system in our country, which now is disjointed, often limiting the ability for life-altering research to reach patients in need. For example, it costs nearly $100 million more— and takes 2 years longer than average—to bring a drug that treats a neurological disease to the market. The combined economic burden of these illnesses and disorders is estimated at $1 trillion annually.

As described earlier, research addressing the concerns most firmly connected to cure agenda types tends to be completely removed from research contributing to the information base for cause-oriented agendas. Murray's statement demonstrates this independence of research agendas.

Expansion of Rights

Cause-oriented discourse was limited, but not entirely absent from, the legislative documents examined. Although not found in documents explicitly discussing neurological difference, a search for documents containing the word "disability" returned discussion of the Lilly Ledbetter Fair Pay Act of 2009. This act, signed into law by President Barack Obama on January 29, 2009, does not exclusively belong to the disability policy subsystem per se. Instead, the bill amends the Civil Rights Act of 1964 to establish that the 180-day statute of limitations for filing an equal-pay lawsuit regarding pay discrimination resets with each new discriminatory paycheck. The intent of the law is to better address the reality that people experiencing pay discrimination may not become immediately aware of the situation.

The act demonstrates that at this point in history disability falls into the standard list of characteristics requiring policy designed to protect rights.

Testimony provided by Senator Jon Kyl on January 22, 2009, included the argument: "Finally, the expansion would not just apply to sex discrimination but to all protected classes of multiple employment laws covering civil rights, age, disability, and so on. So it is a much broader statute than is being portrayed by some who are simply saying this is about employment discrimination and changing the statute of limitations." The status of disability as a standard class in need of attention in general rights policy partly accounts for the absence of specific discourse on disability rights, particularly in a society that is less accepting of collective than individual rights. In considering this as a possibility, it is worth looking at a case of public discourse explicitly focused on the issue of disability rights in a society that is typically more accepting of collective rights. The Canadian Supreme Court case *Auton (Guardian ad litem of) v. British Columbia (Attorney General)* (3 S.C.R. 657, 2004 SCC 78), is an intriguing example of such a situation.

Case Study: Cause, Cure, and the Auton Case in Canada

Any tendency to interpret cure as cause tends to become particularly strong in nations where medical rights exist as part of the basic human or civil rights afforded to either all citizens or all residents of the nation. In the United States, of course, entitlements to medical care currently exist only for specified populations and tend to be articulated in the context of need-based, obligation-oriented care as opposed to rights. In other Western democracies, however, access to medical care represents a central component of rights-oriented policy. In Canada, for example, the Canada Health Act, adopted in 1984, establishes a right to publicly funded necessary health care (defined as provided in hospitals or by physicians).[1]

The right to necessary treatment became a focal issue for the politics of neurodiversity in Canada in the early twenty-first century. In 2004, the Supreme Court of Canada ruled in *Auton* that provinces were not required to pay for a specific therapeutic intervention for autism called applied behavior analysis (ABA; also known as intensive behavioral intervention, or IBI). In so ruling, the Court overturned the decisions of all lower courts. The decision reaffirmed that the Health Act did not require payment for services not considered medically necessary.

The case is intriguing from the standpoint of the politics of neurodiversity and neurological difference because it set the cause- and cure-oriented agendas in direct and public opposition to one another around the question of an established right cherished in a modern democratic context. In the *Auton* case, a group of parents of children with autism brought suit against the provincial government of British Columbia because the province stopped paying for the therapy they considered most appropriate for their children. The parents' argument held that ABA/IBI, while not a completely effective cure for autism, constituted the most scientifically proven intervention for characteristics of autism considered undesirable. As one of the plaintiff parents, Sabrina Freeman, explained in *Science for Sale in the Autism Wars* (2003):

> Parents of children with autism fighting for their children's rights to medically necessary health care for autistic disorder have been at the sharp end of the Health Technology Assessment stick for only one reason: Health Technology tried to convince the courts, at the behest of government, that the science-based standard for autism treatments, Dr. O. I. Lovaas's "Intensive Behavior Treatment" (autism treatment), is purportedly experimental, unsubstantiated therapy unworthy of health insurance coverage. (2)

As part of the argument, these parents explicitly rejected characterization of the treatment as care for individuals with autism, comparing the therapy to, for example, less than 100 percent effective treatments for cancer (Freeman 2003, 25).

ABA/IBI is an intensive program involving one-on-one work for dozens of hours a week. Essentially, it breaks down tasks to their most minute components and forces repetition of those components until the person receiving the therapy can reliably complete that component of the task before moving on to the next step. The process can involve a great deal of time. For example, a three-year-old child engaged in ABA/IBI therapy might spend approximately the same time commitment as in a full-time job, an unusual expectation for any child. As a result of its intensity, provision of ABA/IBI tends to become extremely costly, generally speaking at least at the level of a full-time salary for a certified therapist for each child undergoing this treatment.

Whether ABA/IBI is truly the most scientifically proven treatment for autism is debated. In fact, the British Columbian government once paid for this treatment, but changed its policy as the controversy surrounding the treatment and, in particular, questions surrounding the exclusivity of its effectiveness came to light. The scientific proof of the ABA/IBI therapy rests on studies conducted by O. Ivar Lovaas starting in the 1950s. Although the therapy developed over time, claims of scientific proof of its efficacy tend to rely on early studies that demonstrated improvement in 47 percent (nine out of nineteen) of the children who received ABA/IBI treatment, generally speaking to the point that they became indistinguishable from their neurologically typical peers. Initially the research claimed that the children had "recovered" from autism as a result of Lovaas's 1987 study, however the term *recovered* did not appear in subsequent research.

Most criticism surrounding the research providing scientific proof of the effectiveness of ABA/IBI grows from perceived selection bias in the original studies. Critics held that children less negatively affected by autism to begin with were deliberately chosen as research subjects. The limited replicability of the studies has also been proposed as a potential threat to the validity of the results. In addition, some researchers and advocates expressed concern due to the inability of the children to give consent to the treatment. This argument, however, at least at face value, was less scientifically relevant, as it is common practice to substitute consent of the parent or primary caregiver for consent of the child when involving children in scientific research.

Furthermore, many people, including a vocal community of individuals with autism, object to ABA/IBI therapy on the grounds that it includes the explicit goal of eliminating all autistic tendencies and that the intensity of time involved in the therapy itself deprives children with autism of freedoms normally associated with childhood. After all, the goal of recovering from autism assumes that there is something from which a person needs to recover (Broderick 2009). As advocate Michelle Dawson explained in an essay titled "The Misbehaviour of Behaviouralists":

> Parents, and the industry supplying their demands, have met no opposition in widely diffusing their defamation of autistic people. It has been a successful strategy in meeting their needs, financial and otherwise. In order to continue to grow, prosper, and be paid for by the public, the autism-ABA industry has enhanced then exploited the non-autistic horror and dread of autism and autistics. The parents and their industry have marketed autistics as worthless agents of personal, social, and financial destruction. They have used sensationalism, and emotional and fiscal blackmail, and they have been praised and catered to. The industry— which includes lawyers specializing in ABA cases, and Dr. Sallows' 800-employee corporation—has grown and prospered. (www.sentex.net /~nexus23/naa_aba.html)

Tensions between adults with a particular functional difference and parents of young children with the same diagnosis sometimes emerge in disability policy subsystems. Although society's rights over children have expanded dramatically over the past century and a half, allowing for implementation of policy designed to ensure the basic safety and education of all children, claims to other people's children remain deliberately limited in modern society. Barring unusual circumstances, decisions about children typically stay with their parents. When it comes to disabilities that are not (or at least not entirely) self-replicating, individuals who consider their functional differences a characteristic of community have sought public sympathy for their rights to become involved in decisions surrounding potential members of their communities, including children with the same functional difference. For example, deaf-culture advocates openly criticize parents' decisions to use technology to limit the functional impacts of deafness in their children. Part of the concern, of course, rests with the impression that cure will result in the diminishment or destruction of deaf culture (Brueggemann 2009). Cure, in this case, is seen as in direct opposition to the collective rights of individuals with disabilities.

As mentioned, the parents who sought public funding for ABA/IBI therapy won their case at the provincial level. According to Families for Early Autism Treatment–British Columbia (FEAT-BC), the leading activist group associated with the effort:

> The July 2000 BC Supreme Court decision is the strongest precedent to date in favor of Lovaas-type Intensive Behavioral Autism Treatment (Intensive ABA or EIBI). The court has declared that EIBI or ABA is a "medically necessary" service and must be funded by the government. The BC Supreme Court has ruled that the current failure to fund this treatment constitutes direct government "discrimination" against children with Autism Spectrum Disorder, and is a breach of the Canadian Constitution. (Canadian Charter of Rights and Freedoms, Section 15[1])

The term "medically necessary" became the central factor of the case, symbolizing the opposition between cause and cure agendas underlying the dispute. Such treatment implies that an individual cannot attain health without it. Comparisons to the necessity of chemotherapy to treat cancer abounded in the arguments of the case. However, as mentioned, autism is not normally associated with death and decline. Instead, most individuals with autism develop skills over their lifetimes. In addition, reliable, noncontroversial information about lifespan experiences of individuals with autism can be difficult to come by due to intervening variables such as deinstitutionalization, the expansion of publicly provided special education, and the change in diagnostic criteria for the difference over time. Put simply, no way to reliably predict what the current generation of children with autism will experience as adults currently exists. Whether the interaction of their functionalities and public infrastructures will generally lead to experience of difference, impairment, disability, or (though unlikely) handicap depends upon both the long-term effects of modern special education and therapies and the flexibility of future public infrastructures.

Nineteen individuals and organizations participated as interveners in the case, including the attorney general of Canada and the attorneys general of nine other provinces. In an intervener factum, Dawson stated:

> The Charter does not exist to promote these stereotypes and prejudices by allowing equality, dignity, and participation only to those who succeed in a "medically necessary" treatment to eradicate their differences and render them indistinguishable from Canadians judged to be "normal" . . . The Charter exists to prevent the life, liberty, and security of individuals with differences from being diminished or devalued through discrimination. The Charter does not exist to promote the view that only "normal" Canadians, or Canadians striving to be "normal," can enjoy life, health, liberty, security, and dignity. (www.sentex.net/~nexus23/naa_fac.html)

This case involved dispute over the nature of medical care in the context of generally improved rights of individuals with disabilities. Traditionally, medical care involves efforts to prolong life, maintain functionality, and in some cases return or create a level of functionality approximating the human norm. As a result, large health care systems, particularly public health care systems, tend to be geared toward the needs of emergencies and of maintaining the health of a typical member of a given population. As Diane Pothier testified on behalf of the Women's Legal Action Fund (LEAF) and the DisAbled Women's Network (DAWN)–Canada (www.leaf.ca/legal /facta/2004-auton.pdf#target): "What we have here is a medicare system that is primarily—not exclusively but primarily geared to the typical needs of the able-bodied population . . . it disproportionally meets the healthcare needs of the able-bodied population and, correspondingly, disproportionately fails to meet the needs of the disabled population." As a result, individuals with functional differences experience exclusion from the health care infrastructures similar to the exclusion from other public infrastructures. Equitable access to medical care is as much a natural part of cause-oriented public agendas as access to any other kind of infrastructure.

Furthermore, the need for accommodation exists in medical care infrastructures in the same way it does in other traditionally exclusionary infrastructures. One area of difficulty in accessing medical care for individuals with functional differences surrounds access to appropriate care. Physicians are either specialists or skilled generalists. General practitioners serve as entry points to most medical care. Due to time constraints and the limits of human cognition, training for general practitioners focuses on typical human beings. Especially in the age of the Internet, general practitioners often have little training in functional differences beyond what a motivated, self-taught individual might have learned about a particular functional difference. What training general practitioners do have tends to separate the functional difference from the rest of their medical training, thereby creating a separation of that particular function from the rest of the health (or illness) experience of the individual. As a result, a paradox exists in the provision of care for individuals with functional differences. The functional difference would tend to indicate a need for a specialist, thereby relieving the general practitioner of responsibility for planning and providing care for the individual with the functional difference. However, access to the general practitioner can function as the only path by which an individual with a functional difference has a chance to be treated as a whole, often healthy, person.

Most functional differences stabilize and do not affect the other functionality levels of the individual. As a result, the individual has a need for a general care similar (if not identical) to that required by other members of the general population. Specialists, however, are trained to see every experience through the lens of the functional difference, making for an inappropriate locale for general health care for the individual with the functional difference. People with disabilities can end up caught between the expectation of specializing and the expectation of generalizing, fitting not easily into either location and thereby experiencing difficulty in accessing medical care. Ongoing public debate exists as to whether individuals with neurological differences more appropriately receive routine health care services from specialists or generalists (MacIntyre 2008, 11). As a result, cause in the shape of appropriate planning of accommodation becomes an instrumental goal of care-oriented policy with regard to the question of location of care.

Furthermore, across the industrialized world, people with neurological differences have been found to under-use health care systems as compared to the rest of the general population. As Gillian MacIntyre explained about the United Kingdom: "People with learning disabilities experience more significant health problems—and a greater number of them—than the general population, and are likely to have greater unmet health needs . . . paradoxically, this is a group who tend to access services less often . . . this is particularly true in relation to health promotion and screening activities"

(2008, 62). Relative underuse of the medical system results from a variety of factors, both inside and outside the direct purview of the health care system. In some cases, for example, individuals with neurological differences may find their health care providers and their staff difficult to communicate with. In others, however, the primary infrastructural barrier may be availability of public transportation to the facility.

What the *Auton* case also demonstrates is the implications when cure becomes cause as a mechanism to challenge embedded preferences for traditionally more powerful stakeholders associated with other, more care-oriented medical programs and treatments. Despite increased popularity of cause-oriented agenda types in the disability policy subsystem, public issues relating to disability still more immediately connect to issues of care in the minds of the general public as well as most elected representatives. Indeed, the idea of disability often provokes images of costly long-term care. After all, particularly in recent years, the general publics of industrialized nations have been frequently exposed to rising costs of health care. Longer life expectancy and survivability of disability at both ends of the lifespan are oft-mentioned drivers of these rising costs. However, the social values of modern societies make care-oriented discourse difficult to trump in disability policy subsystems, particularly if there is debate with regard to the appropriate treatment. If a given treatment can be uniquely defined as cure and then linked to cause-oriented agendas, however, potential for trumping other care agendas develops. After all, under such circumstances, expense associated with long-term care is implicitly expected to quickly outpace costs associated with cure. In the *Auton* case, the effort to define a particular form of treatment as cure (and therefore cause) was, to some degree, about taking public attention and resources away from other forms of treatment.

Another confounding factor of the cause versus cure tension as demonstrated in this particular case involves persistence of outdated impressions of ABA/IBI therapy. While little doubt exists that the intervention is intensive and intrusive, it no longer includes forcefully aversive measures. At one point in its development, when a child failed to perform the desired behavior, he or she would receive a punishment (in some cases physical). This was not unusual treatment of either people with disabilities or children during the era of the intervention's invention. However, ABA/IBI never includes this today when practiced by a trained, certified therapist. Such residual impressions of antiquated therapeutic and medical interventions often affect how individuals with disabilities and issue stakeholders representing cause agenda types perceive modern medical care.

Furthermore, a (sometimes deserved) impression of proponents of ABA/IBI is that they think it should be the only intervention used and available for individuals with autism, regardless of their level of capacity and personal goals. For individuals with autism described as being on the higher end of the spectrum, little need for such intensive therapeutic involvement typically exists, even if the individual (or more likely the parents or primary caregiver of the child) requests it. A common concern with services potentially perceived as disability-related advantages such as individualized education surrounds the assumption that entitled parents will seek out the services for their child even if he or she does not really need it. For example, in the United States, the concern frequently arises that some parents might demand an individualized education plan for their child to allow that child more time to take tests or complete modified assignments, not to accommodate an actual disability but to create an advantage. While no credible evidence of such behavior exists beyond anecdotal stories, widespread fear of this practice continues to exist and play a part in ongoing public and political discourse surrounding special education. In fact, such scenarios have been portrayed in popular culture, such as in an episode of *Veronica Mars*.

Another outdated impression of ABA/IBI treatment is that proponents of the treatment believe that it should be applied to every individual with autism regardless of age, demand, and level of capacity. In reality, to some degree, this was the impression given by the proponents of ABA/IBI treatment in the *Auton* case. Nevertheless, even the website of the Lovaas institute (www.lovaas.com) carefully points out that most children transition away from ABA/IBI by early adolescence, toward different therapeutic approaches to managing autism. Furthermore, in the era of deinstitutionalization, forced treatment is becoming less prevalent (though certainly not absent) in modern nations.

Case Study: Autism in
Recent North American Government Discourse

The *Auton* case occurred during a period of rapid ascendance of the public profile of autism. Although the meaning and implication of all neurological differences changed rapidly during the last decades of the twentieth century, autism was perceived at least as experiencing many of these changes (such as incidence, inclusion, and community awareness) in a magnified way.[2] Given this feature of the politics of neurodiversity surrounding cause and cure agenda types, in order to gain a sense of public discourse surrounding neurological differences in Canada and the United States, legislative debates that occurred and reports that were produced between 2007 and 2009 were examined. Because neurological difference and neurodiversity are relatively rarely discussed overtly, it is necessary to use discussions about particular diagnoses as proxies in order to gain insight into how discourse connected to the two agenda types interacts in formal political settings. The case of autism was employed because of the formative role individuals with autism have played in neurodiversity-oriented public discourse.

Recent Legislative Discourse on Cure

On the whole, discourse on autism tended to focus more on cure agendas than on cause. However, even cure agendas received less attention than those concentrating on providing care for individuals (particularly children) currently living with autism. This is not surprising in either Canada or the United States. Despite differences in their health care infrastructures, fiscal outlook, and composition of social services policy and programs, creating effective health care and health-related social welfare services constitutes a public problem on the systemic and governmental agendas of both nations. A repeating refrain of political discourse focused on level of expense associated with currently available interventions for autism. For example, during testimony before the US Congress on September 18, 2008, this element of public agendas regarding autism was explained as follows:

> The National Children's Study will yield benefits that far outweigh its cost. It will be an extraordinarily worthwhile investment for our nation, and it can be justified even in a time of fiscal stress such as we face today. Six of the diseases that are the focus of the Study (obesity, injury, asthma, diabetes, autism and schizophrenia) cost America $642 billion each year. If the Study were to produce even a 1% reduction in the cost of these diseases, it would save $6.4 billion annually, 50 times the average yearly costs of the Study itself.

As this testimony demonstrates, presumed cost savings associated with finding a cure for autism constitute a popular aspect of the persuasive arguments articulated for cure agendas. Similarly, in a report titled "Pay Now or Pay Later," presented to the Canadian Senate's Standing Committee on Social Affairs, Science, and Technology in March 2007, it was stated:

Families with autistic children in Canada are facing a crisis. When a child is diagnosed with autism and therapy is prescribed by a health professional, publicly funded health care insurance does not pay for the cost of the therapy. As a result, families must often pay out of their own pockets for a very large portion of expensive autism therapy—whose cost may reach $60,000 per year—because provincial and territorial jurisdictions offer only limited financial assistance. Families with autistic children across the country are therefore calling on the federal government to take a leadership role with respect to autism. As a matter of comparison, they point to the Combating Autism Act of 2006 in the United States which authorizes the federal government to spend $US 945 million over five years for autism research, screening, intervention and education.

In such political discourse, paying current treatment costs tends to be favorably compared with older policy and programmatic approaches favoring often lifetime institutionalization. The core intention of these arguments involves reaching the conclusion that finding a cure that allows for the transformation of autism from a disability to an impairment or, better yet, a simple difference possibly entirely eradicating outward signs of autism, will be the most cost-effective manner of addressing public challenges surrounding autism.

This topic, combined with references to the rise in measured incidence of autism from its historical rate of approximately 1 in 10,000 individuals, created the platform from which to argue for a sense of urgency for the cure agenda. For example, as Bradley Whitford testified before the US Senate's Appropriations Committee on April 17, 2007:

> 1 in 10,000 kids will have autism. That's what top scientists would have told you little more than a decade ago. Then, it became clear that number was ridiculous. And the CDC [Centers for Disease Control]—with the support of this Subcommittee—started to really look at the prevalence of autism. 1 in 2500, then 1 in 500. By the time the Children's Health Act of 2000 became law, the estimate had become 1 in 250. A few short years ago, the CDC said 1 in 166. Now, just a couple of months ago, the best data ever collected produced the scariest number yet—1 in 150—1 out of 94 American boys.

Testimony such as this seeks to establish growth of autism as an emergency outpacing the ability of government agencies to create effective programs. A similar argument made somewhat more succinctly during a hearing about funding for the creative arts in the United States on March 17, 2007, mentioned in passing, was: "I really want to also talk about a very sad situation in the sense that we've got a high rise of autism."

One procedural step often discussed in cure-related arguments made in public discourse surrounds the search for the etiology of autism. Suspected causal factors fall into two basic categories: environment and genetics. For example, during a hearing before the Education, Labor, and Pensions Committee on March 11, 2008, it was remarked: "I was just a moment ago . . . given this blue wrist band, Autism Awareness Week, and was just talking about . . .what NIH [National Institutes of Health] is funding for them, and environmental causes and all the things we need to look at . . . And the work that all of you do as scientists is so very, very important to us." During testimony before the Subcommittee on Courts, the Internet, and Intellectual Property of the House Judiciary Committee on September 11, 2008, the following statement was made: "I believe, personally, that the number one step right now is to establish a comprehensive plan for autism research that goes from environmental issues to development issues to other issues of definition of what autism really is." Such arguments have become rarer components of cure-related agendas in recent years, however.

This shift in discourse obviously relates to expansion of understanding of the genetic components of autism. However, another element of this type of discourse surrounding the cure agenda relates to environmental causes fundamentally representing something of a departure from the cure agenda. After all, in the final analysis, environmental causes tend to be predominantly linked to environmental and prevention policy solutions, rather than a quest for a cure per se. As a result, environmental elements become deemphasized. For example, on March 2, 2007, testimony before the Interior Subcommittee of the House Appropriations Committee, though purportedly dedicated to environmental aspects of autism, included the statement: "In the case of autism, this is a terrible problem in our country and we must find answers to it. We know there's a genetic component. There still could be an environmental aspect to it and it's our responsibility to have an open mind and continue to look for the answers." The case against environmental factors was even more emphatically made later in the same testimony when a CDC representative argued:

> We have spent a great deal of research effort at CDC and are continuing to do that to look at the whole—the big picture of the association between mercury from any source and a potential relationship with autism, autism-spectrum disorders or other birth defects. And what I can tell you right now is we found no evidence of a linkage in any of the environmental health or epidemiologic studies that have been done to this date. We also know that there's more work to be done at the cellular level to understand how mercury might possibly cause that kind of complication.

Directing discourse within the cure agenda at least subtly in favor of genetic as opposed to environmental causal factors connects cure-oriented agendas more firmly to solutions produced by the traditional medical community. This connection represents an essentialist interpretation of moving the atypical functionalities designated as autism from the category of disability to impairment or difference through direct intervention targeting a person with a difference rather than a society.

Discourse surrounding locating genetic components of autism tends to suggest the penultimate (though elusive) goal of the cure agenda: genetic eradication of autism. References to autism as a birth defect link autism with other neurological differences, especially Down syndrome, which has a completely identified genetic etiology. Kristin Bumiller describes such efforts relating to "genetic citizenship" and explains that "the notion of genetic citizenship is based on the belief that in a biomedical age all citizens are given the possibility and have the responsibility to participate in the creation of healthier societies . . . disability activists have been vocal in their efforts to reveal the reemergence of eugenic tendencies under conditions of biomedicalization" (2009, 885). Of course, given that modern, reasonable individuals tend to avoid discourse in any way suggestive of eugenics, it is not surprising that much political discourse about genetic interventions targeting autism addressed on their surface the potential for individualizing care as a result of improved understanding of the genetic heterogeneity of the set of symptoms collectively described as autism. For example, the following statement was made during a hearing on March 9, 2007, before the Labor, Health and Human Services, Education, and Related Agencies Subcommittee of the House Appropriations Committee:

> In the last two months, we've already launched through a public-private partnership very large-scale studies on ADHD [attention-deficit hyperactivity disorder], autism, depression, bipolar disorder, schizophrenia. And these kinds of studies, which years ago, or even when all of us arrived four years ago, would have taken maybe a decade will now take about 10 to 12 weeks. We can actually do this in very real time. We should have the results of all of this by this summer . . . That will not be the final answer, but it will give us the new set of candidates. And . . . those will help us along this pathway of being able to individualize the way we take care of people.

Statements such as this one leave open for interpretation the nature of the care resulting from ongoing genetic discovery. Discourse surrounding the genetics of autism tends to be at least loosely connected to prevention. Nevertheless, direct connection to the cure agenda tends to be at least cautiously made in these conversations.

Recent Legislative Discourse on Cause

As mentioned, discourse on the cause agenda was found to be much less present in the recent legislative discourse of both Canada and the United States. Furthermore, discussion of cause agendas often had little, if any, relation to neurodiversity. The most prevalent type of discourse relating to a cause-oriented agenda related to increasing public awareness of autism, often as a desperate, growing problem. For example, during discussion of a Canadian parliamentary report describing a national strategy for autism on April 2, 2008, a senator pleaded: "Declaring April 2 World Autism Awareness Day is one small step in a journey to see that all people with autism and their families have the care and support they need . . . I hope that all honourable senators will support me when I table the bill that will provide for Canada's recognition of April 2 as World Autism Awareness Day so that we can take that small step on behalf of all Canadians." Events and efforts surrounding Autism Awareness Day generally involved characterization of autism as a disease. For example, on June 17, 2008, in a statement introducing a private parliamentary member's bill to establish Canadian recognition of Autism Awareness Day, the following persuasive argument was made:

> Honourable senators, April 2 has been declared World Autism Awareness Day by the United Nations. There was consensus among 192 UN representatives that there is a need to draw the attention of people across the globe to this neurological disorder that is affecting more and more families. I am speaking today to inform my honourable colleagues that I intend to introduce a private member's bill so that Canada will also recognize April 2 as World Autism Awareness Day.

Descriptions of autism as a disease represent an anathema for neurodiversity activists who object not only to the association of autism with unavoidable suffering, but also to the implication of deterioration (if not death) that the disease involves. The equation was most emotively made in the Canadian discourse through the invocation of one of the most famous one-man activist actions in Canadian history. For instance, during a debate of the World Autism Day bill on April 2, 2008, one legislator said:

> As I speak tonight, a gentleman by the name of Jonathan Howard is walking across this country. He is not like Terry Fox, to whom we all paid attention. Jonathan Howard started walking a month ago from St. John's

and is walking to Victoria. I do not know who is paying attention to Jonathan right now, but he is walking to try not only to create awareness, which we all want to do, but also to secure a national strategy to deal with autism. He may be in New Brunswick or somewhere in Quebec, but he is still walking.

Terry Fox was a young man dying of cancer with a prosthetic leg who set out to run across Canada in a "Marathon of Hope" to raise money for cancer research. Fox died at the age of twenty-two in 1981 before he could complete his planned journey. Fox quickly became a national hero in Canada. Numerous cancer-related organizations are named after him and statues of Fox can be found in many Canadian communities. Modeling activism efforts on this historical event works toward carving in stone a characterization of autism as essentially similar to cancer.

Another way in which the discourse of the cause agenda departs from neurodiversity involves equating the autism cause with cure. In the United States, the group most famous for having taken this tack is Cure Autism Now (now part of Autism Speaks, the organization arguably most famous for its use of the puzzle piece to represent the need for increased research targeting cures for autism). Part of the efforts of this group involved comparing autism to kidnapping. For example, in a hearing before the Senate Appropriations Committee on April 17, 2007, the common question of this campaign was as follows: "As my friend Jon Shestack has said many times—it's as if 1 in 150 American children [were] being kidnapped. What would this Congress do if that was the case? What must it do to deal with these sad facts, as they truly are?" Posing such a question implies that the only appropriate response to autism is the quest for a cure.

Identification is a core issue upon which cause agendas revolve. Identification can become a sensitive issue for individuals with atypical neurological functionalities because of ongoing discrimination (if not fear) of individuals with these differences. For example, Canadian public discourse surrounding development of a national autism strategy included descriptions of this dilemma such as: "There are people with autistic children who do not like that definition because they think there is a stigma attached to the term." Furthermore, identification can involve routine exclusion believed to be in the best interest of all individuals with autism. For example, during testimony in the United States before the House Committee of Veterans Affairs on December 12, 2007, it was stated: "In May, the Hartford *Courant* ran a series of articles exposing the common practice in this army of deploying soldiers in spite of serious, documented mental health histories, including severe depression, bi-polarity, even autism." The use of the word "even" in this statement is interesting, because it implies that autism is inherently more problematic than the other neurological differences described here as associated (though rarely) with actual problematic events in the military.

Nevertheless, identification embodies a crucial step in becoming involved in discourse on the cause agenda. After all, a fundamental goal of cause agendas embracing neurodiversity is making sure all public discourse surrounding autism includes individuals with autism. Cause-oriented political discourse frequently notes the need for such a presence. For instance, during a debate of the Standing Committee on Social Affairs, Science, and Technology on March 29, 2007, the following request was made: "All stakeholders, including individuals with autism, [should] be consulted on the components that should be part of the Strategy, such as treatment, research, surveillance, awareness campaigns, community initiatives, education, respite care for families." Tellingly, however, statements about the need for the voices of individuals with autism appear much more frequently in the political discourse than do actual contributions from individuals with autism. Since legislative testimony tends to be an extremely formal and selective process, this discrepancy suggests disparity in the level of influence of different types of issue stakeholders in the politics of neurodiversity in cure- and cause-oriented agendas.

Another expression of this element of discourse about cause agenda types involves recognition of autism as a potential defining characteristic for communities. In Canada, during a debate on the national autism awareness strategy on February 12, 2008, this distinction was recognized in the statement: "Every autistic community and organization in this country continues to ask me to keep impressing that we need national leadership. What will it take to simply think outside the box for a second when dealing with the Health Act? There are no boundaries, as we know, when it comes to autism." Similarly in the United States, in congressional testimony on April 1, 2008, it was declared: "And since tomorrow is World Autism Day, I feel it's important to highlight some uses of this technology . . . for example, Autistics.org has created the Autistic Liberation Front . . . it's a platform where men and women with autism or Asperger's are able to find other people with autism, communicate more." Later in this testimony another speaker referenced perhaps the most fundamental aspect of cause agendas incorporating neurodiversity by saying: "To that end, I'd like to introduce this recent article from *Wired* magazine about people with autism and Asperger's and how their creative uses of the Internet is causing some researchers to rethink their conclusions about people with autism." Evidence of understandings of autism involving the possibility that autism might become a valued element of community rarely occurred in the public discourse of either Canada or the United States. Such understandings are not, however, as completely absent as they were when more essentialist conceptions of disability prevailed.

Both the cure and cause agendas of modern political discourse of Canada and the United States that were focused on neurological atypicalities almost always included the goal of elimination of handicap. However, the mechanism of elimination varied depending on the preferred agenda of the stakeholder. In the public discourse of both nations, discussion of cure tended to dominate and even encompass most discussion not exclusively focused on providing care for individuals with disabilities.

Signs of tensions between these agendas were, however, found. These tensions were particularly prevalent in discourse involving disease characterizations, goals of genetic research, and identification. As the average age of the population of individuals with autism increases beyond childhood, such tensions could became more distinctive. As public policy surrounding neurological atypicalities continues to develop, the likelihood of increased scrutiny of underlying assumptions tending toward traditional essentialism rises. Furthermore, should cures for autism continue to prove elusive—thereby curtailing the persuasiveness of the cost-benefit elements found in cure-oriented agendas—deeper discussion of other public agendas is likely to occur. As this examination of Canadian and US legislative discourse demonstrates, roots of both increased tensions between agendas and a higher profile for the cause (if not cultural celebration) agendas are already firmly in place.

When Policies Equate Cause and Cure

As this case study demonstrates, the disability policy subsystem, at least as expressed in the English language, holds the potential to confuse cause with cure both by making cause the cure and by seeking out cure through cause. Part of this phenomenon involves using elements from other agendas as instrumental goals when pursuing one of the substantive goals associated with the four agenda types. When it comes to cure and cause, however, a tendency exists to discuss cause and cure as though they are the same agenda type, which creates a dynamic focused on political survival between the two orientations of political discourse within the disability policy subsystem.

Concern about rising incidence of neurological differences has been growing since the 1970s. Whereas fear that mental handicaps might be spreading or contagious or both has a much longer history deeply intertwined with the goals of institutionalization, since the introduction of policies designed to encourage participation of individuals with disabilities in general society have expanded, so has discourse surrounding concerns about the prevalence of neurological difference (Fenton and Krahn 2007). For example, on March 2, 1975, the *New York Times* ran an article summarizing new research on learning disabilities. The article states: "learning disability takes many forms and that more subtle learning problems are difficult to recognize . . . many experts believe that learning disability is not a rare phenomenon and may affect up to 20% of school population." Such discussion of rising incidences (and prevalences)[3] naturally inspires both public discourse and scientific inquiry into possible causes of the increase. The combined effect of the statistics and the discussion has, in the case of some neurological differences at least, raised the specter of contagion and epidemic.

Epidemics are, by definition, urgent and almost always emergent risks[4] to the general public (Baker and Stokes 2006). The term "epidemic" invokes both unpredictability and a reduced sense of control over human destiny. Furthermore, though the term is often used metaphorically (such as an "epidemic of truancy" in a given school system), in a literal sense the term refers only to diseases with their attendant expectation of deterioration of functionalities, if not threat to continued survival of the individual. For the most part, epidemics are expected to (by implication quite quickly) overwhelm the capacities of public infrastructures to control and combat negative effects. Since public infrastructures cannot expand quickly enough to manage the negative effects of epidemics, the only possible way to fully protect the human and civil rights of the general population in this context is to find a cure or reliable vaccination for the disease.

When discourse in the disability policy subsystems of industrialized nations includes descriptions of neurological differences as epidemics, it thereby combines the force behind cause and cure agendas to garner public interest in the particular neurological difference. On August 30, 2010, a Google search on the term "autism epidemic" produced almost 65,000 hits (5,000 more than in a similar search conducted 3 months earlier). The most popular sites tended to take the term for granted, rather than debating whether or not the autism epidemic existed, and did not consider the accuracy or appropriateness of applying the term to a neurological difference. The designation also frequently appears in newspaper articles and letters to the editor. For example, in a letter appearing on November 20, 2007, in the *Washington Times,* the author criticized the American Academy of Pediatrics (AAP) by writing:

Somehow just diagnosing the problem sooner seems a strange way to address an epidemic. Are we to believe that all those children are born with autism? The AAP doesn't seem interested in why thousands of parents report normally developing, talking, interacting children suddenly regressing into the lost world of autism at age 2. Neither the AAP nor the Centers for Disease Control and Prevention are calling autism a national health care emergency.

Similarly, in a letter appearing in the *New York Times* on June 15, 2007, the author reacted to a previously published assertion of lack of proof of an autism epidemic by stating: "This reminds me of the argument for the last 20 years that there was no 'proof' of global warming . . . Absolute cause-and-effect proof in science takes decades to achieve. Meanwhile, the scientific and political establishment 'fiddled while Rome burned,' and the planet grew warmer." Bringing up the politics of global warming in public discourse surrounding neurological differences represents a fascinating example of the question of the role of falsifiable hypotheses in scientific evidence used in policy development. While seemingly more conclusive than just a few years ago, evidence surrounding global warming can only be highly speculative and difficult to hold to the positivist standard of scientific evidence. Such practices, on the one hand, can represent important developments in the sophistication of the relationship between science and society, including a more accurate representation of actual scientific work than is described by strictly traditional Popperian arguments. As the politics of neurodiversity and neurological difference continue to experience conflict surrounding cause and cure agenda types, managing the nature and standards of scientific evidence employed in discourse is likely to become increasingly complex.

Concluding Thoughts for All Disabilities

No tension is more central to modern disability policy development than the choice to pursue or redefine normalcy. The recognition of neurological differences as legitimate atypical functionalities took a different path through history than that of other disabilities. Nevertheless, negotiating a balance between desirable and nondesirable aspects of functional difference remains a painfully unsettled and unsettling topic in public and political discourse on all disabilities.

Marked imbalances of power continue between cure- and cause-oriented agendas. This power differential exists not only in the politics of neurological difference and neurodiversity, but for virtually all disabilities. From the typical size of faculty in university programs, to the dollars awarded in grants, donated in charities, and provided to legislators, and all the way to the amount of time and energy spent in formal political discussion, resources directed toward cure-oriented agendas almost always outpace those aimed toward the cause of establishing and protecting the rights of individuals with disabilities.

This imbalance may be partially mediated by the inclusion of disability in standard lists of diverse characteristics protected and promoted by modern public policy. Furthermore, the imbalance, while still pronounced, is much less so today than in the past. Nevertheless, this issue of relative resources continues to forcefully shape the relationship between these two agenda types in disability policy development.

To some degree, this distinction is legitimate. As mentioned in Chapter 1, diversity creates strength. Including (and, especially, not deliberately eradicating) nonfatal functional differences in the expected characteristics of some members of society is not only the sole path to justice, but will most likely provide that society with a comparative advantage in the long run. Nevertheless, supporting diversity in society does not include forced continuation of mutable characteristics at the individual level. Of course, strong effort should be made to educate the individual (or their family in the case of children or others with sufficiently compromised comprehension) about the complexity of their choice to pursue an available cure.

After all, just as it would be inappropriate to force an individual to practice a minority religion in the name of the protection of diversity if he or she wanted to make an informed conversion to another faith, forcing an individual to embrace a functional difference against their informed will is oppressive. Cure—or its pursuit—is a part of the inalienable right articulated in the United States as the pursuit of happiness. It is not, however, the same as disability rights, especially when our common belief in our ability to cure functional differences far exceeds our actual ability to do so. Furthermore, in the development of modern disability policy, it is vitally important that responsibility to pursue or accept cure be introduced into public and political discourse only with extreme caution and utmost consideration.

Notes

1. Unlike in other nations that provide publicly funded health care as a basic right, health care in Canada is provided primarily through private entities, and not through a national health service. The majority of health care costs are, however,

paid through public funds designed and implemented primarily at the provincial level of government.

2. This relative popularity of autism in the politics of neurodiversity also extended into the early years of the twenty-first century. Today, however, trauma-induced conditions, especially posttraumatic stress disorder, are beginning to acquire a much higher profile as well.

3. Incidence and prevalence are often confounded in public and political discourse. Incidence describes how frequently people develop a condition in a defined population over a given period of time (usually one year). Prevalence refers to how many people currently have a condition within a defined population at a given time, regardless of when they were diagnosed. When it comes to neurological differences, some debate exists as to whether prevalence (as opposed to incidence) is in fact increasing in populations. For the most part, confusion between the terms makes little difference to current politics of neurodiversity, since both terms are used to inspire the same political action and policy choices.

4. Public risks can be placed on a continuum from emergent to transcendent. Transcendent risks are those perpetually faced by humanity such as natural disasters or hunger. Emergent risks are those that are at least experienced as representing a novel challenge with which humanity has no historical experience. Though epidemics as a class are transcendent, specific epidemics are usually emergent.

5

Securing Civil Rights
vs. Celebrating Diversity

At first glance, cause and celebration agenda types seem most symbiotic of all possible pairings. Proponents of both types embrace a core value of promoting positive attention on issues relating to neurological difference. Also, one could easily expect that positive political and public discourse surrounding one of these agenda types would naturally support the other. Promoting the rights of individuals with neurological differences presumably leads to an appreciation of those individuals as valuable members of society. Similarly, efforts designed to stimulate ways of being human that vary alongside individual neurology, if successful, build a sociocultural environment inherently protective of the rights of those with neurological differences.

Proponents of these two agenda types do in fact frequently work in tandem with one another both in discourse and in resulting programmatic efforts. However, as occurs in the interactions of all agenda types, substantial conflicts have also emerged between issue stakeholders of these two types of agendas. Furthermore, while these efforts might overlap considerably in policy and program goals, they also encompass critical areas of distinction, particularly with regard to historical experiences of individuals with neurological differences and the role of self-activism in the promotion of related political activities. This chapter explores dynamics of the relationships between cause and celebration agenda types by first considering the role of the activist, then exploring emphasis on suffering in rights-oriented discussion, then discussing the role of separatist efforts, and finally presenting an analysis of newspaper coverage of events motivated by differing agenda types.

115

Celebration and Cause: The Activist Effect

Public engagement in policy subsystems includes a variety of archetypical and sometimes mutually exclusive roles. Although no consensus on a standard list of the types of roles generally found in specific subsystems exists, examples of typical categories include legislator, analyst, advocate, administrator, bureaucrat, scholar, and activist.

As a result of these differences in roles, not all actors within a particular policy subsystem engage in the same set of activities or participate in ongoing political discourse employing identical rules of engagement. For example, whereas an advocate would typically take a vocal position on proposed policy, a scholar most often seeks to inject (relatively) unbiased information into the system based on sustained objective study, and a bureaucrat would generally weigh in most forcefully when specifically asked and then implement a policy ultimately designed to the best of his or her ability. No role possesses more inherent value. The efforts of individuals playing different roles ultimately cover all of the work necessary to successfully navigate from the formulation and development to the implementation and evaluation of public policy and programs. Furthermore, within particular policy subsystems, individuals who act out of accordance with their identified role risk losing credibility and, potentially, the goodwill of other issue stakeholders.

Activists rank among expected participants in democratic governance. Archetypically, the role of the activist involves disrupting ongoing activities in policy subsystems in order to inspire fundamental changes in policy agendas or even governmental structures themselves. Activists frequently seek out and destroy stability in public policy and programs in order to achieve their political goals. Except in extreme circumstances, activists generally operate within the bounds of the law, engaging in legal forms of voice and protest. One of the defining characteristics separating activists from other actors in policy subsystems, however, surrounds a lack of concern with regard to bias in information, impact of change on current policy infrastructures, and, often, attention to details surrounding implementation of policy once the desired policy becomes law.

As a result, disability activism can express an ardent version of either the celebration or the cause agenda type. As Tom Shakespeare explained, "the disability activist opposition to charity can sometimes appear almost obsessive, such as the subscriber to Disability Arts in London (summer 2004, issue 182) who withdrew from BCODP and Disability Arts in London mailings because they took advertisements from Scope" (2006, 153).

Natural overlap exists in such efforts, often to the point of superficially re-solving conflict between celebration- and cause-oriented agendas. This be-comes particularly likely at the agenda-setting phase of public policy, where the primary goal becomes gaining public and political attention for a par-ticular issue. Public events combining both celebration- and cause-oriented events have historically represented a particularly fruitful strategy in this vein.

Discussion of Rights Tends to Invoke Suffering

Disability rights efforts connect intimately to other rights-oriented move-ments (Barnartt and Scotch 2001). As a general trend, rights movements moved ever more forcefully onto both systemic and formal government agendas during the late nineteenth century and throughout the twentieth. This sociocultural change powerfully affected nearly all aspects of human existence in the industrialized nations (if not, to some degree, around the world) (Ishay 2008).

The time taken to counter traditions of discrimination is long when con-sidered in terms of human lifetimes. However, given a viewpoint of histor-ical progress, this change can also be perceived as having happened relatively rapidly. For example, in the United States, the transition from con-sidering nonwhites as subhuman, and in many circumstances bereft of even the most basic of civil rights, to electing an African American to serve as president, over a period of less than a century and a half, could be inter-preted as constituting a stunningly quick shift in basic paradigms of the es-sential nature of human beings. Others remain more critical of the pace of change. As Marta Russell described in the late 1990s, "the country has had several hundred years to accomplish equality of results, having sent men to the moon in the meantime . . . if the 'moral' mainstream wanted to solve the problem of inequality, wouldn't it already have done so?" (1998, 230). Re-gardless of one's impression of time taken for change to occur during the evolution of disability policy subsystems in industrialized nations, cause-oriented agenda types focusing on disability rights have been temporal cre-ations to a degree that is difficult to overemphasize (Charlton 2000).

Given this prevailing historical context, cause-oriented disability pol-icy and political discourse often bear stronger resemblance to the policy and discourse of other rights-oriented policy than to the policy and discourse derived from other disability agenda types. In fact, rights-oriented policy focused on human differences sometimes moves beyond the disability policy subsystem, becoming part of the general rights framework in a given society. Demonstration of this takes place when disability appears as part of a list of circumstances explicitly protected from discrimination. For example, the Equal Employment Opportunity statement of Virginia reads: "It is the Commonwealth's objective to provide equal employment opportunity to employees and applicants for employment. All aspects of personnel management and employment practices will be conducted without regard to race, color, religion, sex, age, national origin, disability, or political affiliation (except where a bona fide occupational qualification regarding a particular position applies)" (www.dhrm.state.va.us/hrpolicy/policy/eeo.htm). Such policies treat disability as part of the general composition of diversity rather than as a separate policy subsystem. This can create tension with celebration-oriented agendas, which often seek to maintain a distinction between individuals with disabilities and other members of the general population.

Suffering Supports Rights-Based Claims

One of the core characteristics of political discourse surrounding rights-based policy claims involves emphasis on both historical and ongoing injustice. Specific descriptions of suffering on the part of the harmed party tend to become expected components of injustice arguments. In the case of the disability policy subsystem, those engaged in efforts associated with a cause agenda type would therefore tend to emphasize ubiquitous disadvantages (if not outright harm) associated with living with difference. Such arguments more commonly appeared in the past. However, they still appear in public and political discourse today.

This is not, in the absolute sense, a rhetorical or logical necessity. In more modern, constructivist-oriented cause discourse, disadvantages generally become attributed not only to the difference, but also to the limitations of public infrastructures. For example, regarding disability rights, the American Civil Liberties Union (ACLU) states:

> Despite ample evidence that the ADA [Americans with Disabilities Act] is working, people with disabilities are still, far too often, treated as second class citizens, shunned and segregated by physical barriers and social stereotypes. They are discriminated against in employment, schools, and housing, robbed of their personal autonomy, sometimes even hidden away and forgotten by the larger society. Many people with disabilities continue to be excluded from the American dream. (www.aclu.org/disability/index.html)

The ACLU is a generalist organization committed to protection of the Constitution of the United States of America and the rights of the general population regardless of personal characteristics. Including disability as part of its efforts reflects the position that functional atypicalities represent one of a standard list of potential threats to civil liberties. The Disability Rights Education and Defense Fund, a national organization established in the United States in 1979, also describes its work in constructivist terms:

> The vision of the Disability Rights Education and Defense Fund is a just world where all people, with and without disabilities, live full and independent lives free of discrimination . . . Americans with disabilities make up one of the United States' largest minorities. More than 25% live in poverty and only about 20% have gone to college. Seventy-five percent are unemployed. Such economic and social disenfranchisement is not an inevitable consequence of the physical and mental limitations imposed by disability; it is the result of society's historic response to those limitations: lack of accessibility in the built environment and policies that encourage or even require exclusion, segregation, and institutionalization. The result is a legacy of prejudice and paternalism that is deeply embedded in the social consciousness. (www.dredf.org/about.shtml)

As these statements demonstrate, organizations promoting disability rights agendas tend to emphasize the role of public infrastructures, rather than the essential characteristics of particular conditions, in creating suffering. Articulation of suffering in this manner brings public discourse surrounding cause agenda types more naturally in tandem with assertions made in celebration-oriented discourse than do more essentialist descriptions of suffering.

Arguments of injustice can center around existence of barriers within these infrastructures without invoking specific conditions. In other words, the right to an inclusive society can be understood as a fundamental right of the general population rather than connecting to needs and deficits of individuals with differences. After all, as with diversity more generally, the whole population can benefit from inclusion of the ideas, input, and strengths of all members of the population, just as the existence of unnecessarily dependent groups of individuals might be understood to result in suffering. Most disability studies literature on the subject embraces this conception of rights. However, in terms of political feasibility, it remains generally true that rhetoric of targeted suffering becomes a necessary component of rights-based policy claims, even when articulated in a more constructivist manner. Especially in a civil rights context, claims of suffering require individualization in order to be legally addressed. This practice tends to confuse those who are less prone to thinking about disability in terms of interactions between infrastructures and atypicalities, who might conceive of these provisions as special rights that may (or may not) be owed to lesser members of society. As Jeffrey Dudas explained, "the allegation of special rights propels and amplifies activists' resentment, transforming it from one that is based primarily on competing self interests into one that is concerned with values, morality and national identity" (2005, 723). Given this dynamic, displacement of the goals of both celebration- and cure-oriented agendas can take place.

As a result of these factors, arguments made in political discourse of industrialized nations tend to describe people as "suffering from" neurological differences. One reason for this portrayal, as already suggested, involves the theory that without suffering, no injustice can exist. Furthermore, even when coming from a more constructivist viewpoint, cause-oriented political claims tend to emphasize suffering as an unavoidable result (and often the only result) of interaction between the difference and current infrastructures. Even if the fault lies entirely with society's infrastructures, effects of interactions between political or economic infrastructure and the individual's difference have to be portrayed as predominantly harmful and undesirable in order for the claim of injustice to appear valid. For example, in considering the political implications of neurological differences such as Asperger syndrome or bipolar disorder, the likelihood of sufferers not always fitting in with peers or experiencing periodic incapacity would, in cause-oriented discourse, be emphasized over advantages in recall memory or heightened creativity. Inspiring others to care about a cause depends on a perception of relative suffering resulting from both disadvantage and injustice. Discourse focusing on disability rights rarely highlights positive outcomes of the interactions between infrastructures and functional atypicalities, because of the tendency to create cognitive dissonance in the minds of a general public accustomed to injustice claims rooted in suffering. This focus on suffering can make it difficult for other members of the general population to understand celebration of disability in general, let alone as a matter of public policy or as being an appropriate target for public resources.

Reconciling Suffering and Celebration

This emphasis on negative implications of difference can be difficult to reconcile with celebration-oriented political discourse. First, celebration-oriented agendas conceive of portrayals of inevitable or universal suffering as inherent misunderstandings of the individuality of the experience of difference. For example, in a description of Disability Pride authored by Sarah Triano, the website for the sixth annual Disability Pride Parade, held in Chicago, Illinois, on July 25, 2009, stated:

> Disability Pride represents a rejection of the notion that our physical, sensory, mental, and cognitive differences from the non-disabled standard are wrong or bad in any way, and is a statement of our self-acceptance, dignity and pride . . . It is a public expression of our belief that our disabilities are a natural part of human diversity, a celebration of our heritage and culture, and a validation of our experience . . . Disability Pride is an integral part of movement building, and a direct challenge to systemic ableism and stigmatizing definitions of disability . . . It is a militant act of self-definition, a purposive valuing of that which is socially devalued, and an attempt to untangle ourselves from the complex matrix of negative beliefs, attitudes, and feelings that grow from the dominant group's assumption that there is something inherently wrong with our disabilities and identity. (www.disabilityprideparade.com/whypride.php)

Celebratory events planned and supported by such organizations explicitly reject any connection between disability and suffering. Such rejections can be seen as threatening and unproductive by those most actively engaged in the pursuit and protection of disability rights if interpreted as potentially conveying the message that differences associated with disability are unimportant to the rest of the general population.

Alternatively, celebration agendas may seek to embrace suffering as a source of strength. Arguably a bit stereotypically, celebration involves artists. Though possibly less fashionable than in the past, many artists present creativity as a positive outcome of suffering. Particularly to the extent that art functions as a more or less celebratory expression of separation from the experiences of the general population, celebration-oriented agendas may backwardly benefit from injustice (or claim to do so). Such arguments, however, rarely appear in the public discourse of celebration agenda–type stakeholders in modern disability policy subsystems.

Similitude in Cause- and Celebration-Oriented Agendas

Another core characteristic of cause-oriented political discourse involves an emphasis on the fundamental sameness of human beings. In recent years, there has been increased attention to diversity and multiculturalism, especially in political discourse surrounding ethnic diversity, which has tended to reassert the quality of difference. However, these newer arguments are neither as powerful nor as deeply rooted as those resting on the argument of the essential similitude of human beings. The metaphor of the melting pot still comes into play in public and political discourse in the United States, in spite of evidence of a resurgence of immigrant segregation (Cutler, Glaeser, and Vigdor 2008). As explained on *BBC News* on May 12, 2006:

> Americans take pride in their "melting pot" society (a term coined by an immigrant, Israel Zangwill) that encourages newcomers to assimilate into the American culture . . . But the melting pot imagery has been contested by the idea of multiculturalism, the "salad bowl theory," or as it is known in Canada, the "cultural mosaic," whereby the immigrants retain their own national characteristics while integrating into a new society . . . Some go further . . . According to Professor Huntington the reality of American history is best described as tomato soup: the blending of new ingredients adds spice without compromising the essential character of tomato. (http://news.bbc.co.uk/1/hi/world/americas/4931534.stm)

Such metaphors help explain why cause-oriented discourse often expresses rights in terms of assimilation. Much cause-oriented political discourse seeks to render irrelevant the difference historically discriminated against. For example, arguably the most well-known speech given by US civil rights leader Martin Luther King Jr. is the "I Have a Dream" speech, given on the steps of the Lincoln Memorial on August 28, 1963. One of the most well-known phrases of that speech is: "I have a dream that my four children will one day live in a nation where they will not be judged by the color of their skin but by the content of their character." Such cause-oriented political discourse often promotes the impression of an ultimate goal of rendering irrelevant the foundation upon which distinctions in social, political, and economic discrimination are based.

However, celebration-oriented agenda types pursue improved understanding of the lives of people with disabilities, including how their lives might systematically differ from those of the rest of the general population on a day-to-day basis. Such efforts seek to ensure that individuals with disabilities can live authentically. Myths about disability continue to pervade modern culture. For example, according to Samuel Bagenstos, "many nondisabled people believe that disability benefits programs make disability a *favored* status in society by exempting people with disabilities from the ordinary obligation to work for a living" (2004, 16; emphasis in original). According to the Easter Seals, other common myths about individuals with disabilities include such ideas as: people with disabilities are brave or courageous; people who are blind acquire a "sixth sense"; people with disabilities are most comfortable when with "their own kind"; people with disabilities always need help; and people with disabilities do not lead ordinary lives that include such experiences as sexual relationships, engaging in day-to-day chores, or experiencing the full range of human emotions (www.easterseals.com/site/PageServer?pagename=ntl_myths_facts). Such stereotypes present challenges for cause-oriented agenda types, which sometimes rely on and other times actively contest such interpretations. However, celebrations that emphasize real and potential contributions of people with disabilities can more easily highlight the difficulties inherent in this logic for the general public without alienating broad segments of the general population.

Multicultural Contexts

Another element of discourse surrounding the relationship between celebration- and cause-oriented public discourse involves complications in identifying functional differences in cross-cultural or multicultural contexts. For one thing, historically (and, arguably, all too often in the present), behaviors considered typical or even desirable in one cultural context have been treated as symptoms of disability by members of another cultural context. This becomes especially problematic in circumstances involving cultural oppression. As A. Rosen explained about experiences in Australia, "aboriginal reactions to this cultural oppression are often misinterpreted as mental illnesses, or applied sufficient stress to precipitate them . . . this resulted in a disproportionately high rate of incarceration of Aboriginal people in our mental and 'corrective' institutions" (2006, 82). Under such circumstances, both acceptance and denial of disability motivate misunderstanding and discrimination by the rest of the general population. Historically, the predominant response to this Catch-22 entailed forceful denial of disability and deliberate distancing on the part of advocates for other rights claims from those associated with disability.

The tendency to confound cultural differences and indications of functional differences continues across the industrialized world to this day. For example, in the United States, children from ethnic minorities are more likely referred to special education services than are those from the cultural majorities (Gravois and Rosenfield 2006). Part of this reflects genuine relative difference in academic achievement resulting from social and economic disadvantages still more frequently experienced by members of ethnic minority groups (Hosp and Rechsly 2004). After all, a child who did not have the chance to attend preschool or whose parent remains less aware of the structure of the US educational system becomes less likely to easily achieve academic success in school. However, this difference in referral rate also indicates in some situations a tendency to perceive individuals from racial or ethnic minority groups as automatically less capable, regardless of other indicators of capacity and performance. For example, in a study of the public school system of the United States, Audrey Davis McCray, Gwendolyn Webb-Johnson, and Scott Bridgest (2003) found that children who walked or dressed in ways identified as indicative of membership in African American communities were more often referred to special education services than other children, based on these characteristics alone.

On the other hand, when a person who is a member of an ethnic or racial minority group does have a neurological difference, they remain less likely to receive necessary help. Public discourse surrounding the connection between race and disability often focuses on these disparities (as opposed to overexposure of cultural minorities to interventions). For example, in an article titled "Language, Culture Barriers Can Delay Autism Treatment" that appeared in the *Chattanooga Times Free Press* on June 4, 2008, Claudia Avila-Lopez, coordinator of the Hispanic Program for the Tennessee Disability Pathfinder in Nashville, was quoted as saying: "A lot of Hispanic families think it's normal that their child isn't speaking or that they are misbehaving, which may delay the time when the child is diagnosed . . . many times the doctors say everything is fine, it will go away and they (the parents) don't question it." A music therapist also quoted in the article explained that "autism is a very black and white disability . . . there's no gray area . . . so if the word 'milk' means 'milk,' if you give the word to a child in a different language, you have to explain to him 'milk' equals this white liquid and 'leche'—the word in Spanish—equals this white liquid and that's a very abstract concept for children with autism." Conclusive evidence that children or individuals with autism are less able to understand multiple languages (or even synonyms) does not exist in scientific literature. However, as this quote demonstrates, a sense that current services remain less available to or less appropriate for children of ethnic minorities is commonly expressed in public discourse surrounding neurological differences.

As a result of such tendencies, public support for or provision of celebration of functional differences expressed in tandem with celebration of ethnic or racial differences can become a complicated exercise for celebration-oriented public agendas. After all, celebration is quintessentially positive in nature. Although during the past couple of centuries not all art has sought to please its audience, for the most part in celebration-oriented agenda types the overarching purpose includes promoting positive impressions of functional differences and of the individuals experiencing them. When something considered positive for one traditionally oppressed minority is simultaneously a negative for another traditionally oppressed minority, public support and funding for related efforts can become a politically volatile exercise at best.

Separatism Works Differently in Celebration and Cause Agenda Types

Unlike discourse promoting cause agenda types, discussion of celebration-oriented agendas tends to emphasize differences. This emphasis sometimes extends to the point of creating separate realms for human achievement that are distinct from those in which the rest of the general population competes. The resulting separatism can create tension between cause and celebration agenda types because of the difference in meaning and implications of separate realms of being for the two agenda types.

Separatism in Play: The Special Olympics

Possibly the most famous example of such separate celebration efforts is the Special Olympics. The Special Olympics originated in the efforts of Eunice Kennedy Shriver in the early 1960s. The initial intent of the games involved providing competition opportunities for individuals with neurological differences who were not welcome or considered unfit for traditional arenas of athletic competition. The games now take place in almost all nations of the world and generally involve a total of over 2 million people, making them the largest athletic program in the world for individuals with disabilities (Roswal and Damentko 2006). Historically, the Special Olympics have been nearly universally applauded as a positive source of celebration of the efforts and achievements of people with special needs. Furthermore, research suggests that participation in the Special Olympics associates with positive externalities for participants, such as better dental hygiene (Turner et al. 2007) and increased employment (Roswal and Damentko 2006).

In recent years, some have criticized aspects of the Special Olympics, pointing to the games as (possibly involuntarily) prolonging unnecessary

separation of individuals with disabilities from the rest of the general population (Kellow, Frey, and Sandt 2007). Part of this criticism harkens back
to the concept of special privileges afforded to, but undeserved by, individuals with disabilities as compared to expectation for the rest of the general
population. For example, in a response posted to an article describing the
criticism President Barack Obama received after comparing his skills in
bowling to what one might observe in the Special Olympics, which appeared in the online version of the *Washington Post* on March 19, 2009, one
reader wrote:

> Perhaps an unfortunate comment, but it will give Special Olympics more
> time in the spotlight than they deserve. Personally, I have a problem with
> Special Olympics . . . Less-abled people say don't treat us differently but
> then are more than happy to have an entire event that spotlights they are dif-
> ferent. Seems like the average Joe is left out once again—not Olympic ma-
> terial and yet not special enough to compete either. (http://voices
> .washingtonpost.com/sleuth/2009/03/obama_likens_his_bowling_game
> .html)

Furthermore, specific aspects of the games, such as the presence of people assigned to give hugs to athletes at finish lines, also draw criticism, particularly from younger disability rights activists. Critics point out that such
practices, whether deliberate or accidental, create differences in the social
habits of individuals with neurological differences above and beyond those
naturally attributable to neurodiversity. In other words, the presence of huggers might create (or reinforce) a tendency of individuals with neurological
differences to hug strangers much more frequently than generally practiced
by other members of the general population of a given society.

Another intriguing aspect of the Special Olympics surrounds its balance of separateness and inclusion in the context of functional differences.
Not all of those who compete in the Special Olympics have physical differences that make them inherently less able to compete physically with the
general population of athletes. Eligibility extends to individuals with a wide
variety of neurological differences, including those without any attendant
physical differences from the rest of the general population. According to the
Special Olympics website's description of participating athletes, "though
ability level varies, everyone is welcome, and all grow, building athletic
skills and character traits that help both on and off the field of competition"
(www.specialolympics.org/athletes.aspx). The narrative goes on to emphasize several benefits, such as friendship, that many athletes experience that
have little inherent relation to athletic competition itself and that potentially

contribute to the separateness of the experiences of individuals with disabilities. As the Special Olympics case demonstrates, separateness itself sometimes takes on value in celebration-oriented agendas. This separateness is not without inherent complexities, especially when juxtaposed with the goals of cause-oriented agendas.

Separatist Rights

Despite acceptance of separatist celebration in some contexts, separatist rights less frequently receive recognition as legitimate elements of cause-oriented political discourse, particularly in the United States. For example, although freedom of association constitutes a fundamental right under the Constitution, deliberate exclusion of others as part of this freedom is not habitually considered a viable part of this right. In fact, much of the civil rights movement involved direct contest of the freedom *from* association of the traditionally oppressive majority (Ishay 2008). In the United States, the individual typically represents the relevant unit of analysis when it comes to the articulation of rights, not the community. A claim to protection of a separated community as a matter of right becomes difficult to successfully assert in this context.

Of course, not all nations employ collective rights as individually oriented as the civil rights–based policy found in the United States. Canada, for example, has a much richer tradition of collective rights articulation than does its neighbor to the south. For example, in April 1999, Nunavut officially separated from the Northwest Territories in order to create a territory with a minority majority (First Nations population). Some authors have argued that "minority protection can only operate effectively by transcending the still dominant framework of individual rights and incorporating the concept of collective rights" (Jovanovic 2005, 625).

Regardless of the overarching traditions in rights policy, separatism presents philosophical challenges in the context of neurodiversity, just as it does in other areas of diversity-oriented policies. Forced separation on the basis of difference alone, of course, remains incompatible with modern conceptions of justice, let alone diversity. For example, in the United States, a series of Supreme Court decisions exemplified by *Brown v. Board of Education* (347 US 483 [1954]) and *Loving v. Virginia* (388 US 1 [1967]) established separated institutions as inherently unequal. Any kind of systematic separation, whether voluntary or not, brings complications for cause-oriented agendas. For the most part, voluntary separation of the historical oppressor is seen as contraindicative of diversity and justice. For example, few would argue that venues designed with the intent of exclusive use on the part of people of Caucasian descent would be particularly conducive to diversity or to the general protection of rights in either European countries or their former colonies. Clubs similarly designed for traditionally oppressed groups, conversely, often become interpreted as protective of rights and diversity. Most often, this argument employs direct references to celebration-oriented agendas and their associated public or political discourse.

When it comes to purposeful separateness of the historically oppressed, the relationship between separatism and diversity therefore becomes clouded. In part, a fear of potential assimilation to the point of disappearance on the part of the historically oppressed drives this concern. For example, Native American tribes and the deaf communities in the United States have elected to create and maintain separate (or mostly separate) facilities of higher education, in part with the goal of ensuring long-term survival of a desired cultural difference. Similarly, as explained on the Gallaudet University website, the university's mission involves efforts to "preserve deaf history and use visual media to promote the recognition that deaf people and their signed languages are vast resources with significant contributions to the cognitive, creative and cultural dimensions of human diversity" and "position our community to reach its full human potential and assume its role as a progressive global entity committed to civic responsibility and social justice" (www.gallaudet.edu/mission.xml). In addition, examination of diversity efforts in the workplace, for example, has found that "often organizations in the United States take a benevolent assimilation approach to diversity . . . however, research shows that assimilation does not engage diversity in ways that promote learning, creativity, and organizational effectiveness" (Awbrey 2007, 7). Fully conceptualizing a balance between separatism and assimilation represents largely uncharted territory in the prevailing practices and discourses of both celebration and cause agenda types.

Furthermore, many believe that people with differences—particularly young people—can benefit from occasional more exclusive interaction with others who have the same difference (Johnson et al. 2007). As mentioned earlier, some of those engaged in political discourse on disability consider this perception an all-too-pervasive (and arguably harmful) myth about individuals with disabilities, harkening back to the days of forced segregation. Nevertheless, in some cases, groups of individuals with functional differences continue to seek out exclusion (or periods of exclusion) from the general population as a mechanism of gathering strength and support (Berger 2008; Bruner 2008). Quite often, such efforts also receive support from the rest of the general population (or representatives of the general population) as diversity-oriented efforts. For example, Autism Network International (ANI) hosts a camp, called Autreat, for individuals with autism and their friends. The camp maintains a careful balance of separatist orientation and avoidance of outright exclusion of individuals without neurological differences:

> Typical autism conferences are about autistic people, but are primarily for the benefit of researchers, service providers, or families. Autreat is an opportunity for autistic people and those with related developmental differences, our friends, and supporters to come together, discover and explore autistic connections, and develop advocacy skills, all in an autistic-friendly environment. Family members and professionals are welcome to attend, but the structure and content of this event will be determined by the interests and sensibilities of autistic people. (www.autreat.com/aut03.html)

In addition to this general statement of intent, literature about the camp also advises those who are not autistic to familiarize themselves with the ANI's interpretation of autistic conventions before attending the camp. This is because "Autreat is designed to be 'autistic space' . . . This is sometimes confusing or uncomfortable for non-autistic people attending" (www.autreat .com/aut03.html).

Separatism risks creation of a proverbial slippery slope within the politics of any aspect of diversity. In particular, voluntariness of such separatism often becomes difficult to unequivocally establish and even more difficult to maintain (Shakespeare 2006). This most likely proves true in the case of neurological differences, due to their spectrum nature and the general lack of external evidence of many neurological differences. Furthermore, particularly because sociocultural contexts change over time, distinctions between protecting and strengthening people with a difference and subverting diversity can be difficult to protect in practice. After all, especially in the context of the public sector and exclusive use of resources, no formally established right to solitude or homogeneity generally exists. In this context, interactions between cause and celebration agenda types suggest a need for deliberate improvement of this balance.

Nevertheless, celebration-oriented agendas can easily encompass a variety of separatist-type events that seek to strengthen diversity through permitted (and ideally unobtrusive) educational observation on the part of the general population. Particularly to the degree that design of separatist efforts includes an element of sharing and education, such events can serve the purposes of diversity while not compromising the traditionally oppressed population. Such efforts can only be effectively managed, however, under

conditions including a high level of awareness of both cause- and celebration-oriented agenda types in disability policy subsystems and, at least to a
certain degree, among the rest of the general population. In the absence of
this, too high a potential for caricatures and exploitation or resentment stemming from perception of special advantages develops. Finally, separation
affords one particular challenge in the case of neurological (and other functional) differences in that the differences generally are not transmitted ge-
netically, at least not consistently. This distinguishes neurological
differences from other cultural elements of diversity, which tend to encompass (many) families as a whole and transfer between successive generations of a given family.

Celebration and Cause in the Popular Press

One commonality of cause- and celebration-oriented agendas involves the
tendency to include public events in the exercise of public discourse surrounding these efforts. Obviously, one desired outcome of such events involves increased (or even initial) political and public discourse surrounding
the particular disability-related issue. Given this, examining and comparing newspaper coverage that uses or includes this discourse, especially over
an extended period of time, constitutes one effective way to look at the
relationship between the politics of these two agenda types. This analysis
employs the case of autism, though some of the articles in the sample
included discussion of other differences and disabilities rather than exclusively focusing on autism.

This analysis examined a random sample of 400 newspaper articles,
comprising twenty articles from each year between 1989 and 2008. The
population of articles from which the sample was drawn included all articles retrieved by Lexis-Nexus using the keyword "autism" to search newspaper articles and wire reports published by major outlets in the United
States. The sample articles were then searched for discussion of events or
organized efforts engaging the celebration- and cause-oriented agenda types.
Discourse surrounding these event types appearing in the articles was systematically examined through analysis of quotes from issue stakeholders
included in the articles.

Not surprisingly, the number of articles appearing increased dramatically over time. By the end of the sample period, well over 3,000 articles
were retrieved for each year. The first year of the analysis, 1989, holds sig-
nificance as the year that Dustin Hoffman won an Academy Award for his

portrayal of an individual with autism in the film *Rainman*. Nevertheless, newspaper articles of this time frequently included basic descriptions of autism given with the expressed assumption that most individuals would lack familiarity with the diagnosis.

It is arguable whether or not the honoring of *Rainman* constituted a deliberate action in support of a celebration-oriented agenda. *Rainman* ultimately may have helped the celebration-oriented agendas surrounding autism by raising public awareness through its use of a main character with autism in telling an interesting story. Intentional or not, in the United States at least, *Rainman* became the primary cultural source for public awareness about autism for a number of years after its release (Pitney 2010). Furthermore, although many other causal factors came into play (most notably the recorded rise of both prevalence and incidence of autism in children starting in the early 1990s), public attention toward autism has consistently increased since the release of the movie.

Changing Perceptions of Autism

One change observed in the sampled discourse was in the description of autism over time. As mentioned, descriptions of autism found in the earliest newspaper articles generally appeared to assume an utter lack of readers' familiarity with autism. Not all of the definitions were accurate, and some have passed into history. For example, on September 28, 1995, in the *Times-Picayune* of New Orleans in an article titled "Obsessive-Compulsive Behavior Turns Heads," Stephanie Lyman described autism as "a chemical imbalance that exists at birth but is not usually recognized until the age of 1 or 2." Many neurological differences, such as most that are categorized as mental illnesses, are still understood as chemical imbalances. However, autism is now typically understood as somehow deriving from the structure of the brain itself.

Although the assumed level of knowledge appeared to increase over time, perceived necessity of description continued throughout the period examined. Almost all sample articles, regardless of when the article was written, included a description of autism. This suggests that the politics of neurodiversity and neurological difference remain far from the center of public discourse. After all, in the consideration of other, more politically established areas of diversity, no such definition is given. For example, when writing about gender or racial minorities in the United States, authors do not consider it necessary to define what constitutes a woman or an African American unless the article focuses specifically on such definitions.

Especially in early articles, descriptions often came from the point of view (or perceived point of view) of parents. A description of a press conference that appeared in Portland's *The Oregonian* on April 22, 1991, was as follows: "This was a gathering of the Autism Society of America, composed of parents of those strange and disquieting children . . . they had come to demand education for them . . . there was not posturing or ego on display in Room EF-100 . . . living with an autistic child pares personality down to the bone." In other words, the politics of autism largely took place between people who did not themselves have autism. The political and public actor of interest was the parent, whereas the child with autism became the subject of the discourse.

Articles appearing in the first decade of the sample also tended to emphasize a connection to other neurological differences, especially mental retardation. In general, earlier articles focus more on those at the end of the spectrum of autism disorders most often described as low-functioning. Distinguishing autism from other neurological differences became an increased focus of public discourse over time. For example, in an article titled "Autism Is Mysterious, Baffling" that appeared in *The Oregonian* on November 17, 1997, Alisa Rivera wrote: "The condition is often mistaken for mental retardation, in part because a large number of children with autism are also retarded . . . but even children with 'normal' intelligence have problems communicating and interacting with other people and their environment."

This confusion involved difficulty surrounding the lack of clarity in diagnosing autism and the variety of professionals who become involved in the exercise. In the United States, this is largely a result of special education policy infrastructure. In a commentary titled "Of Mice, Giraffes, and Autism" that appeared in the *Washington Times* on November 10, 1999, Thomas Sowell explained:

> Even when honestly applied, the label of autism can often be a result of incredibly crude check lists, especially when used by people with no medical training nor doctorates in related fields . . . school districts, especially, often have lower-level personnel evaluating children with the aid of checklists—and calling these children "autistic" if the number of items checked exceeds some magic number or percentage . . . if we were to make up a checklist of the characteristics of a mouse—four legs, a tail, fur, two ears, a digestive tract, etc.—a high percentage of characteristics would also apply to a giraffe . . . yet we never mistake a mouse for a giraffe, because we are also aware of the ways in which they differ . . . even if the similarities reach 80 percent or 90 percent, we still will not say: "there's a giraffe under the kitchen sink."

Similarly, in an article titled "Conference to Explore Autism" that appeared in the *Post-Standard* of Syracuse, New York, on March 9, 2000, the following statement appeared: "autism isn't a disease that can be discovered by testing blood or taking an X-ray . . . doctors look for a group of symptoms that includes difficulty mixing with other children, inappropriate laughing or giggling, an aloof manner, hypersensitivity to touch, and the use of gestures instead of words."

As for many neurological differences, defining and bounding autism in a manner easily communicated to the rest of the general population becomes complicated at best. To the extent that neurological difference constitutes an essentialist characteristic tied to an individual as opposed to a characteristic of diversity and community, this complication remains. Unlike either the cure- or care-oriented agendas, policy connected to the celebration and cause agenda types can be designed around such difficulties, because programs and policies do not have to be implemented at the individual level (even though they often are).

More sophisticated descriptions of autism became more common over time. One metaphorical description of autism presented in an article titled "Dealing with Autism; Pasadena Conference Offers Tips for Frustrated Parents" that appeared in the *Pasadena Star-News* on March 17, 2002, held that autism, "often referred to as mental blindness . . . interferes with the normal development of the brain and can affect a person's speech, sensory development and communication skills." Later, on May 15, 2007, in the *Las Vegas Review-Journal* in an article titled "Invisible Disability Leaves Young People Feeling Alone in the Crowd," autism was described as follows:

> The severity of autism varies from person to person. According to Julie Beasley, a Las Vegas psychologist who specializes in children and teens with developmental disabilities, those with severe autism never will be able to live independently. However, many people with autism are high functioning, which means that the person's IQ is within the normal range but he or she has the communication and social skills of someone two to three years younger.

Later descriptions of autism still tended toward negativity. For example, "Autism Risk Rises with Age of Father" (*Washington Post*, September 5, 2006) describes the preliminary research as follows: "Children born to fathers of advancing age are at a significantly higher risk of developing autism compared with children born to younger fathers, according to a comprehensive study published yesterday that offers surprising new insight into one of the most feared disorders of the brain." Interestingly, although more recent articles almost always include a basic description of the characteristics associated with autism in the text of the article, this practice seems more of a rote action rather than part of any concerted intent to increase awareness.

The discourse found in the sample suggests that as time progressed, assumed knowledge of (if not necessarily about) autism increased. Nevertheless, public discourse in this sample supported almost exclusively the premise that autism, as a representative of neurological difference, was an inherently negative element of the human experience. As discussed, some benefit can be gleaned from such portrayals for cause-oriented agendas when such negativity connects to suffering that can be potentially alleviated through social change. Similarly, from the perspective of celebration-oriented agendas, this discourse seeks to establish emphatic need for programs and policies designed to improve and expand awareness of autism on the part of the rest of the general public. Such benefits are inherently limited and limiting, however.

Mixed Expressions of Celebration

The discourse in the sample described many events focusing on autism. As time progressed, both variety and creativity of such events expanded. This constitutes an expected outcome of increased awareness of neurological differences generally and autism in particular. It also reflects a growing trend in the United States wherein public discourse takes on ever proliferating forms, particularly when combined with the entertainment industry. Some of the events, even those found in the early public discourse, were almost exclusively positive. For example, as was reported in Salt Lake City's *Deseret News* on February 20, 1996, the third annual "Possibilities Unlimited" conference, designed to support inclusion of children with disabilities in mainstream classrooms, included "local songwriter Janice Kapp Perry and author Joy Saunders Lundberg [who] will perform at the awards banquet Tuesday evening, during which 10 awards will be presented to individuals or programs that have helped children with disabilities find meaningful involvement in mainstream education." However, as might be expected given the discussion presented earlier in this chapter, expressions of celebration in the form of public events often seemed conflicted and more often than not incorporated some level of focus on cure agenda types.

Celebrity involvement in public dialogue surrounding autism started early within and continued throughout the time frame of the sampled discourse. As most famously demonstrated by Jenny McCarthy during the early years of the twenty-first century, the celebrities who were most prevalent in autism-related discourse tended to be parents of children with autism. For example, in an article discussing recent news about celebrities ("The Lake Effect," *Milwaukee Journal Sentinel,* July 9, 1996): "The man who played Father Francis Mulcahy on the never-say-die TV series *MASH* will be in town Wednesday for the national Autism Society of America Conference at Wisconsin Center . . . William Christopher, who played the chaplain, has a son with autism and has written a book, called 'Mixed Blessings,' on the subject." As the title of Christopher's book suggests, public discourse does not present autism as entirely negative, which can pave the way for celebration agenda types because it does open the door to thinking about the positive aspects of neurological difference.

Similarly, in an article titled "Sadler Carries Colors for Autism Awareness" that appeared in *USA Today* on April 15, 2002, it was described how NASCAR racer Hermie Sadler's daughter's autism diagnosis had inspired him to use his celebrity to raise awareness about autism: "Artie Kempner, lead director for Fox Sports' NASCAR coverage, has a 7-year-old autistic son . . . that bond led the network to make a large ribbon for Sadler's car at last month's race in Bristol, Tennessee, generating more than 11,000 calls to the Autism Society of America." The same article later reported: "Kempner and Sadler are producing an instructional video to help special education teachers better understand autistic children." This position takes on importance by reflecting the lived experiences of individuals with neurological differences and their families, and thereby becomes more difficult to dismiss. This helps open the door for the more exclusively positive and constructivist messages presented by those involved in neurodiversity-related efforts.

As time progressed in the sampled period, more awareness efforts fell under the category of celebration-oriented policy. Some of the celebratory events focused generally on gaining attention for autism. For example, an article titled "Puzzle to Place Focus on Autism" that appeared in Michigan's *Flint Journal* on May 8, 2005, reported that "an enormous 20-by-40-foot puzzle will be constructed at the Family Fun Day Event on June 18 at Creasey Bicentennial Park in Grand Blanc Township in an effort to gain more awareness for autism." Some efforts were highly formal and not necessarily connected to positive interpretations of neurological difference. In February 2005, for example, the Centers for Disease Control (CDC) launched a campaign called "Learn the Signs: Act Early" with the goal of helping parents learn to measure and monitor early social and emotional progress in order to facilitate earlier diagnosis of neurological differences, including autism. In a March 2, 2005, article in *Education Week* titled "CDC Campaign Focuses on Autism Awareness," a spokeswoman for the CDC, Courtney Bolen, is quoted as saying: "if you feel something is wrong and different, you should go to a developmental pediatrician . . . you don't have to wait and see." On the other hand, as time progressed in the sampled period, overtly positive events were found. For example, an event organized by the Autism Action Partnership, detailed in an article titled "Tackling a Tough Topic with Humor" that appeared in the *Omaha World-Herald* on June 3, 2008, was described in part as follows:

> Sunday in Omaha, Elijah Wapner startled the audience by placing underwear on his head and saying "I want to talk about the word 'inappropriate . . .'" people laughed a nervous laugh but listened intently. Elijah, after tossing the underwear aside, told of sometimes being made to feel, as an autistic person, that he is "inappropriate just for being alive" or that it would be appropriate if he kept quiet, "a kind of silence as if I'd never been born."

Despite such efforts to generate positive understandings of neurological differences, however, no instance of efforts focused exclusively on promoting acceptance of neurodiversity was found in the sampled articles. In fact, somewhat ironically, the first sentence of the article describing Elijah's performance is: "Humor, poignancy and sadness mixed at an Omaha gathering about autism, the heartbreaking disorder diagnosed in one out of every 150 children."

Many of the events reported on in the sampled articles focused on fundraising. Earlier discourse tended to focus on programs and services, often including a description of exactly how much money had been raised for the particular target agency. For example, on December 17, 1995, the *St. Louis Post-Dispatch* reported that an auction and dinner at the twelfth annual Festival of the Trees had raised $35,000 for the Judavine Center for Autism. Toward the middle of the time period, however, focus on cure-oriented fundraising increased. According to a report published in *Variety* on August 3, 1997, the post-film party for the opening of *Air Force One* benefited the nonprofit advocacy group Cure Autism Now (whose founder, Jon Shestack, was one of the film's producers).

Like all of the events reported in the sampled articles, fundraisers became more diverse over time. For example, "Riders Get Ready for Fund-Raiser; Proceeds Go to Autism Charity," which appeared in the *Daily News of Los Angeles* on September 13, 2004, profiled the fourth annual motorcycle ride for autism, which raises money for the Jay Nolan community center in Mission Hills. One of the ride's organizers said: "when we received the diagnosis of autism for our young son, Jordan, we were not given a road map to chart a course for therapy or intervention . . . organizations like the Jay Nolan Community Services give much needed support and direction to families in need, and we know how important that is to dealing with and treating autism." Engaging a broad spectrum of the rest of the general population constitutes a fundamental strategy of celebration-oriented agendas. By the end of the period analyzed, a wide variety of sporting, artistic, and cultural events had been enthusiastically described in the public discourse related to autism, indicating a vibrant (if not altogether cohesive) community of stakeholders engaged in celebration-oriented agendas. For the most part, however, the celebration aspect tended to remain secondary to the primary agenda of stakeholders, which over time appeared to increasingly focus on cure.

Limitations of Rights

Questions surrounding cultural differences were also directly brought forth as issues relating to rights. Experiences of discrimination appeared throughout the sample, particularly in the earlier years examined. For example, one mother of a young adult with a disability, quoted December 8, 1991, in an article in the *St. Petersburg Times* titled "Easier Travel for the Disabled," said: "when we check into a hotel, there is outright hostility, indifference and fright . . . they act like he's a piece of furniture, not really capable of human interaction." Other described situations directly involved the legal system. For example, on September 17, 1992, an article titled "New Technique Tossed from Courts" appeared in the *Post-Standard* of Syracuse, New York. The article discussed tension surrounding rejection of admissibility of testimony elicited using facilitated communication, out of concern that the communication did not genuinely come from the person with the disability. Suspicion surrounding this form of communication is ongoing (Biklen and Burke 2006). In the article, family court judge Minna Buck called for increased research into the facilitation communication technique:

> Out of concern for Jenny and all other children who may be suffering from their inability to communicate or possibly suffering from abuse or neglect at the hands of family, their neighbors or others, this Court implores

those individuals who are able to do so, to conduct the necessary studies to determine the reliability and validity of this more interesting technique . . . until this is done . . . we will never know if there is a knocking in the skull, an endless silent shout, of something beating on a wall, and crying let me out.

Routine employment of interpreters exists in the US judicial system. Above and beyond concern about the communication style itself, another legitimate difference in this case involved the fact that the proposed interpreters were not hired by the court but instead included people otherwise involved in the child's life. Nevertheless, this example demonstrates a lack of what Douglas Biklen and Jamie Burke describe as a "presumption of competence" wherein, "with children classified as autistic, it is not uncommon to link early expressive difficulties to a presumption of incompetence . . . delays or perceived deficits in language are taken as evidence of intellectual impairment" (2006, 166).

Another case, involving a young girl named Dina, was described in an article titled "Governor Ratifies a Legal Break for the Disabled; the Fact Remains, However, That Very Few Cases Involving Handicapped Victims Are Prosecuted" that appeared on July 12, 1998, in the *San Francisco Chronicle*:

> She was strong and energetic, a blue-eyed, 10-year-old so full of fun her parents did not shield her from rambunctious play, despite her mental retardation. But when they picked her up later that afternoon, she was hunched in the sandbox, crying, her hair caked with sand. With frantic gestures and the broken phrases that made up her scant vocabulary, she told them two older boys had taunted her. Then followed her into the bathroom. Then raped her. It was a personal tragedy soon to become a legal fiasco. The boys' videotaped confession was ruled inadmissible as evidence in court. Dina was rejected as a witness because she could not testify without help in conveying her thoughts. The case was dropped. The boys walked free. "The judge had this preconceived notion that the case was going to fail," says Dina's mother, Sherri Martin, "because the star witness was handicapped."

The article went on to report that, at the time, people with developmental disabilities were four times more likely to become victims of crime than the rest of the general public, but that the crimes against these victims were only about half as likely to be reported and prosecuted. Establishing and maintaining the dignity of individuals with neurological differences is as much an aspect of celebration-oriented agendas as it is of cause discourse.

Another example of cause and celebration in tension was profiled in an article titled "He Can't Play: Parents Sue After Autistic Boy Is Banned from Playground" that appeared in the *Boston Globe* on June 28, 2004. The article detailed the banning of Jan, a fourth-grader with autism, from an elementary school playground after school officials claimed he had used unacceptable language and engaged in insubordination toward adults. The child and his parents insisted that he had done nothing other than exhibit social skills several years behind those of his peer age-group. The school officials insisted upon the necessity of the action in order to protect the emotional safety of the rest of the children. According to Stephen Shore, then-president of the board of the Asperger's Association of New England, "it doesn't make sense to take someone who already has challenges with social interactions and further isolate them by prohibiting them from playing in the playground with other children." The article also argued that "some advocates for people with autism say Jan's case highlights a resistance to accepting 'invisible' neurological disabilities, especially in small, homogenous communities such as Falmouth . . . the Falmouth school system's student body of about 2,200 is 96 percent white and there are 10 autistic children."

Access to health care was described during the sampled period as a neglected right, especially in later articles. For example, an August 6, 2007, article titled "Madison/Doyle, Dems Push for Autism Coverage" that appeared in the *St. Paul Pioneer Press* of Minnesota described how insurance companies were opposing bills requiring coverage of autism treatment. The article quoted Amy Masek, director of development and outreach for the Wisconsin Early Autism Project, as saying: "at the end of the day, this is really a fairness issue . . . individuals with autism should have the same access to health insurance coverage everyone else has." According to the article, "most insurance companies don't cover autism because it is classified as an emotional disorder rather than a neurological medical condition . . . as a result, many people wait more than a year for state services that treat delayed speech and other social and motor skill problems characteristic of autism." Another article, titled "Florida: Committee Clears Autism Bill" and appearing in *American Health Line* on March 24, 1999, succinctly described opposition to such measures. According to the article, "arguing against the measure, AVMED and Florida Association of Managed Care Providers lobbyist James Moffat said, 'If you mandate treatment for autism, next year it's going to be attention deficit, hyperactivity and all the myriad disorders that afflict children.'"

Of course, what Moffat suggests as catastrophe, others would enthusiastically embrace as policy goals perfectly appropriate for both cure and care agenda types.

Cost of Cause

Concerns about cost appeared frequently in the sampled period in public discourse surrounding cause-oriented efforts, particularly regarding special education. This type of public discourse became especially common during the middle to late 1990s, a time during which the fundamentals of public education in the United States were being questioned, often as part of efforts associated with the Contract with America. This set of initiatives, promoted largely by Republicans under the forceful leadership of Newt Gingrich, included unfunded mandates as a focal point. The provisions of the Individuals with Disabilities Education Act generally came to be considered under this category of policy. In public discourse, the argument was often made that special education policy unfairly placed the good of the few with disabilities above the needs of the many. For example, in an article titled "Spillane Slaps Hill on Special-Ed Funds" that appeared in the *Washington Times* on May 30, 1995, Mari Koklanaris reported: "in Montgomery County, recent changes in state law regarding the placement of special-education students in private schools—required by federal law if there is no suitable public school—have cost that county an extra $750,000 the past two years . . . the state did not pick up those costs." Similarly, in an article that appeared in the *Times Union* of Albany, New York, on June 27, 1996, titled "Equal Opportunity Needs a Few Limits," Arthur Chaplan wrote: "Sometimes the price of being fair is high . . . once in a while it is so high that it becomes unfair. That is what has happened as a result of America's desire to make sure that children with severe disabilities get an equal chance at education." The article went on to describe a comatose boy brought to a regular elementary school every day for five months even though he never regained consciousness. Later in the article, without making any kind of distinction between the two situations, Chaplan stated:

> In South Portland, Maine . . . the public schools deal with a bill of more than $120,000 per year to cover the costs of education for children with severe autism . . . every child deserves an education, even an expensive one in the case of a child with a disability . . . but at some point, providing education for a few begins to infringe on the rights of too many oth-

ers . . . Congress should take another look at what its 20-year-old under-funded mandate is doing to the nation's public schools.

Of course, this public discourse fundamentally views education as a private rather than a public good, divisible at the level of the student in terms of both expense and benefit. This interpretation is more in keeping with cause-oriented discourse focused on civil rights interpretations and on essentialist understandings of disability than with more constructivist understandings of disability and democratic understandings of education.

Another concern brought forward, especially in the early years examined, related to whether or not children actually benefited from inclusion. Education professionals were especially likely to voice this concern. For example, in "All Children Are Special," an article that appeared in the May 1, 1994, edition of the *Post-Standard* of Syracuse, New York, Janet Bass, a spokeswoman for the American Federation of Teachers, stated: "the problem with inclusion is the unfortunate trend to just put these kids in regular classrooms regardless of whether they can function or not, and that is very troubling." This represented the official position of the organization in 1994, owing to the belief that "if the practice continues, teachers will be overwhelmed and the majority of students in such classes will suffer academically," as reported in "National School Matters Notes Ideas, Trends in Education" (*Atlanta Journal Constitution,* January 2, 1994). Such statements reinforce the necessity of both celebration- and cause-oriented efforts, particularly when examined from the perspective of the politics of neurodiversity.

Discussion of inclusion continued in the later articles, but tended to embrace a more nuanced look at the question of inclusion of individuals with neurological differences into general education programs. For example, in an article titled "School Plan Highlights Autism Debate: Integrated or Separate Classes?" that appeared in the *Philadelphia Inquirer* on April 15, 2005, Paula Lieb, executive director of the New Jersey coalition for Inclusive Education, said: "we're really over-segregating kids into separate schools . . . we're kind of training kids to live a separate kind of life." Later in the article, Barbara Gantwerk, director of New Jersey's Office of Special Education, was reported to have said: "New Jersey has a problem in that we have an overreliance on separate programs for students with disabilities." Such progress on the question of inclusion of individuals with disabilities is hardly complete or necessarily pervasive, but does demonstrate increasing comfort with inclusive education over time as a result of successes in both cause- and cure-oriented policy efforts.

Community Inclusion

Challenges (and to a more limited degree benefits) of community inclusion were also discussed in the sample. In the earliest articles, public discourse surrounding community resistance was especially common. For example, in an article titled "Group Home Proposed for Fayetteville," published in the *Post-Standard* of Syracuse, New York, on December 3, 1992, one potential neighbor was quoted as saying: "I don't think they'll be able to blend in here . . . I don't think they could play games with the kids or socialize with the adults." However, even in early articles there was no consensus on exclusion. Later in the *Post-Standard* article, a different community member was quoted as follows: "we all have disabilities of one kind or another—nobody's perfect . . . as long as it's people with disabilities and not criminal records, I wouldn't mind." Of course, a certain amount of irony exists in that statement as well. Public discourse surrounding community inclusion also included conflicted statements on the part of parents of children with autism. For example, an article titled "Calla's Story: Music Therapy Helps Autistic Child to Blossom," published in the *Richmond Times Dispatch* on November 8, 1995, included the following quote from Calla's mother: "accepting the fact that Calla is autistic—instead of denying it—really made a difference . . . I think the fact I didn't lament a lot over it was important." Later in the article the mother added: "I think it's sad for Calla to not have had certain experiences . . . she's never been invited to a birthday party . . . she doesn't have any friends . . . as a mother, that saddens me . . . but in the overall picture, that's not a big deal . . . she's loved, and she knows she's loved." This quote highlights the tension between the goals of celebration and cause that often underlies the day-to-day lives of individuals with disabilities and those closely connected to them, in that it demonstrates how seeking out one goal can mean, temporarily at least, abandoning the other.

Concluding Thoughts for All Disabilities

Similarity does not always imply symbiosis, particularly given the intervention of politics. Fortunately, when it comes to the celebration- and cause-oriented agenda types in modern disability policy subsystems, the goals of these two agenda types tend to orient basically in the same direction. Nevertheless, as has been explored in this chapter, there are areas of tension with the capacity to both enrich and threaten progress in the development of disability policy. These areas of tension are possibly especially pronounced in public and political discourse surrounding neurological difference and neurodiversity because of the relative novelty of many of these differences as compared to disability at large. This relative amplitude serves to emphasize tensions extant in public and political discourse surrounding all disabilities.

In particular, difficulty arises as a result of insufficient differentiation between the two agenda types in the minds of both activists and the rest of the general public. A failure to recognize any distinction between celebration and cause agenda types sometimes creates too limited a space for proponents of either agenda type to function effectively in the face of the other. Such crowding-out involves competition for often already quite scarce resources. Time, talent, expertise, and funds that might be otherwise expended productively toward creating or maintaining real progress in disability policy go to a rivalry between these two agenda types that is hardly noticed by the rest of society.

Cause- and celebration-oriented agenda efforts engage in an intricate dance in disability policy subsystems of modern democracies. Though intents and purposes of these agendas tend to appear in tandem, specifics of goals and purposes of these two agenda types often come into tension or outright conflict. Partial management of this reality results from a recognition of different roles in the disability policy subsystem. This involves acceptance of the fact that not all who are engaged in the public and political discourse surrounding neurodiversity and neurological difference need to (or even should) become activists. The same holds true for all functional differences, whether or not they are typically associated with disabilities in a given society at a given moment in time.

Some questions underlying tensions between celebration and cause in disability-oriented policy, such as those surrounding separatism in the context of disability, will likely be best answered through an agreement to disagree for the time being. Informed individuals on both sides of the argument are likely to better serve the disability policy subsystem as a whole if they endeavor to understand those who take well-thought-out (rather than anachronistic or reactionary) but different positions on separatism as being members of a loyal opposition rather than as potential oppressors of individuals with disabilities.

Another key is to consider more deliberate separation of cause- and celebration-oriented efforts. Slippage of intent leads to confusion and, sometimes, misunderstandings or outright lack of appreciation for the efforts of those pursuing different agendas. As was seen in the analysis of newspaper coverage, over time the general understandings of neurological difference have increased, but have also become more complex. Such complexity represents strength for a policy subsystem, but only when combined with a deliberate creation of space for alternative agendas that address the same issues without compromising one's own agenda. This type of distinction might be especially difficult both for the activists and for those with the (stereotypically at least) creative temperament. Negotiating this distinction, however, is absolutely key, not only to the politics of neurodiversity, but also to the development and implementation of policies and programs that support all characteristics conducive to diversity in modern societies.

6

Providing Care
vs. Finding a Cure

More than any other of the agenda type pairings, care and cure frequently become mistaken for one another both in the casual thinking of the general population and, to a more limited degree, in the more deliberate public and political discourse of those actively engaging the politics of neurodiversity and neurological disability. Medical care, after all, can be interpreted as administration of a cure for a particular neurological difference. Furthermore, in most formal discussion of medicine and health policy, both care and cure tend to fall under the more general category of treatment. In such discussions, while medical distinctions are maintained, distinctions in policy intents and political goals tend to be blurred or ignored.

With a little reflection, however, distinctions between these two agenda types become apparent. For one thing, it does not take much information about the disability policy subsystem to realize that care policy typically extends well beyond health care policy in the modern world. The medical literature surrounding disability itself includes discussion of interactions with other policy subsystems such as social welfare, employment, and education policy. Furthermore, despite impressive medical advances in recent decades, cures, even when desired, remain much rarer than popularly assumed. After all, though our understanding of our brains has recently improved considerably, unknowns still thoroughly outweigh information reliably known about the human brain. Finally, the interaction of these two agenda types includes a pronounced impulse to design a hierarchical relationship between care and cure in which one becomes subsumed by the other. The tendency is partially a legacy of late-nineteenth and early-twentieth-century institutionalization and professionalization and partially the legacy of later efforts to design community-based care in

145

a way that controlled or eliminated remnants of the so-called medical model of disability.

Differentiating Between Care and Cure in Practice

The line between care and cure is not always abundantly clear in program development or in the day-to-day lives of individuals with neurological differences. This is particularly true when it comes to neurological differences in the modern world. For example, as Kristin Bumiller explains about the expectations of today's parents of children with autism, "most recently, the capacity to use the most up-to-date medical understanding of autism is becoming necessary in order to know about and prove eligibility for social services . . . in this way, geneticization raises the standards for good parenting and places high expectations on parents' ability to utilize medical knowledge" (2009, 893). Proper implementation of policy connected to the goals of either agenda type can involve more direct interaction with professionals than with most of the rest of the general population, particularly given a well-planned relationship with members of the health care community. In theory, however, there are three primary differences between the outcomes of policies and programs from the two agenda types in practice: completeness, duration of application, and permanence.

First, cure is assumed to be total. Care, on the other hand, is understood as alleviating only negative manifestations of a condition. Care often addresses only some aspects of a condition considered undesirable. Care also tends to involve ongoing balancing of side effects and inconveniences against the observed benefits attributed to treatments. In other words, the concept of a cure invokes the expectation that the individual to whom the cure has been applied has no residual aspects of the difference being cured, while care assumes the condition continues to be present, sometimes to no lesser extent than before should care become discontinued for whatever reason. Because of the tendency to involve behavior-based diagnoses, when it comes to neurological differences a person would generally be considered cured when they become (permanently) indistinguishable from their neurotypical peers. Figuring out when and if this has happened is difficult at best. As a result, cure becomes defined through convention and professional deliberation (Campbell 2005; Haupt et al. 2007) and is often driven by the varying opinion of members of the health care community and other professionals engaging the individual with the neurological differences. Such opinions tend to be profoundly affected by the hazards of fate, family and life circumstances, and the nature of the public infrastructure surrounding the individual. As a result of this requirement, a hesitancy to talk in terms of cure often develops inside the medical community, which tends to further confound cure and care discourse.

Second, for the most part cure is anticipated to be of a limited duration with regard to the period of time an individual is directly engaged in treatment. This is the primary (largely theoretical) reason that cure is assumed to be less expensive than care. In other words, the time it takes to undergo a cure, while variant, is assumed to be measurable and finite for each individual. At some point a person will be cured. Care, on the other hand, may or may not be finite depending on whether the combinations of flexibility of infrastructure and limitation of functionality are expected to continue for the foreseeable future. Though by no means always (of even most often) the case when it comes to neurological differences, care can involve services a person might reasonably be expected to need for a long period of time up to the full duration of his or her life.

Finally, cure is assumed to be more or less permanent. Care, even medical care, on the other hand, is understood as being effective for a limited period of time. For example, while there are a variety of medications an individual with asthma might take that can sometimes result in the complete absence of symptoms so long as the individual continues to take the medication, no medication currently exists that, once taken, will permanently eliminate the underlying differences that result in asthma in the individual. There is therefore no cure for asthma. Heated political debate surrounds the question of the existence of a cure for some neurological differences. For example, some have publicly claimed to have cured their children of autism through medical interventions. For example, the actress Jenny McCarthy received substantial public attention in her discussion of her son's recovery from autism. Many have interpreted her comments to mean that she believes her son was cured of autism, demonstrating the confounding in many people's minds of cure and care. As McCarthy described on CNN on April 4, 2008:

> There are some who wonder what we mean when we say "recovering" from autism. They confuse the word recover with cure. While you may not be able to cure an injury caused in a terrible car accident, you can recover; you can regain many skills that you once lost. In the case of autism, we think there are treatments that often bring about such healing, so that the observable symptoms of the condition no longer exist. Even though we may no longer see any symptoms of autism, we can't say a child is "cured" because we do not know what they would

have been like had they never been injured. (www.cnn.com/2008/US
/04/02/mccarthy.autismtreatment/index.html)

Such claims are typically deemed deeply suspect by members of the
health care community and others engaged in autism-related policy, including many members of the neurodiversity movement. Often criticisms of
such claims extend to the point of stating that the individual in question did
not really have the neurological difference to begin with. For the most part,
however, according to the accepted medical consensus, cures for neurological differences are simply not (yet) available.

The Role of Time and Event Horizons
in Interactions Between Care and Cure

Outright conflict between care and cure agenda types results less from differences in basic understandings of disability than from questions of timing.
Publicly provided care seeks to address, almost by definition, immediate
concerns of those with atypical functionalities and their families. Needs and
services are understood as being required in the present to serve the current
population of individuals with functional differences. Political discourse on
the subject tends to emphasize urgency and a desire to put a stop to long-
term neglect of needs. Delay of care often links to unnecessary stagnation
or decline in functioning and an increased potential for onset of disease
(Levine et al. 2007; Hill and Phillips 2006). Care-oriented public discourse
tends to emphasize an urgent need for access to care and the importance of
investing in the current population of individuals with disabilities.

Cure agendas, on the other hand, are almost unilaterally focused on the
future. Though some discourse in cure agenda types focuses on access to existing cures, especially given the current state of science, the preponderance
of the conversation addresses the need to invest in development of cures
(see, for example, Rizza, Eddy, and Kahn 2008). As a result of the long
event horizon involved in the creation of new cures, current investments of
public funds into scientific research focused on finding a way to eliminate
a particular functional difference are not generally expected to impact the
current population in any meaningful way other than to provide a distant
sense of hope.

While progress in the medical sciences has proceeded at a stunning pace
in recent decades, innovations remain elusive and take a long time to become available for general use. Such long timelines exist for both thera-

peutic and pharmaceutical interventions. In addition, though calculating exact price tags is complicated at best, estimates of the cost of new drug development run into the hundreds of millions of dollars (Adams and Brantner 2006). Not only does it take time to develop cures, but substantial time, interest, and effort also go into making sure the necessary primary research is conducted. This becomes especially true with regard to differences with less well-understood etiologies, including most neurological differences (Patterson 2009). As a result of such time differentials, tensions between care and cure agenda types often center on debate between spending on those with needs in the present and investment in hope for a different needs structure in the future. As Kristin Bumiller explained while discussing the search for genetic etiology of (and by extension, possible cures for) autism: "coupled with the high personal and financial costs of caring for a child with autism, this has created an unusually sharp divide between advocates for genetic research and others who are focused on responding to the immediate concerns of (usually female) caretakers" (2009, 876).

Cure Is Assumed to Be Less Expensive as an Article of Faith

Despite this high expected cost of development (and possibly production), cure is generally assumed to be the least-expensive option when it comes to publicly provided interventions for undesired neurological differences. In political discourse, often the argument is made that while care expenditures are ongoing, money spent on locating a cure represents a onetime investment. As Murray Levine explained, "the medical model assumes that once the illness is diagnosed and treated that all else will be well" (2007, 64). Unless cure is in fact total, such thinking about the disability policy subsystem is incomplete. As such, the academic field of disability studies was founded in part to "challenge the notion that disability is primarily a medical category" (Linton 1998, 2). Such arguments fit more naturally with essentialist understandings of disability than with understandings that include some role of public infrastructures (and external private practices such as family circumstances or trauma) in the creation of neurological differences.

Of course, this argument often overstates the simplicity and completeness of quests for cures. Research directed at finding a cure for disease—let alone for more complex and less well-understood conditions such as neurological differences—generally requires substantial capital investment and repeated failures (Weimar and Vining 2005). Many other conditions and diseases also compete for the time and resources of primary researchers and for funding to target such primary scientific research. Especially in the United States, where a substantial share of biomedical research is conducted within the private sector, the question of potential profit also looms large in decisions about directing efforts toward pursuit of cures. Cost-benefit analyses of cures for neurological differences may not compete successfully with the pursuit of cures for other conditions. This reality is particularly relevant to the case of neurological differences, as genuine cures for neurological differences have proven elusive despite many advances in neurology and modern medicine.

Cure Is Assumed Preferable Where Possible

A fundamental assumption of modern medicine is that, given a choice that does not involve extraordinary costs but that does involve a certain amount of scientific certainty, cure is always preferable to care. But scientific certainty comes at a high cost and can be difficult to achieve in our modern, increasingly politicized version of scientific study, findings, and progress. As Roger Pielke explained, "our time is characterized by new demands upon scientists in policy and politics . . . but experience and research shows us that science is well suited to contribute directly to the resolution of political conflicts only in the most simple of decision contexts" (2007, 8). Care, particularly in the form of medical treatment, is understood as being a relatively pale stand-in until there is a cure. As a result, one ongoing dynamic between these two agenda types is an articulation of choice between the present needs of those with neurological differences and the needs of individuals who might experience the neurological differences in the future. Under many circumstances, individuals of the future tend to be "silent losers" (Weimar and Vining 2005) in policy choices, as they are by definition unable to exert direct political pressure on policymakers. However, because of the level of attention given to both the real and imagined health care and service costs associated with neurological difference, this typical element of political discourse asserts itself less powerfully in the disability policy subsystem.

In the case of neurological differences, care and cure agendas are sometimes set in explicit conflict with one another in both scientific discussion and political discourse. As noted in Chapter 3 in the discussion of the period of institutionalization, neurological differences historically were sometimes attributed to the type or quality of care the individual received from natural caregivers. Mothers, in particular, were blamed (and to some degree continue to be blamed) for the neurological differences experienced by their children. The description of mothers of children with autism as "refrigerator mothers" by Bruno Bettelheim, prevailed for several decades (Smukler 2005; Bumiller 2009). As Ken Garber explained, "until the mid-1980s, experts considered autism a strictly environmental disorder, with most of the blame falling on faulty parenting" (2007, 190). Bettelheim, in fact, argued that autism was the result of a child having parents who wished their child did not exist (Grinker 2007). The effect of this theory on public and political discourse surrounding neurological difference was chilling. As John Pitney points out, "But whereas agenda-setting books convince readers that a policy response is necessary, [Bettelheim's] *The Empty Fortress* pointed in the opposite direction by blaming maternal coldness. Instead of spurring demands for effective public action, it made a generation of autism mothers feel guilty. Its fraudulent research and bogus conclusions spread popular misunderstandings that would take years to correct" (2010, 5). Such thinking became surprisingly popular, particularly among members of the medical professions. In an article titled "What Can You Learn About Mental Illness from the Aviator?" that appeared on Cox News Service on March 13, 2005, Gregory Ramer explained:

> When in college, I was taught that cold, rejecting and rigid mothers were responsible for autism . . . since these mothers did not bond with their infants, the children retreated into their own world . . . they developed self-stimulating behaviors to compensate for the lack of love and attention they didn't receive from their mothers . . . in some instances, it was recommended that autistic children [be] removed from their parents and placed with families who could give them the affection they were lacking.

Public discourse surrounding autism took quite a while to change completely, often requiring that the difference be overtly explained. For example, in a *Contra Costa Times* article titled "Autistic Children Thriving in Program That Emphasizes Structure" that appeared on February 18, 1997, Gayle Vassar Melvin wrote:

> Autism used to be considered an emotional or mental illness caused by poor parenting . . . but in the last 30 years, autism has been recognized as a developmental disorder that affects about 15 out of every 10,000 births in the United States . . . Two treatment methods have come to the forefront: one an intensive one-on-one method for 40 hours or more a week, and the other the TEACCH [Treatment and Education of Autistic and Communication Related Handicapped Children] method, which can be used in a classroom or center.

Although such dramatic versions of blaming parents for children's neurological differences have largely receded from modern public and political discourse, remnants of these arguments continue to exist. For example, in recent years some of the political discourse surrounding the push for publicly provided early childhood education aims in this direction (Klebanov and Brooks-Gunn 2007). The argument that a large proportion of children arrive at kindergarten unprepared is sometimes at least close to stating that the environment provided for (typically underprivileged) children by their parents causes learning disabilities. Given such attitudes, the perception emerges that at least some kinds of care and cure cannot coexist. In fact, the argument is based on a now dated understanding of neurology that held that certain periods in a child's life were the only times at which certain types of neurological development could take place. As Jonah Lehrer explained, this understanding involved the expectation that people did not develop new neurons past infancy. In recent years, however, neurologists have discovered that "the mind is never beyond neurogenesis . . . as long as we are alive, important parts of the brain are dividing . . . the brain is not marble, it is clay, and our clay never hardens" (2007, 42). Despite this new knowledge, the old understanding of neurons as finite, particularly after the first three years of life, dominates political discourse. As a result, cure becomes, at least in part, the antidote to incorrectly designed care, making reconciliation of the interests of these two agenda types more complicated.

Care Is Reflexively Assumed to Be Medical

In modern disability policy subsystems, not all care is medical care. In fact, care-oriented policy focuses on supports for all aspects of daily living, many of which have no relation to disease or the management of long-term health concerns per se. Nevertheless, publicly provided care either is typically assumed to be medical or is managed by medical professionals, at least at the level of gate-keeping in terms of deciding which individuals receive services under what circumstances. As Samuel Bagenstos put it, "because our society's response to disability has historically been so heavily medicalized, many of the services people with disabilities need for independence and labor force participation—personal assistance and assistive technology being the most obvious—are typically regarded as 'medical' services for which the health insurance system is responsible" (2004, 26).

Such assumptions create challenges in modern disability policy subsystems. First of all, because of the economics of disability, care can be (and is even more often perceived as) relatively expensive. This is especially likely to be the case when it involves assistive technology or programs with intellectual property restrictions. As a result, particularly in health care systems that include a strong role for privately held corporations (most notably the health insurance companies of the United States), resistance to paying for such services can be built into the system, causing increased exclusion of individuals with disabilities.

Finally, at least in the United States, confounding care and cure into a general category of medical treatment has a tendency to increase other challenges that individuals with disabilities face in relation to public infrastructures, particularly employment. As Bagenstos put it, "far and away the most significant barrier to employment for people with disabilities is the current structure of our health care system" (2004, 26). Two archetypical reasons exist for this phenomenon. First, in the United States, most employers have a legal obligation to pay for (or at least subsidize) the health care insurance of their full-time employees. As is to be expected both within a profit-seeking environment and under the circumstances of perennially limited resources faced by both public and nonprofit agencies, a strong incentive exists for employers to minimize health care costs. Even though it is illegal under the Americans with Disabilities Act to discriminate in hiring on the basis of disability, it is notoriously difficult to detect whether or not employers have allowed such considerations to enter into their hiring practices (McMahon and Hurley 2008). This is likely to be particularly the case when it comes to neurological differences, due to the perceived heightened levels of unknowns when it comes to providing for the medical care needed to target atypical neurological functionalities (O'Brien and Brown 2009).

Furthermore, ongoing care needs that are considered medical or distributed through the consent of physicians are often not covered in private health care policies. For example, private health policies routinely exclude home-based nursing services, limit the number of therapy appointments a person can receive on an annual basis, and arbitrarily restrict the number of days in behavioral health hospitals that insurance will cover (often to ten per year), regardless of the health status of the covered individual or the medical opinions of his or her providers. As a result, individuals with complex needs requiring ongoing care become either hesitant or unable to become employed because of the associated loss of funding for care through publicly provided health insurance that is available to some of the unemployed. Some recent changes in policy have attempted to address this issue by allowing individuals to maintain their eligibility for publicly provided care after becoming employed. Such policies are neither universal nor comprehensive at this point in time in the United States, however.

Balancing Care and Cure: Nonprofit Organizations

Nonprofit, or third-sector, organizations constitute a vital category of stakeholders in the politics surrounding neurodiversity and in the provision of publicly funded services to individuals with neurological differences. In modern societies, nonprofit organizations proliferated dramatically over the past couple of centuries as the dominance of established churches became less common and societies became more complex. The missions and scope of such organizations range from the wildly ambitious to the highly specific. The size of these organizations ranges widely, from tiny groups of individuals involved in charitable or activist work, to hundreds of individuals employed globally across numerous countries. Nevertheless, as with any organizational type, nonprofits have a tendency to both formalize and specialize over time. As a result, organizations focused on the specific agenda types extant in the disability policy subsystem have developed. An examination of mission statements of organizations directing their efforts (primarily) toward neurological differences highlights aspects of the dynamics between cure and care agenda types.

As the disability policy subsystem developed, the variety of disability-focused nonprofit organizations grew dramatically across industrialized nations. A Google search on the keywords "nonprofit" and "disability" returned over 2 million hits in 2009. Traditionally, nonprofit organizations associated with public challenges attributed to disability have designed themselves around a particular type (or a select few types) of functional difference. For example, the Association for Retarded Citizens (ARC) was originally designed to represent the concerns and serve the needs of individuals identified as having mental retardation. By 2009, however, the organization had evolved its mission statement: "The Arc of the United States advocates for the rights and full participation of all children and adults with intellectual and developmental disabilities" (www.thearc.org/NetCommunity/Page.aspx?pid=266). As this example suggests, in more recent years, organizations with the explicit mission of serving a broader scope of individuals with disabilities have proliferated. At the same time, the development of the Internet also facilitated creation of a much broader variety of nonprofit organizations targeting ever more specific segments of the population of individuals with neurological differences.

As is the case with policy stakeholders, nonprofit organizations are not conveniently identifiable as being oriented toward one agenda type or another. However, unlike with individual stakeholders or specific policy products, the mission statements of organizations tend to explicitly state their aspired goals. Whereas this analysis requires judgment in determining the nature of some organizations, most can be relatively easily categorized as care-oriented, cure-oriented, or both, according to their self-described purposes. A sample of seventy-five organizations focused on neurological differences is examined here.

Care-Oriented Organizations

Care-oriented organizations are an incredibly mixed bag. This reflects the deep roots of this agenda in the politics of neurological difference and neurodiversity. It also serves as a reminder of the fact that caring for individuals with disabilities arguably encompasses the oldest of all collective social responses to the presence of disability in society. Furthermore, most of the organizations in the sample expressed a distinct orientation toward care, and the majority of those that focused on other agendas—even those not in the business of providing or organizing services—referenced care as one of their primary concerns. Nevertheless, organizations with care-oriented missions remained distinct from those targeting cure agenda types in some key ways.

Perhaps the most striking way in which care-oriented missions differed from those focused on cure surrounds the question of innovation and potential. First, cure-oriented organizations, when speaking of innovation, discuss innovations in treatment expected in the long term. Care-oriented missions point to innovation in the present tense, highlighting modern approaches to services expected to improve the lives of individuals with neurological differences in the here and now. The underlying assumption of such statements appears to be that the potential for success already exists in individuals with neurological differences and the public infrastructures surrounding them. For example, the Federation of Families for Children's Mental Health declares that its mission is to offer "services, support and advocacy to children and families of children with mental, emotional, or behavioral disorders to empower them to lead happy and productive lives." Similarly, the Chrysalis Foundation for Mental Health declares that its mission is "to develop resources to meet mental health needs of adults and children in our communities. The vision of the Foundation is to be a leader in the support of mental health in North Carolina, facilitating innovative and successful programs and needed services to enable individuals living with mental illness and disabilities to live life to their fullest potential." Another organization, the nonprofit Family Mental Health Foundation, targets a quite different population of individuals (those who experience more short-term neurological differences) and employs the concept of potential as recovery in "serving women, babies, fathers, families, the medical community and the general public. We are dedicated to helping people live with and recover from mental health problems, especially those who suffer from Postpartum Depression. We feel no one should suffer alone and everyone is deserving of compassionate care." As mentioned earlier, care agendas are most concerned with the present and the long-term implications of actions taken today on the lives of the current population of individuals with disabilities.

Second, this concept of potential is frequently found in care-oriented organizations that appear to take an overtly constructivist approach to understanding disability. Though both care- and cure-oriented agendas target the potential of individuals with neurological differences, organizations focused on care lean toward making at least some changes that are external to the individual with the neurological difference. Another organization, the all-volunteer Daniel Jordan Fiddle Foundation, which focuses on autism, declares that its mission is "to develop and award grants to programs that enrich the lives of adolescents and adults with Autism. Our expertise encompasses developing, identifying, supporting and supervising exemplary programs throughout the United States." Again, this mission rests on the assumption that the knowledge needed in order to achieve care-oriented agendas already exists. The basic theme of realizing existing potential is articulated similarly in the mission of the Grand Avenue Club, which seeks "to provide people who have experienced mental illness with all the ingredients for a satisfying life—opportunities to get ready for work, paid employment, education, housing, as well as recreational and cultural opportunities." However, the simplest expression of such intent found in the sampled organizations came from Spectrum: "we form relationships which support individuals with disabilities to achieve their life goals." The realization of potential represents the modern version of the care agenda, which once was mostly limited to either infantilizing those with neurological differences or encouraging behavior "passing" as neurologically typical, but now has become more focused on bridging gaps perceived as more or less continually existing between those with neurological differences and surrounding societies. This changes the nature of the relationship between cure and care agendas from one of ranked hierarchy to something more proximate to partnership.

One way in which some care-oriented missions specify the concept of potential is through the concept of self-sufficiency. The ideal of a level of independence presumed to exist for most adults in modern democracy fits easily within care- and cure-oriented agendas. For care-oriented missions, however, the self-sufficiency tends to rest on the assumption of an approached rather than a fully achieved goal. As mentioned, the concept of cure generally involves a short period of targeted intervention, whereas care presumes an ongoing need. Self-sufficiency becomes, then, an individually optimizable characteristic as opposed to a homogeneous state. An example of expression of this concept in an organization's mission statement reads:

> Opportunity Partners supports people with disabilities and other special needs in their effort to improve their self-sufficiency at work, at home, and in the community. The range and depth of services offered by Opportunity Partners means that clients have flexibility among programs and can select the services that meet their needs. Currently, Opportunity Partners provides personalized education, housing and employment to more than 1,300 clients with developmental disabilities, brain injury, autism and other special needs.

Although medical intervention also involves a degree of personalization given the needs of the patient, discussion in the public and political discourse surrounding cure more often than not surrounds a singular cure (*the* cure) rather than the flexibility described in the preceding care-oriented statement. This distinction is also found in another mission statement:

> QSAC [Quality Services for the Autism Community] is an award winning non-profit dedicated to meeting the needs of individuals with autism and their families throughout New York City and Long Island. QSAC offers programs and services that provide support to individuals with autism throughout their lifetimes. Services from Early Intervention to Residential Programs ensure that QSAC is available to assist persons with autism in leading independent, productive, and fulfilling lives.

This flexibility, however, tends to involve discussion of a particular set of ingredients. For example:

> Established in 1970, KYC's [Kenneth Young Center] mission is to help people feel good, do better and find solutions. We counsel adults, children and families through difficult times. We help elderly people manage in their own homes. We guide people with serious mental illness back to independence and hope. Our values include: Respect for clients, volunteers, staff and community . . . recovery oriented, goal-directed intervention [and] incorporation of individual, family and community strengths.

Each of these value statements represents current outcomes of ongoing political conversations (if not outright debates) between stakeholders in modern disability policy subsystems and their surrounding political infrastructures. Referring to those served by care-oriented organizations as "clients," for instance, is a popular political act connected to privatization movements in democratic governments in the 1990s and early twenty-first century.

Another goal connected to potential involves deliberate removal or control of barriers to the effective participation of individuals with neurological differences in the socioeconomic systems of societies. Often this comes from recognition of extraordinary burden. This concern is perhaps currently most prevalent in the United States, as a result of its more limited public health and social services systems (which, ironically, do not necessarily translate into a lower level of public expenditures on such public programs). Third-sector organizations have a long history of stepping in to fill part of the gap between the economic potential and needs of individuals with disabilities. The mission of the Doug Flutie Jr. Foundation, a care-oriented organization involved in this effort, is "to aid financially disadvantaged families who need assistance in caring for their children with autism; to fund education and research into the causes and consequences of childhood autism; and to serve as a clearinghouse and communications center for new programs and services developed for individuals with autism." Such missions demonstrate a conception of care with deep roots, and the notion that disability in one member of the family should not be allowed to devastate the economic security of the entire family. This assumption that the third sector has a responsibility to help in this capacity predates the existence of public institutions, which, as discussed in previous chapters, were founded partly to address this economic argument. It is important to remember that the implications of this assumption are not necessarily inherently oppressive, even if they do tend to highlight negative aspects of disability. Fundamentally, the goal is economic survival, which does not necessarily divorce the individual with the disability from the rest of their family in an economic sense.

The care-oriented organizations examined also included organizations "of" individuals with disabilities (as opposed to those created "for" individuals with neurological differences). The mission statements of such organizations also targeted self-sufficiency, typically with a focus on empowering individuals to locate existing services and, in many cases, to advocate for programmatic and policy change. For example, the mission statement of the Advocacy Center for Adults with Asperger Syndrome, Autism, and Related Disabilities says that the center is founded by a person with Asperger Syndrome, who himself, now an adult, faced several challenges before being properly diagnosed with the disorder, and now understands the consequences that an undiagnosed and untreated adult faces. We want to make sure that the lives of those with such disorders are productive by guiding such individuals to services provided by specially-trained professionals in handling cases of autism-spectrum disorders, particularly those who do not initially appear to have such disorders . . . Objectives of the Organization are to provide such services as needed, raise public awareness of such disorders, train professionals, especially law-enforcement and correctional staff and lawyers to handle individuals with such disorders, who often get into unfortunate situations because of misunderstood behavior, and criminal activity incited by a normotypical "bully" in order for the autistic person to be "accepted" by him. Our objective is also to handle complaints by these individuals of abuse, neglect or exploitation, such as in the example mentioned above.

Clearly this mission reflects a very constructivist viewpoint, challenging assumptions typically expressed in cure-oriented discourse. The care agenda type, however, has room for such statements, since in its modern incarnation it more easily takes into account the aspects of disability resulting from inflexibilities in socioeconomic and political infrastructures.

Not all organizations "of" individuals are so completely constructivist, however. In fact, many are formed by those who might use language such as "survivors" to describe their experience with neurological difference. Such statements involve less tension—and perhaps even symbiosis—with cure-oriented political discourse, since part of such organizations' goals includes the alleviation or even elimination of the neurological difference. For example, the mission statement of one such organization reads:

Freedom From Fear was established in 1984 by Mary Guardino as an outgrowth of her personal experience of suffering with anxiety and depressive disorders. Freedom From Fear has expanded from a local support group to a nationally recognized advocacy voice for those who suffer from mental illness. Freedom From Fear provides many programs including national education/outreach programs, turnkey kits for professionals to organize educational/screening programs, national programs to decrease stigma associated with mental illness, research to learn more about the causes, treatments and the barriers to treatment for individuals with mental illness and local support groups and training programs.

As discussed earlier, the differences in tone and intent of these statements result from fundamental distinctions in the experiences of those with neurological differences writ large. One defining element of such distinctions tends to be whether the neurological difference is perceived to be an acquired or an innate condition. Both care and cure agendas as currently expressed in modern disability policy discourse (and in disability studies academic literature) insufficiently address the implications of this element of diversity. All too often in fact, this inconvenient aspect of attempts to aggregate the experiences of individuals with neurological differences for the purposes of public and political discourse becomes deliberately ignored so that stakeholders can simplify their positions and arguments.

Finally, many organizations with missions focused on health care were also located in the sample. As previously noted, these organizations generally do not fall into the cure agenda types because they do not seek to eliminate the neurological difference itself. Although in the minority of cases this results from purely constructivist approaches that interpret part of the experience of neurological difference as worth preserving, for the most part this comes about because cure for the particular neurological difference is understood by the organization as unavailable for the foreseeable future. For example:

> The Treatment Advocacy Center (TAC) is a national nonprofit organization dedicated to eliminating legal and clinical barriers to timely and humane treatment for millions of Americans with severe brain disorders who are not receiving appropriate medical care. Founded in 1998, TAC serves as a catalyst to achieve proper balance in judicial and legislative decisions that affect the lives of persons with serious brain disorders. TAC works on the national, state, and local levels to educate the public and civic, legal, criminal justice, and legislative communities on the benefits of assisted treatment, also known as involuntary commitment, in an effort to decrease homelessness, jailings, suicide, violence and other devastating consequences caused by lack of treatment.

Such care-oriented organizations are likely to remain particularly common in the United States so long as the country lacks a public health care system, but also in other democratic nations where such services are not included in the national health care system. One example of a mission statement of such an organization reads: "Crider Health Center is a critical resource to the communities we serve: the Missouri Counties of Lincoln, Warren, St. Charles, and Franklin. Our goal has always been to assure every citizen of this area has the health care they need, at the time they need it, delivered in the setting in which those services will be most effective and efficient." Discourse within care-oriented agendas may work quite closely in tandem with cure-oriented discourse because of the working relationships that can exist between the professional stakeholders actively involved in this part of the disability policy subsystem. As discussed earlier, however, this can also result in a tension surrounding the event horizon that pits the needs of the current generation of individuals with neurological differences against the hope for elimination of such neurological differences from future generations.

Cure-Oriented Organizations

Cure-oriented organizations were less prevalent in the sample. As might be expected given the clarity of the goals of public and political discourse of cure-oriented agendas, the mission statements were also much less varied than those addressing care agenda types. After all, when it comes to cure discourse, easy consensus on the ultimate goal inherently exists. Most of the debate surrounds the most promising approach to locating cure, which is (ideally at least) a scientific rather than a political question and which is therefore resolved through traditional scientific methods rather than through public or political discourse.

As a result, the mission statements of cure-oriented organizations tended to be shorter and simpler than those of organizations involved in care. For the most part, the mission statements focused unequivocally on cure. For instance, the Anxiety Disorders Association of America characterized itself as "a national nonprofit organization dedicated to the prevention, treatment, and cure of anxiety disorders and to improving the lives of all people who suffer from them."

Similarly, the Michael J. Fox Foundation, created by the popular actor following his own experience with Parkinson's disease, characterized itself as "dedicated to finding a cure for Parkinson's disease through an aggressively funded research agenda and to ensuring the development of improved therapies for those living with Parkinson's today." In this statement, the potential for effective partnership with care-oriented organizations is evident, albeit with the assumption that care agendas and solutions are inherently inferior to cure. This assumption also underlies the mission statement of the National Eating Disorders Association, which "supports individuals and families affected by eating disorders, and serves as a catalyst for prevention, cures and access to quality care." Another, less disability-specific organization, the Foundation of Hope, also shares this characteristic, in its mission "to promote scientific research aimed at discovering the causes and potential cures for mental illness in order to develop a more effective means of treatment. Additionally, the Foundation is committed to raising community awareness and supporting effective treatment programs."

Finally, some cure-oriented organizations expressly focused on specific negative experiences sometimes associated with certain neurological differences. For example:

> The Kristin Brooks Hope Center is a non-profit organization dedicated to suicide prevention, intervention and healing: by providing a single point of entry to community-based crisis services through innovative telephony and internet based technologies; by bringing national attention and access to services for post partum depression and other women's mood disorders; through education and advocacy; through formal research and evaluation of crisis line services; and, by championing the need for national funding for community-based suicide prevention crisis services.

In other words, such statements demonstrate a focus exclusively on symptoms, essentially bypassing the question of cure of the neurological difference itself. Such an approach would tend to more easily operate in symbiosis with other disability policy agenda types.

Organizations Targeting Both Cure and Care

Some organizations in the sample affirmed a relatively equal commitment to both care- and cure-oriented agendas in their mission statements. Some appeared to be highly generalist in nature and therefore not particularly associated with any political agenda type. For example, the mission of Autism Speaks is to "change the future for all who struggle with autism spectrum disorders." Similarly, the Dan Marino Foundation's mission is to "'open doors' for children and young adults with special needs by supporting comprehensive integrated treatment programs, providing outreach services, advancing scientific research, and fostering independence through transition programs." Another mission statement in the sample read: "The Child & Adolescent Bipolar Foundation educates families, professionals, and the public about pediatric bipolar disorder; connects families with resources and support; advocates for and empowers affected families; and supports research on pediatric bipolar disorder and its cure." The work and intentions of some organizations span multiple agenda types, often without questioning why or complicating the day-to-day operations. As discussed earlier, however, a crucial factor in this symbiosis is the tacit assumption of a ranking of disability policy agendas wherein cure is universally understood as being the ultimately preferable social and political goal. Care, in particular, is seen as a second-best stand-in for cure.

Finally, for the subset of neurological differences understood as men-

tal illnesses, the concept of recovery has gained substantial popularity in recent years. This is not to suggest that in earlier times, society's tolerance
of mental illness was such that recovery was deemed unnecessary. Rather,
mental illnesses tended to be thought of as lifelong, increasingly debilitat-
ing diseases that all too often fully took over the lives of those who experienced them. At best, a person with a mental illness could expect to spend
a lifetime in treatment. During the early years of the twenty-first century,
however, an expectation of (at least potential) temporariness of mental illness developed, largely in the absence of the development of reliable cures.
This change in expectation appears in mission statements. For example:
"Mental Health America is dedicated to promoting mental health, pre-
venting mental and substance use conditions and achieving victory over
mental illnesses and addictions through advocacy, education, research and
service." Similarly:

> Skyland Trail is an Atlanta-based 501(c)(3) nonprofit serving adults aged
> 18 and older with serious mental illness that impairs their thinking, be-
> havior, relationships, and ability to hold employment. The mission of Sky-
> land Trail is to promote recovery from mental illness. Our programs foster
> community reintegration and empower adults to live independently with
> dignity. In partnership with families, clinicians, and the community, we
> deliver excellence in treatment and education, and provide a model for
> replication.

As a result of this change in popular philosophy, cure and care agenda types
have been brought into closer proximity with regard to mental illnesses over
the past decade.

Toward the end of the first decade of the twenty-first century, public
and political discourse surrounding these two agenda types rested closer to
one another with regard to mental illnesses than with regard to other kinds
of neurological difference. Intriguingly, this history led to an emphasis in
some organizations on the optional nature of treatment. For example: "The
mission of the Depression and Bipolar Support Alliance (DBSA) is to provide hope, help, and support to improve the lives of people living with depression or bipolar disorder. DBSA pursues and accomplishes this mission
through peer-based, recovery-oriented, empowering services and resources
when people want them, where they want them, and how they want them."
Deliberately asserting the optional nature of treatment and services mini-
mizes (though perhaps fails to eliminate) the perception of the primacy of
the cure-oriented agenda in how organizations engage the politics of neurodiversity and neurological difference.

Concluding Thoughts for All Disabilities

Time and timing demarcate perennial political challenges for all policy sub-systems. Pacing, prioritizing, and defining event horizons are never simple tasks for modern democratic systems. The politics of neurological difference and neurodiversity encompass few (if any) exceptions to this general rule. The same is true for the development of policy addressing any kind of disability.

Negotiating time, timing, and prioritization is particularly relevant to the relationships between cure- and care-oriented public and political discourse. In fact, as shown in this chapter, this dynamic tends to be powerful enough to extend well beyond formal politics and, often, into the operations of third-sector organizations serving those with disabilities.

An intriguing factor of the relationships between cure- and care-oriented agendas is the usually strong prevalence of unquestioned assumptions in the surrounding political and public discourse. First, and perhaps most important, is the almost completely unquestioned assumption of superiority of cure over care. The belief that care is considered inherently less desirable by all stakeholders and more costly across a variety of measures tends to be tacitly assumed. Regardless of the type of disability or, for the most part, the nature of the services received, care is interpreted as undesirable dependence even if creating benefits such as jobs, social capital, and increased social engagement for both caregivers and care recipients, whereas cure is assumed to foster independence even if associated with lifelong dependence on medication or monitoring by health care professionals.

Second, under the assumption of primacy of cure, a tolerance for political and public discourse preferencing care depends almost entirely on the observation that cures tend to be both elusive and a long time in coming. Public and political discourse emphasizing care agendas tends to focus on need. This need comes about as a result of an absence of other ways to alleviate barriers to participation in society. More often than not, this absence is established by the statement that no cure is available for the functional difference in question.

Third, particularly in health care settings, care and cure are treated as synonyms, or at least as part of a singular effort rather than as distinct political efforts. In the extreme version of this model, care becomes nothing but a less than perfect cure applied only in the meantime while everyone waits for something better to come along. Under such circumstances, apart from the effort to increase funding for primary medical research, no political question exists (let alone one that might support multiple viable agenda types). Weighing care and cure becomes, then, an exercise in balancing the needs present in the current population of individuals with disabilities, with the needs expected to be present in the future.

Despite the strength and prevalence of these assumptions, however, recent years have shown an increased complexity of the interactions between these two agenda types. A prime and rapidly evolving example of this phenomenon involves the recent discussion of simultaneous recovery from and more or less permanent identification with diagnoses of some mental illnesses, as demonstrated in the claiming of a diagnosis as a life choice. In coming years, especially given the growing sophistication with which we understand ourselves, the dynamics between cure- and care-oriented agendas are likely to unfold in particularly fascinating and largely unpredictable ways across modern democracies.

7

Providing Care
vs. Celebrating Diversity

The politics of care and celebration surrounding neurological atypicalities naturally overlap to a great degree. Both deeply connect to the questions of identity and identification of individuals with neurological differences. Both also are ideally designed to make possible self-actualization of individuals with neurological disabilities and the realization of inclusive societies. Although care of individuals with disabilities might historically have tended toward paternalism, as discussed in previous chapters, such tendencies are not immutable components of publicly provided care. At least to the degree that care is person-centered and designed with as full as possible consideration of preferences of individuals receiving care, providing care to individuals with neurological differences comes to include some celebration of those neurological differences.

Despite this natural potential for overlap, substantial areas of tension exist in the politics of care and celebration agenda types in modern disability policy subsystems. These originate particularly around issues of identity of both individuals with neurological differences and those of the rest of the general population, starting with caregivers, who enter into often complicated relationships with individuals with neurological differences. Control and direction of identity construction can become especially divisive. In addition, in the political discourse of disability of modern democracies, care often takes place only in the context of established need for sympathy and obligation. Such rhetorical efforts are all too easily undermined by celebration of disability. Another outcome of interactions between care and celebration agendas is the potential for celebration-oriented politics to become or seem patronizing. For example, as is mentioned in Chapter 5, practices such as the presence of huggers at the finish lines of events in the Special

Olympics are referenced by some disability scholars and activists as a prominent example of the tendency for celebratory efforts to appear disingenuous or to infantilize the individual with the neurological differences when put into practice.

Potential for Preferencing
Those Considered Higher-Functioning

A perennial challenge in the interaction between celebration and care agenda types surrounds the perception that celebration-oriented agendas tend to focus on those considered higher-functioning. This focus is perceived as often being detrimental to lower-functioning individuals with more pronounced needs for care. As has been explained about diversity more generally, "the potential of escaping a low-status group actually induces more competitive behavior toward fellow group members" (*Harvard Law Review* 2008, 2164). In other words, celebration-oriented agendas offer possibilities of better incorporation into the rest of the general population of individuals with functional differences, through a deliberate minimization of challenges experienced by a minority of those individuals.

One strategy by which individuals pursue this goal is through active competition with other people with disabilities that is designed to ultimately reinforce a difference between the victor and other individuals with the same or similar diagnoses. Such practices are sometimes described as the "supercrip phenomena" in the case of individuals with disabilities, wherein those who do remain less typical are interpreted by other members of the general public as having, as described about the United States, "somehow failed the test of American wholesomeness" (Fleischer and Fleischer 2000, 4). As a result, some individuals with disabilities who achieve success become active opponents of some policies designed to assist minority groups. For example, Ward Connerly, a successful African American businessman and former regent of the University of California, gained attention as one of the more vocal opponents of affirmative action policies. To the degree that differences might be made to seem irrelevant through such strategies, surface inclusion of individuals with neurological differences becomes easier. Such "heroes of assimilation" (Sewell 2008) might under some circumstances serve celebration-oriented agendas well. However, their success often conflicts with the goals of care agenda types. To the extent that celebration-oriented agendas pave the way for some individuals as opposed to the minority group as a whole, they tend to be in tension with care-oriented agendas because ultimately they include at least tacit denial of the necessity of publicly provided care.

Another way of preferencing those considered higher-functioning or those with extraordinary talents is through celebrity status. Though defining characteristics and mode of selection of celebrities vary across time and space, all societies include the phenomenon of selective fame. Heroes with whom individuals with neurological differences might identify represent as natural a need as they do for any other individual or group. However, to the extent that luminaries such as Bill Gates or Thomas Jefferson are promoted as examples of individuals with neurological differences, concern arises that the experiences of others who are less celebrated by the general population will be ignored. As Andrew Fenton and Tim Krahn (2007) described this "show-casing" of exceptional individuals with autism:

> Though important for disabusing some of the misconceptions surrounding ASD [autism spectrum disorders], showcasing the successful among the neurodiverse risks two untoward implications: (i) that the cognitive capacities of the neurodiverse (minus the exceptional cases) are still seen as typically lying outside of what is properly regarded as normal or functional for humans; (ii) that the cognitive capacities which are to properly qualify as functional, or at least non-pathological, must enable successful living in the world of those described as normal. (2)

In other words, under such conditions, neurodiversity becomes tolerated only for the value it can provide to the predominantly neurologically typical general public. Furthermore, in the context of perennial resource limitation in the disability policy subsystem, some argue that expenditures on celebration-oriented efforts represent luxuries given to individuals already better-off while shortchanging individuals requiring publicly provided care.

Another concern that develops as a result of this surrounds the possibility that celebration-oriented policies will also only enable the already more-able while leaving those with more extreme functional differences ignored, even if there is no heroic and celebrity status conferred on specific individuals as a result of celebratory efforts. This concern has been expressed with regard to the goal of promoting cultures organized around specific disabilities. As Kristin Bumiller described, "some argue that only high-functioning individuals have the incentive to focus on autistic culture and that this emphasis fails to consider the needs of children with autism for more support and funding to compensate for social and educational difficulties" (2008, 970). After all, organization of celebration-oriented activities typically requires sustained effort and a surplus of time not dedicated to the pursuit of more basic needs. These activities also tend to require a so-phisticated understanding of human interactions and infrastructures, con-cepts that some individuals with neurological differences find more elusive. As a result of these factors, celebrations organized primarily through the ef-forts of individuals with neurological differences will typically be led by those who are understood as being higher-functioning. When such concerns are voiced, often a backlash concern is also voiced, that the needs of those who are high-functioning are systematically neglected in favor of those with more complex care needs.

Making a Place for Celebration in Public Policy

Celebration agendas tend to fit somewhat awkwardly into modern public policy subsystems. Issue stakeholders of celebration-oriented agendas are continually required to make the case for the basic legitimacy of the agenda type. This limited acceptance of the necessity of public celebration is not unique to disability policy subsystems. As a result, public resources dedi-cated to celebration-oriented policies and programs tend to be scarce, even by comparison to other aspects of social policy. This dynamic naturally con-cerns those who engage in care agenda types, who when forced to choose become inclined to emphasize the needs of those considered lower-func-tioning as more urgent (sometimes even to the point of inadvertently creat-ing circumstances that might result in the decline of those currently considered higher-functioning).

Furthermore, celebration-oriented policies and programs hold great po-tential for triggering a reliance on competition due to the mechanisms by which celebration is publicly practiced. For example, if public fiscal support exists to promote the artistic accomplishments of individuals with particu-lar neurological differences, under many circumstances this raises the ques-tion of who is being left behind. Often this concern extends to include the assumption of deprivation of those without neurological differences of spe-cial opportunities provided to individuals who do have disabilities.

Part of the concern surrounding potential influence of celebration-ori-ented events on support for care-oriented policies and programs emerges from the competitive nature of celebration-oriented agendas. As mentioned, in general, public funds and programs oriented toward celebration tend to be severely limited. For example, while there are public funding sources for arts in many cities, the level of funding tends to be relatively low as compared to the level of interest in participating in this kind of celebration.

Furthermore, unlike as is often the case for policy and programs focused on other agenda types within the disability policy subsystem, celebration-oriented policy is almost exclusively funded through discretionary (as opposed to entitlement) spending (Lewis and Rushton 2007). Policy developments in many societies over the course of the twentieth century resulted in an ever decreasing proportion of public budgets available for discretionary spending. As a result, funds and other opportunities are routinely assigned on a quite competitive basis to those wishing to engage in publicly funded celebration. For example, selection of a sculpture for display in a local park or on the campus of a state-run university generally involves a competition held with the intent of fairly distributing the opportunity among the interested population. It is usually reasonable to assume that those who are already more capable more frequently succeed under such auspices.

In addition, competition itself is celebrated in many societies. The mere fact that a process is competitive is, in and of itself, often believed valuable. Competition is also believed to be a formative element of communities—if only at the level of imagination—as is the case, for example, with the currently popular televised national singing and dancing contests (Reijnders, Rooijakkers, and van Zoonen 2007). Especially at the highest levels, winning in competitive events often includes formal recognition by and increased access to elected officials. In fact, individuals who have been successful competitors in one arena (such as sports) have even been known to employ these accomplishments as qualifications for elected office.

Competitive arenas are, generally speaking, constructed in accordance with the skills of elite members of the population. In other words, competitive arenas tend to be constructed around the preferences of the historical victors. As a result, competitions are rarely designed around advantages associated with disability (at least not purposefully so) (Berger 2009). In fact, when a person with a disability appears to have a competitive advantage resulting from their difference, the so-called fairness of the competition is routinely questioned in public discourse. Societies do not comfortably tolerate situations where disabilities create advantages, especially in formal arenas of competition.

When it comes to neurological differences, individuals considered higher-functioning typically more easily "pass" as neurologically typical or can downplay challenges associated with their differences while at the same time highlighting any competitive advantages. In some situations, the successes of competitors with neurological differences are portrayed through heartwarming, archetypical stories emphasizing perseverance, but only when these competitors are well established as successful. For example, on September 18, 2008, *Business Day* of South Africa included the following account in its section on the economy, business, and finance, in a short article titled "Overcoming a Major Disability on the Road to Success":

> Mallen Banda has suffered from muscular dystrophy all her life, but was determined not to let that stand in her way. In 1998 she joined the Tupperware sales force and in 2004 became a unit manager and an executive manager in 2007. Her lifelong dream was to drive, as she had to rely on public transport, enormously difficult given her physical condition. "Through her commitment to the business, Mallen earned the right to drive a vehicle. The company presented her with a customised vehicle in March," says Allan Dando, MD of Tupperware southern Africa. "She is well on her way to becoming a million-club manager. She is a warm caring person who embraces life and is an inspiration to us all."

Similarly, in a tribute given in the US Senate February 25, 2009, Patrick Leahy stated:

> In the early years of his career, Leon Fleisher astounded audiences with a golden sound. His career then seemed tragically cut short when he began suffering from a rare neurological condition that rendered his right hand unable to play. Instead of withdrawing from the musical world, Leon Fleisher remained in close contact with music through conducting, teaching and playing scores specially written for pianists who lost use of their right hands. He persisted in the effort to play the full concert repertoire, and some novel medical treatments eventually helped him regain full use of both hands . . . It is a classic American journey, tracing a path out of despair to triumph. In Leon Fleisher's sense of determination, dedication, vision and skill, there is much for all of us to both admire and emulate.

Such narratives of success in the face of adversity are, of course, vital to modern, well-rounded understandings of disabilities as being more than just simple disadvantages. They also demonstrate the important role of celebration-oriented political discourse in countering negative effects of discriminatory attitudinal infrastructures on the self-esteem of individuals with functional differences.

However, concern has arisen that such celebratory agendas promote minimization of challenges experienced by many people with functional differences in today's societies. For example, in a comparison of representations of people with intellectual disabilities in the British press in 1983 and 2001, Penny Wilkinson and Peter McGill found that the more modern press "systematically under-represented complexity and severity of need" (2009, 65). Particularly among those pushing for care-oriented policies, concern arises that the popularity of such narratives with the general public creates false impressions of difficulties faced by individuals with neurological differences in current social, economic, and political infrastructures.

Furthermore, public discourse surrounding celebration agenda types sometimes describe neurological differences as nothing more (or less) than a treasured artistic temperament or some other relatively rare talent valued by society. As Philip Patson (2007) described:

> Each of us has a different capacity to function at different times in different situations. Many activities involve functioning in several ways. For example, elite athletes need to function at a very high capacity physically and cognitively. Scientists may need only cognitive capacity to perform well. Artists' aesthetic appreciation requires motor, sensory, and creative capacity. We would forgive an athlete's temporary lapse in concentration or a scientist's dubious aesthetic discernment. We would not judge an artist's capacity because of a tendency to be reclusive or lack social skills. In fact, society forgives people for these deficits because of their successes. (1626)

Such statements suggest that because deficits are forgiven on the basis of a record of success, acceptance of difference rightfully depends on the existence of an extraordinary characteristic. Essentially this amounts to paying society back for any efforts made to include the individual with the perceived deficit.

In the face of such positive descriptions, conflict with the necessity of focus on challenge found in care-oriented public discourse naturally arises. This tension can be beneficial to the degree that it helps emphasize the diversity of experience for those with neurological differences. Such awareness ultimately helps create more flexible policies that serve the interests and needs of a broader scope of the general population. However, when an imbalance exists that strongly favors stakeholders who more or less exclusively pursue one agenda type or the other, real threats to the ability of either so-called lower- or so-called higher-functioning individuals with neurological differences tend to emerge. Especially in situations of public financial distress, which by nature involve a need to trim programs and cut costs, polarized coexistence of these two agenda types can weaken all claims made by disability policy subsystem stakeholders.

Celebration Agendas
Can Involve Apologizing for Care Efforts

Celebration-oriented agendas can also involve official apologies for past policy and public programs. For example, in 2002, the state of Virginia formally apologized for its sterilization programs, including official honoring of the memory of Carry Buck through such measures as a highway marker in her name. As Steven Noll describes, "Governor Mark Warner offered his 'sincere apology' for the 'Commonwealth's past mistakes'" (2005, 38–39). Similarly, on December 3, 2003, the governor of Oregon issued an official apology for the state's involvement in the eugenics movement (Kitzhaber 2002):

> Oregon has made remarkable progress in treating citizens who suffer mental illness or disabilities. But even as we celebrate the progress we've made, we must also acknowledge the realities that darken the history of our state institutions. The time has come to apologize for misdeeds that resulted from widespread misconceptions, ignorance and bigotry. It's the right thing to do, the just thing to do. The time has come to apologize for public policies that labeled people as "defective" simply because they were ill, and declared them unworthy to have children of their own . . . To those who suffered, I say, The people of Oregon are sorry. Our hearts are heavy for the pain you endured.

Organizations with a long history and therefore a history of involvement with care now described as at best paternalistic and at worse associated with attempted genocide of individuals with disabilities can find themselves in awkward situations in the face of such celebratory political actions. Playing the villain of the story—even the villain of history—is not comfortable for anyone seeking to make a positive difference in society. Furthermore, particularly in the context of modern public media that are often more focused on sensationalism and pain than depth and reconciliation, the narrative templates available for organizations and individuals seeking to make amends are often scarce at best.

The role of the scapegoat constitutes an expected component of the practice of bureaucracy. After all, this practice of placing the blame allows for continuation of public infrastructures and preservation of organizational strength rather than dismantling of infrastructures and starting over completely whenever significant errors in judgment are recognized. However, scapegoating can complicate the formation of positive identity at both the individual and the organizational level. Convincing others to change attitudes and practices, regardless of how genuine the attempt, is complicated.

In particular, including organizations (let alone individuals) with such pasts in celebration-oriented agendas often creates cognitive dissonance on the part of target populations and the rest of the general public. When modern incarnations of these organizations are still involved in the direct provision of public care of other individuals with neurological differences, proponents of care and celebration agenda types can find themselves at odds, especially at the more local levels of governance. Statements made as part of such conflicts can be especially confusing to members of the rest of the general public, who are often called upon to support (or not to support) such organizations at the local level by passionate activists and advocates on both sides of the debate.

Objectification Through Celebration

Just as concern exists that celebration-oriented efforts authentically rooted in the hearts and minds of higher-functioning individuals with neurological differences could lead to misunderstandings regarding the severity of negative implications of neurological differences for some people, a parallel concern exists that celebration of individuals with neurological differences can result in their objectification in many of the more mainstream efforts. Sometimes concern about the potential for (or realization of) such objectification develops around celebrations organized by caregivers involving individuals considered lower-functioning. Other times this concern arises when aspects of neurological difference are woven into pop culture media, particularly those that are part of the entertainment industry.

Concern also arises when language used to describe neurological difference is used as metaphor for other social conditions, concerns, or even desirable characteristics of aspects of the human experience that have no relation to observed differences in brains. For example, though certainly rarer than in the past, the presence of a neurological difference is sometimes used as an insult against a rival in political discourse. For example, according to the BBC in October 2006:

> A charity has criticised George Osborne after he appeared to suggest Gordon Brown could be "faintly autistic" . . . The shadow chancellor, who denied the charge, was criticised by the National Autistic Society after a light hearted exchange at a Tory fringe meeting . . . Mr. Osborne had been recalling his ability to retain odd facts, when the journalist hosting the event joked he might have been "faintly autistic." (http://news.bbc.co.uk/2/hi/uk_news/politics/5399072.stm)

This remark, which bears some similarity to the remark about the Special Olympics for which President Barack Obama drew criticism during an appearance on *The Tonight Show with Jay Leno* early in his presidency, was immediately criticized and not defended. Nevertheless, though such remarks are perceived as unacceptable enough in the current era to inspire criticism and even the occasional public apology, they have not yet reached a taboo status, in that popular (as opposed to extremist) politicians still feel comfortable making them in their less guarded moments.

Objectification and Disability Arts

Such concern becomes especially relevant in the production of arts, where the line between being the subject of artistic effort and being objectified by it might be no more solid than the subtleties of perceptions of the observer and the sophistication of the audience with regard to paradigms of disability. Substantial discussion of the meaning and impact of the profession and public "gaze" directed toward individuals with disabilities has highlighted the potential of cultural norms to objectify the individual being unapologetically stared at because of his or her observed difference (see, for example, Lau et al. 2007; Shakespeare 2006; Ware 2008). Inviting the gaze is a different matter, but must be understood as being different for the observer compared to the observed in order for the distinction to be meaningful. However, this concern extends to all celebration-oriented political discourse, agendas, and both organized and spontaneous events focusing on the achievements of individuals with neurological differences.

When it comes to both popular culture and most celebration activities of the past, this type of objectification often involved insincere or pathos-driven responses on the part of the rest of the general population. For example, when attending an event in which the artistic efforts of individuals with neurological differences were on display, well-intentioned individuals might have praised (or even purchased) such pieces as an essentially charitable act as opposed to as a response to the art itself. Of course, such transactions commonly existed, and continue to exist, in all artistic endeavors, particularly those run by nonprofit organizations. A person might very well purchase a piece of art from a student art show with the goal of supporting the school rather than out of genuine appreciation for the particular piece of art, for example. To the extent that the action goes in tandem with feelings (expressed or otherwise) of infantilization of individuals with neurological difference, however, the celebratory intent of the exchange may not be realized as intended. Furthermore, the act itself could undermine ongoing efforts to move care-oriented agendas away from their historically paternalistic tendencies in the construction of policies and programs designed to publicly provide necessary care for individuals with neurological differences.

Such complications arguably become most likely to arise when celebratory activities are undertaken by or for organizations more fundamentally engaged in care-oriented agendas. For example, an organization might produce holiday cards with images created by individuals with neurological differences with the express purpose of raising funds for care-oriented activities during the holidays. While the intent of the effort is, in the modern context at least, presumably associated with celebration-oriented agendas, an effect of the exchange can be objectification of the individual with the neurological difference, since it is connection to the individual objectified as their disability rather than the art that becomes the real product of the commercial exchange.

Objectification in Mainstream Arts

Objectification also describes situations in which people are used as means to an end (Gruenfeld et al. 2008; Kruppers 2007). Mainstream arts, particularly movies and novels, have often employed characters with functional differences as simplistic plot devices. Traditionally, characters with disabilities are rarely developed into three-dimensional characters. Rather, they exist either as caricatures (especially of the villain) or as sources of humor, or are employed to artificially invoke emotion into a piece of work that might otherwise fail to move its audience. For example, the revelation that a character's child has dyslexia could be used as a way to inspire more sympathy for that character's situation when she hears that her child has been teased at school. Rather than having to understand the reasons behind the targeting by other children, the audience is left to assume that the functional difference was the motivating factor.

Arguably, this concern is particularly relevant in the case of some neurological differences in which individuals might be less able to actively counter representations that objectify them. As Anupama Iyer explained with regard to fictional descriptions of individuals with what she described as intellectual disabilities, "literature both reflects and shapes societal attitudes to people in this vulnerable minority group . . . people with intellectual disabilities are seldom able to determine, confirm or counter narratives about themselves . . . this situation, in which the subject is fundamentally unable to participate in their representation, raises unique ethical considerations" (2007, 127). Well-articulated celebration-oriented political discourse involves direct consideration of these ethical dilemmas at least at the level of acknowledging their existence. Furthermore, efforts associated with care agenda types become at times affected by these representations because they tend to shape the impressions of the lives of both individuals with disabilities and their caregivers among the rest of the general population.

In public portrayals of disability, the more pronounced the difference, the more emotive the situation becomes without having to introduce additional details into the plot of the story. In such portrayals, a tendency to focus on those at the lower end of the spectrum usually arises, often for no reason other than the fact that this can heighten the dramatic tension introduced into the piece through the employment of a character with a disability. In addition, such portrayals frequently involve either miraculous recovery or a reduction of observed effects of the functional difference as part of the resolution of the story, at least in the case of the hero. For example, as Lori Breeden (2008) points out, films featuring individuals with autism that are made for mainstream populations tend to include increased eye contact and affect on the part of the character with autism as the film progresses, without including any discernible explanation for the change other than the audience's increased (expected) connection with the character and the development of the story itself.

In the case of the villain, an opposite portrayal is frequently employed. A character's disability might become more pronounced and obvious to other characters during the resolution and dénouement, often resulting in a confounding of the character's efforts to hide their functional atypicalities and their villainous acts. For example, in *Something About Mary* (1998), one of the men interested in romantic involvement with the main character is revealed late in the film to have a disability. The level of difference, including the character's tendency to stutter, increases in tandem with the unfolding revelation of his villainy. By the end of the film, the character has transformed from a well-spoken, well-educated gentleman to an individual who is almost completely unable to express himself through discernible speech and is prone to violence. The character of Mary's brother, on the other hand, who is portrayed as having a relatively nondescript form of mental retardation, becomes somewhat less affected by disability as the film progresses and his connection to the story and other main characters increases.

The introduction of characters with disabilities also becomes used as a form of artistic shorthand when stereotypes are deliberately manipulated in the hopes of inspiring particular responses and understandings in the audience. These understandings are generally based on limited understandings of disability rooted in a tradition of lack of exposure to individuals with disabilities on the part of many members of the general public. For example, since individuals with mental retardation are stereotypically assumed to be good-natured and unlikely to hold their tongues, a character with this functional difference might be introduced into a piece of art in order to create situations of humor wherein the humor derives from the voicing of an uncomfortable truth or when, for example, a family holiday scene might be made more touching by the presence of an uninhibited individual. As Iyer explained about the use of individuals with neurological differences in fictional literature, "in essence writers use figures with intellectual disabilities as a narrative device, where they function as contrasts to the other characters, various marginal groups or the world they find themselves in" (2007, 131). These characters serve as a descriptive extension of the narrator's voice as opposed to a separate, more independent element of the story, even when the character is a major one.

Interestingly, such characters tend to be invoked in political discourse. This phenomenon of using fictional characters as anchors of real world political discourse is hardly unique to the disability policy subsystem. For example, the fictional character Murphy Brown was repeatedly brought into the political discourse surrounding public challenges believed by many to be associated with single motherhood during the 1990s as a result of her character's choice to bear a child out of wedlock. Similarly, individuals taking political posts in real life have been described in the media in terms of who held the appointment on the television show *The West Wing*. Part of the motivation for this strategy is the (generally correct) assumption that a wide spectrum of the general population will be familiar with fictional characters and stories found in popular culture. Also, because the character is fictional, there is—at least at face value—less risk that those who are making use of the character as an element of their political argument will either publicly contradict themselves or suffer the repercussions that might result from defaming a real person.

Some recent disability scholarship points out that stereotypes are not necessarily inherently harmful if used in a more enlightened way in popular culture. In fact, as Rebecca Mallet (2009) explains, constant search for and focus on negative aspects of stereotypes has led to a stereotyping of stereotypes that has ultimately stilted celebration-oriented policy agendas and resulted in missed opportunities to more fully engage members of the rest of the general population. For example, Mallet describes how the television show *South Park* employs many disability stereotypes in a fashion

that deliberately raises questions and points out absurdities of the stereotypes themselves, arguably much more efficaciously than direct activism
would for some members of the general population:

> It seems that how we read representations of disability is contingent on
> where we are and this recognition is helpful when it comes to debating
> what we want the future of disability-criticism to be. Like the study of
> gendered, racialised and sexualised representations before it, disability-
> criticism has to balance its theoretical potentials with its political expedi-
> ency . . . As "stereotypes" have demonstrated, the choice of tools is
> necessarily a choice about the theoretical and political effectiveness of the
> resulting criticism. (9)

Since the final years of the twentieth century there has been, at least in
the United States, a (re)discovery of the potential of humor as a deliberate
vehicle through which to educate members of the general population more
effectively about political issues. Though the practice has been around for
a long time (at least since the writings of Voltaire in modern Western societies), the potential of humor as a reliable source of political engagement
was less completely employed in the extended past. The tremendous popularity of television shows such as *The Daily Show with Jon Stewart* and *The
Colbert Report* forcefully demonstrate how humor might be used to inspire
increased political awareness and public engagement, particularly among
relatively apathetic groups.

In the context of the politics of neurodiversity (and disability policy subsystems at large), potential for conscious and effective use of stereotypes in
this way exists, and represents a particularly promising strategy for negotiating and maximizing the positive outcomes of tension and conflict between
celebration- and cause-oriented agendas. After all, issue stakeholders directing their energies toward these agenda types tend to have expansive and
rich histories of direct observation of interactions between social infrastructures and individuals with neurological differences and the effect stereotypes play in shaping and complicating such personal experiences.

Case Study: *Autism: The Musical*

Consideration of a specific case helps to illuminate the nature of identity
and identification as they relate to public discourse surrounding care and
celebration agenda types. Over the past couple of decades, dozens of films,
novels, and other pieces of popular culture have addressed themes relating
to neurological difference, many times speaking at least implicitly in the

context of the politics of neurodiversity. Quality, audience, and authorship of these products are as varied as they are for any other topic of interest to modern audiences. Some are produced by individuals with neurological differences while others appear to have been created by individuals unlikely to have consciously interacted with anyone with atypical neurology. Some are fiction whereas others are based on true stories or documentary presentations. Some are produced for limited, specialized audiences while others aim for mass distribution. In selecting a piece of work to consider as a case study for the purposes of this book, one that in many ways falls between these extremes was deliberately selected.

In 2007 a documentary titled *Autism: The Musical* premiered at the Tribeca Film Festival in New York City. The film was produced and directed by Tricia Regan, whose other works include *Psychic Kids: Children of the Paranormal* (2007), *Soldiers Pay* (2004), and *A Leap of Faith* (1996). The film chronicled the creation and performance of an original musical by children with autism living in the Los Angeles area. In addition to its reporting on the unique creative process employed, the film profiled the parents (and to some degree the families and close friends) of several of the children involved in the production. After the festival, the film was shown in limited release and then extensively on HBO. From there the film gained a high degree of popularity, largely as a result of word of mouth and through publicity provided by public and nonprofit organizations focused on autism.

In 2008, the film won two Emmy Awards. In a written reflection on the Emmy win that originally appeared in the *Huffington Post* and was subsequently posted on the Autism Speaks website, Elaine Hall (2008) wrote:

> Today, I received an email from a 14-year-old boy in Virginia who said that after seeing The Miracle Project in Autism: The Musical, he is now proud to say he has autism. I have received over 3,000 emails from others whose lives have been changed after watching this film. Those who chose to devote their time to this film and newsprint to covering our "little" miracle are those who have made a difference, not only in my life and those of my students living with autism, but to our global tribe who has seen and experienced the boundless beauty of mothers, fathers, neighbors, volunteers, educators, community members and children of like mind and heart, joining an effort to build bridges and hope.

As this reflection suggests, the film garnered a relatively substantial amount of public attention for a documentary of its type.

Three aspects of the film strengthened its appeal for general audiences. First, the children featured most prominently in the film were depicted as spread across the spectrum of autism differences. Although it was made clear that each of the children starring in the film had a neurological difference, the uniqueness of the difference experienced by each child was also emphasized and held up for celebration. For those who were relatively uninformed about autism, this represented an intriguing discovery, inspiring increased curiosity about both the individual children and the nature of neurological difference. For those more aware of the nature of autism, it represented a welcome choice with which individuals could relate, serving as a bit of a counter to the tendency for all of autism to be understood in the terms of *Rainman*. In other words, because children from across the autism spectrum were featured, autism became understood as both more compelling and less potentially subject to unwelcome stereotype. This aspect tended to be positively received by stakeholders interested in both celebration- and care-oriented agendas for whom the issue of diversity within single diagnoses has been a source of political challenge and tension with other disability policy agenda types.

Second, the children most prominently featured were also quite charismatic. Although autism-as-intriguing is a commonly used plot device, the potential for (and uneven assignment of) personal charisma is a less well-considered aspect that individuals with autism share with other members of the general population. In particular, individuals with autism are often universally described as having flat affects (little or no facial expressions) and a tendency not to emote in ways that individuals without autism can understand. The film effectively demonstrated variance in personal charisma between individuals with autism. In several of the cases, the charisma itself may be a familial trait. Though it was not revealed at the outset, many of the parents of the children starring in the film were successful members of the entertainment industry. Though the parents' fame was unquestionably a secondary aspect of the film, connection to fame tends to lend an element of interest for the general public. After all, in modern society, there is a general attraction to fame that extends well beyond the reason for public notice. This aspect of the film may feed into some of the tensions between celebration and care agenda types. As is discussed earlier in this chapter, implications of fame tend to be quite different for proponents of celebration and care agenda types. From the perspective of care-oriented agendas, one criticism of the film could be that in featuring privileged children with autism, day-to-day difficulties of children with less well-connected parents might become underestimated. Use of celebrities is generally assumed to be a positive strategy in celebration-oriented agendas, but tends to be employed in a much different way in care-oriented efforts (through appearances and other public calls for attention to fundraising events, for example).

Third, at least according to some who reviewed the film, *Autism: The Musical* was different because it presented autism in a positive (or at least not completely negative) light (Zeitchick 2007). In fact, reviews of the film routinely mentioned this aspect as remarkable. This observation is intriguing because of the rapidly growing popularity of characters with autism in both popular fiction and commercial entertainment in the 1990s and early 2000s. Most of these characters are not villains. What this response demonstrates, however, is the degree to which autism has been used in art as a plot device as opposed to a well-developed character trait. Though exceptions to this rule, such as *The Curious Incident of the Dog in the Night-Time* (Haddon 2003) exist, this observation on the part of reviewers demonstrates Iyer's observation that individuals with disabilities tend to be employed as narrative devices in popular culture. Individuals with autism are often used as a metaphor of tragedy, for example, even to the point of harkening back to old theories about the causality of autism that placed the blame on either personal catastrophe resulting in permanent emotional shutdown or long-term, pronounced emotional neglect on the part of a mother with a child with autism. Reviews of, publicity for, and other public discourse surrounding the film therefore involved (deliberately or not) celebration agenda–type activities in that they highlighted this observed difference in the tenor of the film on the subject of autism.

Autism: The Musical is not a musical per se. Rather, the film chronicles the experience of making an original musical using the talents of children with autism. Although some of the reviews and other public responses to the film reacted somewhat negatively to what they considered a bait and switch, the vast majority of public discourse about the film either simply noted this fact in passing or congratulated the filmmakers for a clever marketing device. In fact, the film itself includes what is presumed to be a drastically edited version of the titular musical and focuses, even during the performance of the musical, on the drama surrounding the production of the musical rather than the musical itself. While the musical is being performed, one of the parents of the children with autism is shown experiencing frustration about her son's performance. The film frequently cuts away from the musical itself in order to follow this mother's (and to a lesser degree other parents') experiences and actions. *Autism: The Musical* is a piece of art about art production. This characteristic increases its potential contribution to public discourse surrounding both care and celebration agenda types because it contextualizes the production in a way that is hoped to increase understanding rather than just evoke a particular emotional response in its audience.

Tricia Regan, the director of the musical, stated her purpose in making the film in this way: "I have no idea if they're going to be able to pull it off. Autistic kids, by nature, are isolated, not supposed to be able to be spontaneous, imaginative; sounds can be too loud, so how can you have kids singing? I want to have a musical! An all-out musical! There's all these myths about what a child with autism can do . . . I plan to shatter those myths" (Grant 2008). In other words, the primary intellectual and artistic interest of the director was the possibilities and drama surrounding the process more than the artistic product produced by the children with autism. This purpose diverged to some degree from the traditional narratives of overcoming diversity and commonly associated stories about the accomplishments of individuals with disabilities. At least initially, audience members were taken by surprise by this fact. As was explained in a review of the film that appeared in the *New York Times* on March 25, 2008 (Genzlinger 2008):

> It promises a feel-good let's-put-on-a-show story with autistic children in the roles usually played by plucky singers and hoofers. And eventually the film makes its way to the inevitable standing . . . But in the process it exposes you to a story that is not feel-good at all, but instead full of stress and frustration and despair. It's a story of what it's like to be the parent of a child with autism or any other serious disability, a tale that deserves to be told even if it is difficult to watch.

In typical versions of disability success stories, adversity is emphasized at the beginning and then strategically included during selected plot points. Audiences are thereby brought to a predictable (and comfortable) feeling of more or less inevitable progress toward a familiar form of celebration. Of course, this ritual of celebration creates tension with care-oriented agendas owing to a resulting (at least perceived) need to reconvince members of the rest of the general population who are exposed to such forms of celebration of the ongoing and lifelong needs for publicly provided care experienced by some individuals with neurological differences.

Because *Autism: The Musical* diverges somewhat from this artistic convention, it manages to communicate a more sophisticated message. As public discourse, works such as this particular piece of art bridge this tension between disability agenda types. For example, in a review that appeared in New York's *Daily News,* David Hinckley (2008) wrote:

It's impossible not to root for all of them and not to feel triumph at their achievement. But at the same time, director Tricia Regan also conveys the breadth and depth of the impact an autistic child can have on the family. This isn't the child's fault. It isn't anyone's fault. But in talking to the parents of all these children to fill in the backstories and the context, Regan details the ways in which the strain of caring for an autistic child tears parents and families apart. (62)

Autism: The Musical, like most theatrical documentaries, walks a fine line between deliberately planned performance and unexpected outcome. Mary McNamara (2008) described in her review for the *Los Angeles Times:*

The fact that autism is a neurological disorder having little to do with intelligence is proven with throat-closing finality when some of the least-verbal children use keyboards to express their thoughts. "I am going to put mom on the spot," writes Neal, who has spent much of the film with his heartbreakingly handsome face devoid of emotion or even recognition of what is going on around him. "You need to be a better listener," he writes, and though no doubt Elaine, like any mother, would rather hear something other than criticism, she receives the words in rapture, as if they were the first images from the moon. There he is, her son Neal. And he's been with her, this whole time, after all. (E9)

In looking at pieces of art in the context of care- and celebration-oriented public discourse, two important themes to consider are those of spectrum and objectification. *Autism: The Musical* addresses the first by including children with a wide spectrum of autism disorders. Despite this, some critics of the piece did not feel that the representation was accurate enough. For example, Chris Georg, in a statement demonstrating the tension in celebration-oriented agendas wherein emphasis is placed on those considered higher-functioning, wrote about Regan's efforts to shatter myths about the limitations of autism: "She pulls it off, but it wasn't fair game: most of the children are not representative for what actual autism sufferers are like. Some of them have ASDs, Autism Spectrum Disorders, which are milder forms of autism affecting people to a lesser degree and allowing for some communication" (2008). Emphasis on those who are higher-functioning, to the exclusion of those who appear to be less so, is a common source of conflict between celebration- and care-oriented agendas. Still, like this critic mentions, the film does include children who are less high-functioning than others, even if possibly excluding those at the most extreme end of the spectrum. Especially since neurological differences are interconnected with individuality, fully including people representative of the full spectrum would presumably be impossible. Maintaining balance of representation between strengths and skills is an ongoing challenge for artists, audience members, and stakeholders representing all disability agenda types alike.

Furthermore, examples of public discourse such as *Autism: The Musical* that suggest that those perceived to be at the higher end of spectrums of neurological difference face no negative consequences as a result of these differences, since they are not "actual sufferers," serve to create the impression that policies and programs targeting either the full spectrum or specifically the needs of those considered higher-functioning are unnecessary. Especially because individuals considered to be higher-functioning often interact more intensively with public infrastructures on a day-to-day basis (and often with less direct assistance), promotion of this impression creates further challenges for agenda setting within the politics of neurodiversity and neurological difference. Public challenges associated with neurodiversity that typically affect those considered to be higher-functioning are discussed directly by the children participating in the film. For example, as Caroline Grant (2008) describes:

> Wyatt speaking with sad sophistication about the bullying he endures in elementary school, and what he foresees for the future: "Maybe if I got into a regular class then I'd show the bullies that I—how—how I can deal with a regular class, they're not going to bully me, maybe. You think that's why? You think it's because I'm in a special ed class?" He pauses, and then continues more quietly, "They'll still be cruel in a main-stream class. I know that. I know they will."

Wyatt is one of the most charismatic children featured. During the course of the film, audience members find it easy to connect with him and understand the pain he feels in his attempts to socialize effectively with his neurologically typical peers. His self-expression helps to illuminate the nature of some of the challenges faced by children (or individuals) who appear to be higher-functioning. The empathy invoked also helps to lay the ground for potential support for related programs and policies among audience members.

Autism: The Musical also serves to highlight that not all needs associated with neurological difference can necessarily be confined to the individual with the neurological difference. One challenge faced by care-oriented policy, particularly in the United States, relates to the fact that while a preference for policy employing the individual as the unit of analysis exists across all policy subsystems, challenges associated with differences often manifest at more collective levels, particularly at the level of the family. As well, as a result of becoming natural caregivers for individuals with disabilities, parents and other family members also experience difficulties with public infrastructures and, often, increased public needs as part of their connection to an individual with a neurological difference. Challenges and discrimination are not completely contained in the person with the neurological difference. This realization can create conflicts with celebration-oriented agendas, which would tend naturally to minimize potential impacts on natural caregivers due to the dangers and negative implications associated with acceptance of connected effects. Furthermore, using a unit of analysis other than the individual also tends to invoke habits of blame that tend to objectify and otherwise dehumanize either the individual with the neurological difference, the natural caregiver, or both.

In *Autism: The Musical* an attempt is made to walk this fine line between honesty about potential challenges and the potential invocation of blame responses (or other forms of lazy thinking) on the part of the audience. For example, in a description of the challenges articulated by mothers, Grant (2008) describes:

> The children blossom under Elaine's attention, so proud of their achievement, but it's the moms who especially riveted me. They are wearing themselves out for their kids, even just to get a proper diagnosis. Hillary recounts asking a doctor, "Does she have autism?" And getting the unhelpful response, "Well, I wouldn't go so far as to say that, but it is organic." "And I thought," Hillary remembers, "Organic is good. Organic is healthy! Organic is pesticide-free! I mean, organic doesn't mean anything to me."

Focusing on the infrastructure challenges, such as the language employed in health care settings, as opposed to simply starting and ending the story with the negative effects on the caregiver attributed to the neurological difference in an essentialist way, helps to balance tensions between the purposes and goals of celebration- and care-oriented agenda types.

Similarly, one review directly tackled the fact that the movie does not overtly address the question of cure. As Jennifer Merin (2009) wrote:

> Right up front, the film gives us the stats: in 1980, one out of 10,000 children were autistic, now it's one in 150. Shocking. But this film doesn't hammer home the need to find a cure. The message is presented in a much more subtle, much wiser and, ultimately, much more effective [way]. Not that it's easy to watch these kids—they behave strangely, they have inexplicable tantrums, their needs are overwhelming. And it's difficult to imagine what their parents—Stephen Stills, the rock star, happens to be one of

them—contend with off screen. But, ultimately, this film connects you to the way that autistic kids can and do learn, communicate and enjoy their lives.

This is not to say that this particular piece of public discourse takes a purely constructivist tack, thereby ignoring or overtly denying any legitimacy of cure-oriented agendas. After all, a portion of the profits generated by *Autism: The Musical* are donated to the nonprofit organization Autism Speaks. Also, one of the executive producers of the film is a former board member of Cure Autism Now. Furthermore, Grant (2008) describes how the film explicitly touches upon cause oriented-agendas:

> Finally, Roseanne draws parallels to the Civil Rights movement. Speaking to the other parents at The Miracle Project—and in doing so, pointedly addressing the film's audience—she says, "It's not enough for you to be doing better, the whole tribe has to do better, or else you really can't do much better, believe me, and I see all of your kids as my son's tribe." Roseanne's words resonate with me. Autism doesn't touch my family directly, but that doesn't matter. Every parent worries about how their kids are treated outside the safety of their own family, how their children function in a group of their peers, and even how they'll manage life without us.

Whereas *Autism: The Musical* speaks most deliberately to celebration agendas and, in the course of the movie, reveals or suggests many realities about care-oriented agendas, in the end public discourse related to all four agenda types is incorporated into the film.

Concluding Thoughts for All Disabilities

Construction of modern identity unavoidably involves politics at many levels. Especially as domestic policy expands and becomes more sophisticated, governments become increasingly involved in the construction of the individual identity. Furthermore, as political discourse surrounding construction of an element of an individual identity moves beyond the simply interpersonal toward community identification, policy subsystems hold relevance to identity (and vice versa). In modern disability politics and policy, dynamics between care and celebration are the most involved with the question of disability identity. The typically more pronounced role of this relationship in construction of identity holds true not only for neurological difference, but for all disabilities as well.

One key element around which tension between these two agenda types revolves involves perceived divisions between those considered to be higher-functioning and others with the same (or similar) diagnosis. As has been the case with other interactions between disability agenda types, public and political discourse surrounding neurological difference and neurodiversity simply reflects with greater intensity what takes place with regard to all disabilities. Depending on the circumstances, preferencing (or the perception thereof) of either end of a functional spectrum can manifest in public or political discourse and in the development of public programs. Most frequently, care-oriented agendas are believed prone to preferencing so-called lower-functioning individuals, whereas celebration-oriented agendas do the opposite. This distinction inserts distance between the public and political discourse surrounding the two agenda types. Neither focus is particularly helpful for modern disability policy. Deliberate and thorough consideration of such created spaces can, however, spark much needed and intricate conversations between proponents of these two agenda types (as well as other disability policy stakeholders).

Especially under circumstances of limited or declining public resources, it is vital to be mindful of the potential for misinterpretation of public and political discourse surrounding both celebration and care agenda types. Nevertheless, public and political expression of tensions between care- and celebration-oriented agendas can help the general public attain a better understanding of disability. This is because expression of these tensions brings into focus the diversity of experiences with disabilities, even within the population of individuals sharing a diagnosis. Articulation of these tensions also has potential to both expand support for and inspire the diversification of celebration-oriented policies. As a result, at least in the long run, celebration-oriented policies could become much more supportive of other types of disability policy than is currently the case.

8

Finding a Cure
vs. Celebrating Diversity

Of all of the agenda types in disability policy subsystems, cele- bration and cure seem to fall into the most natural of tensions. Taking pride in the presence of something is difficult to do while simultaneously at- tempting to eradicate it. In considering cure-oriented agendas, it is impor- tant to keep in mind that curing something fundamentally represents an all-or-nothing preposition. Curing, at least as usually discussed in political and public discourse, typically implies elimination of all traces of a neuro- logical difference, not just characteristics considered undesirable. On the other hand, celebration tends toward the opposite interpretation of neuro- logical differences, focusing as much attention as possible on positive as- pects of atypicality, including possible benefits derived from both suffering and overcoming challenges. Given this natural opposition, it can hardly be surprising that these two agenda types wind up in conflict with one another in public and political discourse. These tensions, nevertheless, create in- stances in which the politics of these agenda types work in (or can be made to work in) symbiosis as well.

Pursuing Cure Is Assumed to Be Simple

One area of tension between celebration- and cure-oriented agendas in- volves the decision to undergo cure. For the most part, cure agenda types rest on the unquestioned assumption that the decision to accept cure is a rel- atively easy one in the absence of a specific set of factors. Unless the cure has a high rate of failure or involves extraordinary pain, expense, or effort (which many cure agendas do), then many people believe that few accept- able reasons for rejection of cure exist. Furthermore, particularly in the case of neurological differences associated with mental illness, refusal of treatment can be understood as being as much a symptom of disease as it is a necessary right (Jacob et al. 2005). In practice, refusal of available cure is generally interpreted as nothing short of an irrational and irresponsible act most often guided by fear, ignorance, or, more charitably, eccentric religious or cultural beliefs. Often, mainstream public and political discourse have little tolerance for such decisions, especially to the degree that they become perceived as simultaneously threatening public support for other types of disability agendas. In other words, in the minds of many, if a cure is available, an individual with a functional difference has an obligation to accept it or else to opt out of demand for any policy targeting neurological differences, because the individual is believed to be passing up the more rational opportunity to exist without a neurological difference.

Individuals who have undergone cures tend to strongly support these sorts of arguments. Rarely do individuals who have undergone cures articulate regretting this decision. This is hardly surprising but not inherently convincing as an argument upon which to base policy or program decisions. As Tom Shakespeare argued about physical disabilities, "evidence that those who have undertaken surgery are glad that they have done so is also problematic: after so great an investment of time and endurance of pain . . . it is hard for any individual then to admit it may have been a mistake, or to say that they are not happy with the result" (2006, 115). Especially if the change is irreversible and if the consensus of the rest of the general public is that the cure is highly desirable, there is little room for a sense of loss associated with cure. After all, individuals without functional differences routinely overestimate suffering associated with functional differences and rarely, if ever, express genuine understanding (let alone envy) of advantages associated with functional differences. For example, whereas the creativity of artists known to suffer with mental illnesses might be celebrated in the abstract, with the exception of some adolescent seekers of angst, people do not generally deliberately attempt to take on mental illnesses. As a result, the decision to undergo cure tends to be a one-way street that allows for little possibility of regret in the case of success and nothing other than sympathy in the case of failure.

In the context of the politics of neurodiversity and neurological difference, the question of refusing to accept cure (or treatment in general) becomes further complicated by questions of capacity. Not all individuals with neurological differences have the ability to fully understand implications of refusing or accepting treatment for the effects of their neurological atypicalities. Owing to barriers in society's infrastructures, limitations in the communicative abilities of the rest of the general population including health care providers, and prejudicial interpretations that lead some to believe that attempts to discuss implications would be futile, an even greater proportion of individuals with neurological differences are treated as being incapable of making such decisions. Furthermore, review of research on determination of capacity reveals far from perfect consensus among professionals with regard to how to define and measure capacity to make informed decisions about treatment at the individual level (Okai et al. 2007). Also, many individuals with neurological differences for whom cure might be considered are children, who are often insufficiently mature to effectively contemplate long-term effects of decisions. Finally, another substantial proportion of the population of individuals for which treatment (and less often cure) for neurological differences is considered are the elderly who have acquired neurodegenerative conditions late in life, an experience their loved ones naturally associate almost exclusively with unwelcome deterioration and loss. As a result of these factors, cure decisions frequently fall to others involved in the lives of individuals with neurological differences. This introduces additional ethical challenges for those working on implementation of policy addressing cure-oriented agendas. It also complicates the relationship with celebration agenda types, which those making decisions for loved ones with neurological difference sometimes interpret as introducing unrealistic and over-idealistic complications and interventions into already difficult decisionmaking processes.

While few examples exist in the case of neurological difference, ex post facto consideration of potential downsides of cure might become even more complicated, particularly as an element of political discourse. By definition, changes in neurological status would involve fundamental changes in the way in which individuals consider data and make decisions. As mentioned, part of the concern associated with cure focuses on the potential that the individual's personality might be lost in the process. In other words, if a person has lived a significant portion of his or her life as an individual with a neurological difference, undergoing cure involves consideration of destruction of fundamental components of identity, personal relationships, and socioeconomic circumstances. When this concern is combined with the question of whether or not the particular individual holds the capacity to understand implications of making this change or even the existence of a choice in the face of substantial public pressure toward neurotypicality, effective consideration of potential downsides both before and after the introduction of cure could become impossible at the individual level. As a matter of public policy, it is also especially difficult to consider implications of these choices at the collective or population level, which makes for unbounded and unorganized public and political discourse on the subject.

Even when such tensions surrounding feelings about cure resolve more completely, consideration of cure conflicts with celebration agenda types. For one thing, as already mentioned, under some circumstances application of cure might result in a (possibly total) loss of any unique strengths or benefits associated with neurological difference. This creates conflict, especially as benefits of neurodiversity become recognized. As Walter Glannon explains, neurodiversity inspires new politics because "it forces us to consider the extent to which pathological traits can be balanced by salutary traits and whether and on what grounds individuals with a combination of these traits should be treated . . . but how do we decide whether a person's general set of mental traits is normal or abnormal and thus indicative of pathology?" (2007, 1–2). For example, some public discourse maintains that attention-deficit hyperactivity disorder (ADHD) includes potentially positive traits. According to Susan Smalley (2008):

> The neurobiological research in ADHD suggests several neural systems that may contribute to putative strengths . . . For example, the atypical right/left cerebral asymmetries and a right hemisphere "bias" observed in ADHD may contribute to insight problem solving, intuition, or creativity, as well as self-transcendence (a character component of personality) . . . Adults with ADHD have been shown to score more highly on measures of self-transcendence . . . a trait associated with improved survival after illness or end-of-life stages, although this finding requires replication . . . Novelty-seeking, a temperament trait, is associated with ADHD, and this construct may be associated with creativity and innovation, while daydreaming (a common behavioral feature of ADHD) may be associated with creativity and learning. (3–4)

As our understanding of neurological diversity within humanity continues to develop alongside generally increased expectations of neurological capacity for participation in the economy and social life, the boundary between neurological difference and different versions of neurological typicality may become increasingly blurred, especially with regard to public policy. This presents challenges for both cure- and celebration-oriented agendas, both of which depend to a degree on the ability to identify observed differences at the individual level as identifiable (and presumably problematic) communal categories. Unless specific differences can be fully defined as atypical, consideration of cure and, to a lesser but still important degree, cause for deliberate, identity-oriented celebration cannot be easily justified, particularly as appropriate targets for public intervention. This challenge is not unique to the politics of neurodiversity and neurological difference. Other categories of difference considered relevant for public policy (such as gender, racial ethnicity, and sexual orientation) have begun to be understood as having more permeable lines between taxonomic categories in modern societies than was traditionally assumed to be the case. Such blurring of boundaries may ultimately make necessary more innovative (if not completely nonincremental) thinking about diversity-oriented public policies in general.

In some situations, association, including familial association involving shared neurological difference, might become changed or compromised as a result of availability of cure. This becomes even more likely if related individuals make or support divergent decisions with regard to cure. Such concerns have been expressed with regard to the decision to use cochlear implants to reduce the physiological effects of deafness. As Shakespeare (2006) described:

> The dilemma for deaf children of Deaf adults is that the maximum benefit of a cochlear implant comes when the child forgoes sign language and concentrates entirely on learning to speak and hear and lip read. Therefore if Deaf parents implant their deaf child, they are sacrificing their best hope of communicating with their own child, who will additionally suffer from having parents whose speech is probably limited. For this reason, the opposition of Deaf parents to implanting their own children is understandable, but it should not prevent hearing parents from using this technology to improve the life chances of their deaf child. (115)

Though less exploration of this question with regard to neurodiversity and neurological difference exists in current research, the same cultural factors likely come into play in families with several members with the same or similar neurological differences. Furthermore, disability activists would typically assert that being able to hear, even if it improves life chances, is an undesirable characteristic of exclusionary societies rather than an immutable characteristic of collective human experience.

The fact or impression of the undesirability of living under conditions of systematic discrimination, however, does not necessarily mean that those making the choice of whether or not to individually select out of an oppressed category will choose not to do so in the name of social justice. As discussed earlier, not every person is by nature an activist, and effective democracy in fact depends upon the presence of people who engage politics from distinct roles and employ dissimilar strategies (Woshinsky 2008). Historically, consideration of questions surrounding "passing" as a member of a nonoppressed category has been strained at best. However, in public (and undoubtedly private) discourse, discussions of individual choice to take an opportunity to select out of an oppressed category portray such situations as lucky or, at least realistic, given the pressures faced on a daily basis involved in living a difference out loud. Social change tends to move at a slower pace than that of a human life, after all. As a result, elective suffering in the name of social justice must remain optional, at least in the context of free societies. Even so, when it comes to political discourse and development of public policy, any temptation to require cure should be avoided. Though historically this approach was used, other characteristics are not typically managed this way in modern society, at least not overtly. In other words, people are not told (or at least not explicitly told) to change their gender, race, or religion in order to avoid discrimination or because it will improve their life chances.

On the other hand, the politics of neurodiversity become even more complex surrounding balancing cure with celebration when it is perceived that society benefits (or could potentially benefit) from the positive outcomes of a particular individual experiencing an undesired neurological difference. As Glannon (2007) described:

> One might argue that, for creative individuals with bipolar disorder, lithium would not diminish one's intellectual or artistic creativity. On the contrary, it would enhance this ability by enabling one to be more organized, focused, and productive . . . Treatment may not always be in the best interests of people with bipolar disorder, however . . . In moderate forms of this condition, an affected individual may rationally decide that any benefits from pharmacological intervention would not be worth the cost of losing certain abilities. (3)

To the extent that this rationality also includes a public perception of community benefit resulting from the particular skill, this question becomes more complicated, especially with regard to children or others whose talents have yet to be fully developed. This is a source of tension with celebration-oriented agendas and questions such as whether or not the art of Van Gogh is by some measure worth the suffering he experienced as a result of his mental illness. Questioning of the potential benefit of difference has appeared in democratic political discourse for some time. For example, a 1946 court case involving the dismissal of a researcher with a physical disability stated:

> President Henley in a letter to respondent not only clarified appellant's position with respect to the immateriality of the physical handicap but indicated that he deemed it a probable advantage. That letter in part is as

follows: "We were very pleased to receive your letter indicating your desire to serve on our staff. You mention a physical handicap. As long as it does not interfere with your research abilities, we would not have any objections whatever. In fact, we can think of some physical handicaps which would even improve one's ability as a research worker." (*William P. Canavan, Respondent, v. College of Osteopathic Physicians and Surgeons [a Corporation]*, Appellant Civ. No. 15158 Court of Appeal of California, Second Appellate District, Division Two 73 Cal. App. 2d 511; 166 P.2d 878; 1946)

Such issues also bring forth some of the tensions discussed in the context of celebration and care because of a resulting tendency to set the needs of those considered to be higher-functioning in opposition to the needs of those considered to be at the lower end of spectrums of neurological difference.

A Further Complication for Cure:
Refusal of Desired Treatment

A further complication involved in public and political discussions involves refusal of desired medical care in modern Western democracies. Refusal of medical treatment by individuals with disabilities has been, at least by disability scholars, less often described as a public or policy problem than as a refusal of medical establishments to provide treatment to individuals with disabilities. For decades, individuals with disabilities found themselves subjected to limitations to access to lifesaving (and other) medical treatment, particularly in emergency, birth, and end-of-life situations (Shakespeare 2006). Physicians often asserted or simply practiced without question a right to limit care to individuals with disabilities based on the impression that living with certain disabling conditions constitutes a life not worth living. While this may have been more generally accepted, given situations such as persistent vegetative states as experienced by Terri Schiavo prior to her death (Perry, Churchill, and Kirshner 2005), individuals with a broad scope of disabilities frequently reported difficulties in getting physicians to provide them with care, even to the point of "do not resuscitate" orders being issued without their consent.

In some circumstances, refusal of treatment extends to the point of deliberately causing death. For example, some countries, such as Holland, engage in routine euthanization of infants with severe disabilities. This practice and, to a somewhat lesser degree, other forms of nonvoluntary euthanasia, though not at all a popular topic in recent scholarship, have been occasionally positively discussed in the academic literature in recent years (Uniacke and McCloskey 2008). Given this context, both individuals with disabilities and health care providers find themselves in murky situations with regard to the application of cure, particularly when associated with the question of a right to choose death. As Margrit Schildrick (2008) explained in the context of feminism:

> Conflicts between bioethicists and disability theorists often arise over the permissibility of euthanasia and physician assisted suicide . . . Where mainstream bioethicists propose universalist guidelines that will direct action across a range of effectively disembodied situations, and take for granted that moral agency requires autonomy, feminist bioethicists demand a contextualization of the circumstances under which moral decision making is conducted, and stress a more relational view of autonomy that does not require strict standards of independent agency. (209)

Given this, disability activists find themselves in an awkward situation that sometimes involves advocating for medical treatment in the case of declining functionality, but not in the case of potential for improved functionality.

Organizations such as Not Dead Yet argue that "though often described as compassionate, legalized medical killing is really about a deadly double standard for people with severe disabilities, including both conditions that are labeled terminal and those that are not" (http://notdeadyetnews commentary.blogspot.com). This has been presented as particularly true in countries, such as the United States, without widespread access to public health care and where pressure can build up around the extreme economic burden placed on families as a result of a decision to continue seeking medical care. Especially given the diversity of functional differences, this can create a fine line for health care providers to negotiate. Figuring out when, how, and who will make decisions with regard to the right to refuse medical treatment is extraordinarily complicated (Rothman 2003). In such contexts, conflict with celebration-oriented agenda types becomes frequently reduced to the level of caricature, and has even been so used as a plot device in popular medical dramas such as *House, Grey's Anatomy,* and *ER.*

To a more limited degree, interpretation of "do not resuscitate" orders also directly affects members of nonmedical professions, including those presumably more habitually connected to celebration- than to cure-oriented agendas. For example, as Todd DeMitchell and Scott Fletcher discuss, increased inclusion of students with disabilities in schools resulting from late-twentieth-century innovations in special education policy occasionally puts teachers in the position of having to implement "do not resuscitate" orders for some students with disabilities and illnesses. According to DeMitchell and Fletcher, "a do not resuscitate order for a student challenges the legal duty to protect and the professional demand to act ethically . . . unfortunately, this situation occurs within the special education community of our public schools with heart wrenching frequency" (2008). By design, the teaching profession focuses on child development (and hopefully celebration) rather than becoming directly involved in consideration of health care, particularly at the terminal stage. Public and political discourse motivated by celebration-oriented agenda types frequently enters into the formulation and development of special education policy.

However, owing to the traditional separation between health and education policy subsystems, cure-oriented discourse has been largely left out of the conversation surrounding special education policy, except by those who initially asserted that inclusion would be dangerous to the health of students with disabilities or with regard to contagion concerns surrounding communicable illnesses. Greater inclusion of individuals with disabilities in mainstream society is, however, likely to broaden the scope of professionals who become involved in implementation of policy affecting both treatment and end-of-life decisions.

When Neurological Differences Are Considered Diseases

Furthermore, celebration and cure come even more into tension when neurological differences are (or are understood as) acquired diseases or injuries. In many circumstances, changes in neurological status very clearly relate to disease or injury—a person experiencing a decline in neurological functionality after, for example, a motorcycle accident or stroke can confidently assert (or have asserted for them) that the change resulted from an identifiable, generally unplanned, and presumably unwanted event. Such circumstances involve no necessary conflict with celebration-oriented agendas, which then tend to focus positive energy on survival and perseverance of the individuals experiencing such differences. In fact, under such circumstances, the rhetoric of heroism may be in fact more or less reflexively welcomed by the individuals experiencing the neurological difference and their families.

For other observed changes in neurological functioning, connection to accident or disease is far less clear and in fact may be a primary source of political conflict within the disability policy subsystem, especially between cure and celebration agenda types. In the case of autism, for example, some issue stakeholders believe that autism is in fact a form of mercury (or other) poisoning (Austin 2008; Schechter and Grether 2008). After all, a substantial proportion of children with autism do not appear to be born with the condition. Most often in public and political discourse, this poisoning has been attributed to the use of thimerosal in childhood vaccines, which increased dramatically in the decades after World War II. This proposed connection has been adamantly and repeatedly denied by government agencies such as the US Centers for Disease Control and by the majority of mainstream health care academics. Even so, in a case filed in November 2007 in the US vaccine court, the court decided that "the government said the child had a pre-existing mitochondrial disorder that was 'aggravated' by her shots, and which ultimately resulted in an ASD [autism spectrum disorder] diagnosis" (Kirby 2008).

Proponents of the causal link between the widespread use of thimerosal in vaccines and increased prevalence of autism point out that the cumulative dose of mercury administered through an ever increasing number of vaccines did not enter into the decision process surrounding the creation of mandatory (and voluntary) changes in recommended vaccine schedules over time. As described on June 4, 2008, in an article released on PR Newswire titled "Jenny McCarthy & Jim Carrey Host the Historic Green Our Vaccines March and Rally in Washington DC":

> McCarthy, author of the best-selling book *Louder Than Words: A Mother's Journey in Healing Autism,* and Carrey have joined forces with national advocacy organizations in the battle to eliminate toxins from childhood vaccines and to encourage national health agencies to reassess mandatory vaccines schedules . . . while they do support immunization, like many parents and experts in the medical community, McCarthy, Carrey, and their many allies feel that children are receiving too many vaccines, too soon, many of which are toxic . . . their goal is to demand a safer vaccine supply and schedule for children.

Vaccine safety was tested using the individual vaccine as the unit of analysis as opposed to the combination of vaccines consequently received by children. Active policy stakeholders, including public interest groups and policy entrepreneurs, continuously promote the policy goal of establishing safety protocols that do not include grandfathering and that consider the vaccine schedule as a whole when determining the safety of vaccines. For example, the mission of the nonprofit group Safeminds is "to end the devastation to human health and function from early life exposures to man-made sources of mercury, the second most toxic substance on earth. Our mission will be achieved through scientifically based internal and externally-funded research, increased awareness, and advocacy in the public policy and legal arenas" (www.safeminds.org/home/mission_strategies.html). Although the mission does not explicitly identify autism as the devastation, most other statements made by the organization describe autism and related neurological differences as the avoidable negative outcome. Furthermore, the founders of the organization include parents of children with autism who are convinced that their children fell victim to mercury poisoning through vaccination (Kirby 2008).

Those who oppose the causal link frequently express frustration with the ongoing public and especially the political discourse surrounding vaccines. Virulent public and political discourse is frequently employed. For example, in an article titled "Politicians, Celebrities Flaunt Scientific Illiteracy" that appeared in the *Orange County Register* on March 15, 2009, Henry Miller, a physician and molecular biologist working at Stanford University, wrote:

> Deciding how to vote in the November election was excruciatingly difficult: I was so put off by the pronouncements on scientific issues by Barack Obama, John McCain and Sarah Palin that, in the end, I didn't vote for a candidate for president. Every politician cannot be a genius (possibly the understatement of the millennium), but the leader of the free world should know what he doesn't know . . . Both Sens. Obama and McCain made unfortunate misstatements about the safety of the measles-mumps-rubella vaccine during their campaigns. "We've seen just a skyrocketing autism rate," Obama said. "Some people are suspicious that it's connected to the vaccines. This person included. The science right now is inconclusive, but we have to research it." These sentiments were echoed by Sen. McCain: "It's indisputable that [autism] is on the rise among children, the question is what's causing it. There's strong evidence that indicates it's got to do with a preservative in the vaccines."

As a matter of political discourse, opponents of vaccine theories typically describe a scientific consensus surrounding the matter, more often blatantly ignoring rather than bothering to discredit other research. Proponents of vaccine theories at times employ mobile hypotheses or less established forms of research to make their arguments. Neither strategy represents the idealized, Enlightenment version of scientific research, but both are in keeping with the (arguably troubling) trends in modern scientific protocols that are increasingly employed in studies relating to politically controversial topics (Pielke 2007).

Descriptions of poisoning necessarily imply injury and disease. Poisoning, by definition, often produces negative outcome unless cured. However, from the perspective of the politics surrounding public aspects of neurological difference, especially to the extent that scientific causality remains in question, interpretation of the implications of the description of difference as tantamount to disease is far less clear than in the case of stroke or vehicular accident. As Kristin Bumiller explained, "neurodiversity proponents argue that there is limited evidence to advance the claim that autism is a form of mercury poisoning, but their most fervent objections arise when 'mercury mothers' describe autistic children as damaged in the course of lobbying against pharmaceutical companies producing vaccines" (2008, 972). In other words, one complication of the description of neurological differences as diseases in the context of cure-oriented public agendas is the presence of issue stakeholders more focused on celebration agenda types who might, by their very existence, threaten acceptance of an already tenuously accepted proposed causal link.

Furthermore, even the effort to differentiate disease from neurological difference is understood by some as problematic in the context of the politics of neurodiversity. After all, as mentioned earlier, disability rights movements have been stigmatized over time owing to the fact that those who advocate for diversity argue their own case for rights by pointing out they are not disabled. By extension of this logic, individuals with disease tend to differentiate disease from disability, which creates a similar dynamic, in that it supports discrimination against those with disease in the name of promoting the rights of people with disabilities.

The Advocacy Effect: Fundraising and Events

One of the various archetypical roles that exist in public and political discourse is the role of the advocate, which involves efforts to speak for interests of a particular population without calling for dramatic change to the surrounding social or political infrastructure. Often advocates see themselves as serving an educative role that seeks to rather gently guide society in the desired direction. Though the dividing line between activist and advocate is frequently identified as the willingness or lack of willingness to break the law in the name of achieving a desired goal, the event horizon is just as prominent a distinction, as advocates tend to think in terms of much longer-term change. Also, within a given population of issue stakeholders, advocates tend to include a greater proportion of individuals who are not themselves members of the target population. Advocates tend to speak for others. The relationship between celebration- and cure-oriented agendas is particularly shaped by the role advocates play in this area of the politics of neurological difference and neurodiversity.

A sense of distinction between the exercise of cause and celebration agenda types can be gleaned from consideration of advocate efforts to raise money for a cure and those designed explicitly to celebrate neurodiversity. As mentioned earlier, comparisons between events directed toward cause agenda types does not include all events self-described as being causes, because events designed to raise resources for quests for cures often employ the word "cause" as a rallying point.

Fundraising for political purposes is a form of political discourse. Both the intent and the outcome of political fundraising are not nearly as clear-cut as they are popularly imagined to be (Eom and Gross 2007). In modern Western democracies especially, popular mythology posits a direct relationship between the ability to raise and expend funds and the political influence as observable in policy output. The presumed mechanisms are twofold: political contributions and marketing expenditures. While it is certainly true that contributions to politicians matter, evidence suggests the direct impact on the votes of the politicians themselves is less than popularly imagined (Woshinsky 2008). However, while contributions may not have direct effects on the votes and therefore the essential likelihood that a given bill will pass into law, contributions have been shown to affect the specifics of the policy content itself (Figueiredo and Edwards 2007). Since both celebration- and cure-oriented policy tend to be dramatically affected by subtle differences in policy that may or may not be discernible by any but the most engaged issue stakeholders, this impact of fundraising arguably matters more for the relationship between these two agenda types.

The influence of advertising and marketing expenditures is even more complex. Contributions to politicians or political interest groups are often used to produce advertising and marketing materials for either the general population or supporters. Such materials have the potential to affect public thinking on a particular issue and thereby shape public and political discourse. Voters have been found to respond differently to materials produced by special interests as opposed to those produced through publicly funded campaigns (Houser and Stratmann 2008). On the other hand, there is always the potential for backfire if the message is not in keeping with the sentiment of the general population. Even so, the ability to raise resources in the name of a particular agenda (or even agenda type) represents a vital form of political discourse in modern policy subsystems.

Periods of Awareness

An intriguing interaction between celebration- and cure-oriented agendas occurs during periods designated by (more or less) formal policy as being dedicated to a particular neurological difference. Formally dedicating periods of time to disability or to specific forms of disability is a popular strategy in celebration-oriented agenda types. For the most part, these policies started out being largely symbolic in nature, without any direct programmatic implications either within or outside the disability policy subsystem. Such symbolic policy, though often frustrating for its lack of immediately visible programmatic change, is nevertheless vital to creation of conditions supportive of neurodiversity. After all, as Richard Scotch explained, "symbolic contexts are not inherent to any given policy problem, but rather are socially constructed, sometimes inadvertently and sometimes deliberately" (2001, 159). Symbolic policy serves to create deliberately constructed symbolic contexts.

In recent years, a wide variety of groups have used awareness months as catalysts for calls for other, less symbolic policy changes. In addition, particularly as the politics of neurodiversity and neurological disability have expanded, they now invoke public commentary from a broad scope of groups and individuals. Symbolically dedicating periods of time to autism, for example, has become popular over the past couple of decades. In September 2010, a Google search on the phrase "autism awareness month" returned over 1 million hits and a search on "autism awareness day" returned over 13 million. Examples included the Centers for Disease Control website, with an announcement that April was Autism Awareness Month followed by a basic description of autism and the agency's involvement in autism-related research. The majority of the statements included in their first paragraph a reference to the incidence of autism (usually 1 in 150) followed by a list of the major behavioral indicators of autism.

This form of policy is now practiced on a global scale with regard to autism. On December 18, 2007, the United Nations adopted a resolution declaring April 2 of every year World Autism Awareness Day. According to the official statement of purpose:

> This UN resolution is one of only three official disease-specific United Nations Days and will bring the world's attention to autism, a pervasive disorder that affects tens of millions. The World Autism Awareness Day resolution encourages all Member States to take measures to raise awareness about autism throughout society and to encourage early diagnosis

and early intervention. It further expresses deep concern at the prevalence and high rate of autism in children in all regions of the world and the consequent developmental challenges. (www.worldautismawarenessday.org/site/c.egLMI2ODKpF/b.3917077/k.186A/About_World_Autism_Awareness_Day.htm)

Several world leaders released statements of support for World Autism Awareness Day in its first year. The majority of these statements primarily described autism as problematic and invoked, if not explicitly the need for cure, at least the need to control autism through treatment and early intervention. World Autism Awareness Day appears to be not about celebrating autism but about calling for a common response to an international problem. For example, the statement from the prime minister of Canada, Stephan Harper, included the following:

> On this day, I salute the thousands of families in Canada who confront the unique challenges of autism on a daily basis. This is also an opportunity to recognize the tireless work of all those who are championing the cause. I commend Autism Speaks Canada for providing a strong voice to those affected by autism through your ongoing efforts to increase autism awareness, service delivery and research . . . On behalf of the Government of Canada and my wife Laureen, I invite all Canadians to reflect on the lives of those living with autism and to recognize their valiant efforts to overcome the challenges of this disorder with compassion and perseverance. (www.worldautismawarenessday.org/atf/cf/%7b2db64348-b833-4322-837cdd9e6df15ee%7d/prime%20minister %20of%20canada's%20statement%20for%20waad.pdf)

As such statements demonstrate, awareness policies provide an opportunity to call attention to a broad spectrum of disability agenda types. In doing so, they involve a degree of constructivist thinking, but tend to rely on more traditional thinking not explicitly including expressions of neurodiversity.

President Barack Obama's statement issued on World Autism Awareness Day 2009 involved a more proximate description to the politics of neurodiversity than was typically found. The statement was somewhat unusual in that it did not focus on cure, nor did it start with the commonplace reference to the prevalence and incidence of autism or the behavioral characteristics of autism:

> We must build a world free of unnecessary barriers, stereotypes and discrimination. Policies must be developed. Attitudes must be shaped, and we must ensure that everyone has a chance to live independently as full

citizens of their communities. For too long the needs of people and families living with autism have gone unrecognized and underappreciated. That is why my Administration supports increased funding for autism research, treatment, screenings, public awareness, and services for ASD. We must also remember that children with autism become adults with autism who deserve our support, our respect, and the opportunity to fulfill their potential.   (www.worldautismawarenessday.org/atf/cf/%7b2db64348 -b833-4322-837c-8dd9e6df15ee%7d/president%20obama%20 waad%20statement.pdf)

While still obviously invoking cure-oriented agendas, President Obama's statement took the unusual step of explicitly reminding the public not only of the existence of adults with autism, but also of the importance of respecting individuals with autism, a mainstay of celebration agenda types. An underlying source of tension between cure- and celebration-oriented agendas is the tendency of cure-related public and political discourse to speak only of children with autism, sometimes to the point of creating the impression that adults with autism do not exist. Such impressions help to solidify the understanding of autism (or other neurological differences) as disasters, as opposed to (even if only sometimes) manageable characteristics that become a part of the adult's personality, thereby raising the question of legitimacy of cure in some cases. By avoiding adults, such discourses avoid the question. Compared to other statements of support, President Obama's therefore is somewhat more in keeping with the fundamental goals of celebration-oriented agendas.

Periods of awareness fit quite naturally into celebration-oriented agenda types. Of course, the degree of fit depends quite substantially upon who is crafting and promoting the material surrounding the issue. When awareness materials are produced by those more inclined toward other agenda types, the more cultural aspects of neurodiversity and neurological difference may go less noticed. As Stephen Drake discussed in April 2009 on the blog of the Center for Disability Rights, awareness is often less about celebration than it is a quest for cure when it comes to neurological differences (http://cdrnys .org/wordpress/?p=187). Since awareness programs and events tend to employ celebratory policy strategies, this can create tension between celebration and cause agenda types in disability policy subsystems. According to Drake, "these problems make many people, including myself, dread the month more than I dread the Jerry Lewis/MDA [Muscular Dystrophy Association] Telethon, which lasts a mere 24 hours." Drake went on to describe the tension as follows:

The most succinct statement of that dominant pitch can be found in this press release promoting Autism Awareness Month, from Autism Speaks, the most influential autism advocacy group in the country: "Autism Speaks is dedicated to increasing awareness of the growing autism epidemic and to raising money to fund scientists who are searching for a cure." To be fair, the press release mentions "advocating for the needs of affected families" and the need for "treatments," but the main focus is on a cure—the idea that some research will result in a "silver bullet" that will magically erase the neurological differences associated with autism and leave a "neurotypical" child behind . . . Obviously, anyone familiar with the controversy over the Telethon's focus on "cure" will see some similarities. When "cure" is put forward as the "solution" to autism—or any disability—the real need for access, supports, accommodations, and inclusion fade far into the background in the "awareness" efforts. (http://cdrnys.org/wordpress/?p=187)

Similarly, in an Associated Press article released on March 20, 2007, titled "Alabama Leaders Push for Autism Task Force," state representative Cam Ward was quoted as saying in response to the recorded rise in incidence of autism: "with any other disorder or disease, this would be considered an epidemic." Such framing of awareness messages can ultimately be completely counterproductive for those engaged in celebration-oriented agendas. Members of the rest of the general population are often left behind in the political discourse, largely confused about any negative responses to awareness efforts. Particularly when they have participated in awareness events, people tend to respond defensively about their participation and interpret complaints made by individuals with neurological differences and other celebration-oriented stakeholders as either selfish or misguided. Awareness events are frequently not the most successful venues when it comes to inspiring communication about differences in understandings and goals relating to disability.

Some public discourse directly addresses the immediacy of the connection between awareness and the quest for cure. Thus far, these expressions of public discourse have tended to be less publicized and to come from currently less powerful players in the politics of neurodiversity and neurological difference. This does not, however, mean that they are irrelevant or without potentially influential audiences. Often such statements are located on blogs written by individuals with autism (or related conditions) or their family members. Some who are engaged in neurodiversity public discourse have produced artwork in opposition to the more prevalent public expressions on autism awareness. For example, in March 2009 on the blog page

Asperger Square 8, an artist displayed a series of posters titled "What Passes for Autism Awareness" (http://aspergersquare8.blogspot.com/2009/03 /autism-awareness-month-posters.html). These posters stated to viewers that, "while they were walking" for autism awareness, the prevailing public and political discourse continued to support the use of shock therapy for children with autism in schools, vaccine research remained dedicated to the self-described greening of vaccines rather than focused on preventable diseases, and employment policy remained insufficiently supportive.

The artist indicated on her website that she would be displaying a few of these posters at autism awareness events, and gave explicit permission for others to do the same. While the audience of such artistic products was undoubtedly minuscule by comparison to those produced by national and international organizations (most notably in this case Autism Speaks), such works are vital components of celebration-oriented agendas. Authentic messages found in original pieces of art tend to be potentially quite powerful in the context of public discourse, particularly when produced by members of a group perceived as being oppressed by the general population. While it may take some time for their messages to come to the attention of members of the rest of the general population or to attain real relevance in the political discourse of the policy subsystem, they are not easily permanently refuted by those proposing other interpretations of awareness (especially, arguably, when the other interpretation represents a push for annihilation).

Furthermore, some writers openly questioned the utility of periods dedicated to awareness. This is not surprising given the cure-oriented interpretation of awareness most commonly found in the public discourse surrounding such symbolic policies. As described earlier, celebration-oriented agendas, more than any of the other agenda types, find themselves perennially at risk of becoming subject to successful denial of their ultimate relevance. Even when the discourse is more or less in keeping with the understandings of disability embraced by proponents of other agenda types, celebration-oriented efforts can be perceived as not working and as a luxury at best and a waste of resources at worst, because celebration-oriented policy does not appear to directly impact ongoing programmatic efforts at first glance and because repetition becomes necessary to transform traditional attitudes of the rest of the general population. Concerns about relevancy become even more pronounced when stakeholders believe unhelpful misinformation that becomes part of celebration-oriented efforts. On another blog, Silicon Valley Moms, a mother of a child with autism wrote in May 2009:

> But a "cure" isn't really "awareness." In fact, it would be much nicer if the buzzword were "acceptance" not "awareness." Plus, I can't help thinking that many of the folks who are truly impacted by autism don't have the time, energy, or child-care options to throw themselves into the various public events surrounding autism unless it is the quite literal bringing one's child into a public place with the resulting tsk-tsk of those disapproving parents of perfect children. (www.svmoms.com/2009/05/april-was-autism-awareness-month.html)

As this piece of public discourse demonstrates, celebration-oriented efforts run the risk of being seen as pitting the needs of those considered higher-functioning against the needs of those considered lower-functioning. In addition, as the preceding blog entry demonstrates, public displays of autism, for some people, can be potentially interpreted as modern incarnations of traditional practices of putting individuals with disabilities on display as part of "freak" shows or other forms of ritual entertainment for the rest of the general public.

To be fair, such intentions are almost never included in modern celebration-oriented efforts, the vast majority of which deliberately articulate respect for individuals with neurological differences at some point in their description of purpose and which increasingly (though still relatively rarely) seek the input of individuals with autism and their families into program design. Furthermore, the message of purpose communicated at such events is definitely not one of either shock or mockery. These intentions, however, cannot completely erase in the short term either the historical legacy of events that were so intended or the instances of discrimination (including public shaming such as that referenced by the Silicon Valley Moms mother) still frequently experienced by individuals with neurological differences and their families in public settings. After all, one fundamental characteristic that celebration and cure agenda types share is the long time horizon wherein goals are ultimately expected to be accomplished, usually over the span of several decades or even generations.

Finally, another topic frequently included in public discourse surrounding the policies that create symbolic periods of awareness relates to the cause (etiology) of autism. While at first glance this element of discourse may seem a somewhat strange fit for celebration-oriented policy, the question of where autism comes from and the degree to which it is a novel experience for humanity is both scientifically and politically volatile. Such concern is hardly limited to the politics of neurodiversity and neurological difference, since origin stories represent a fundamental human need. This is especially true when there is debate surrounding origin. For example, in an

April 2009 article titled "Autism Awareness Month: What Did We Learn?"
Melissa Rowley wrote:

> Over the last three decades, a handful of theories about what causes autism
> have been put on the table for debate. Autistic traits often run in families.
> This trend has prompted experts to search for genes that may carry the
> catalyst. Some medical professionals believe autism is caused by a child's
> surroundings or another biological condition. And others speculate that
> childhood vaccines such as the measles-mumps-rubella, or MMR, elicit
> the disease. (www.causecast.org/news_items/8351-autism-awareness-
> month-what-did-we-learn)

The question of origin of autism is a tricky one for both cure- and celebration-oriented agendas. Arguably, the question of origin of neurological
differences holds more relevance for cure and celebration than it does for the
other two agenda types. However, reasons for importance are both conflicted within the agenda types and ultimately in tension between the agenda
types. For celebration agenda types, the question of history of neurological
differences is important in the context of neurodiversity, particularly to the
degree that autism and other neurological differences are interpreted as ever
present aspects of human diversity. This is also a popular strategy for countering epidemic or environmental injury theories of the origins of autism.
Disability history (including, but not limited to, the presence of individuals
with disability in history) is therefore key to creating a comprehensive set
of celebration-oriented policies. One response to this, as mentioned in Chapter 1, is the practice of identifying well-known historical figures as individuals with autism. However, this tendency retains the potential for
divisiveness in terms of its implications across the spectrum of individuals
with autism.

For cure-oriented agendas, the question of origin is largely a scientific one. As such, it is a vital component of creating complete cure-oriented agendas. First, part of cure policy is prevention. In the absence of an
ability to fully cure a condition, after all, another medical strategy is eradication through prevention. Somewhat ironically in the context of autism,
vaccines are the prime discursive examples of such approaches to cure.
Furthermore, though not strictly necessary in some treatment research, understanding the origin of a condition that is viewed as a disease can help
in the creation of a cure. Accomplishing this goal tends to be easier given
a complete disease model. Finally, questions of etiology become political
lightning rods in the context of cure agenda types. Part of the challenge is
that whereas causal explanations are in their infancy, the general public

does not tend to understand the limitations of our current understandings of neurology. Public discourse explaining this is relatively rare. One example, which appeared in the Ascribe Newswire on February 13, 2003, in an article titled "Dealing with Reams of Data, Scientists Work Toward Unraveling Gene Expression in the Brain," came from Jonathan Pevsner, an associate professor of neurology at Johns Hopkins School of Medicine. Pevsner explained: "in some conditions, like autism, the biological cause is still unclear, but even with Downs Syndrome, which we know is the result of having an extra copy of chromosome 21, we don't know exactly what genes or processes lead to the neurological changes." Different causal factors tend to suggest different treatment strategies, thereby preferencing some research agendas over others. As a result, researchers pursuing cures associated with the more politically successful (and, ideally, though not always, the most scientifically established) causal explanations will have an easier time procuring research funding, publishing, speaking engagements, and other benefits attendant to and necessary for pursuing a research agenda. As a result, stakeholders pursuing different cure strategies may find themselves at odds with one another politically.

Another largely unexpected implication of politics of causal factors within cure agenda types is the tendency in certain situations to oppose environmental explanations for autism and other neurological differences. This outcome, though certainly not true for all cure-oriented researchers and possibly particularly relevant for those engaged in genetic research surrounding autism, exists because environmental explanations tend to suggest that environmental policy solutions might either partially or completely replace efforts to find cures. As a result, otherwise unexpected partnerships between entities accused of creating environmental factors that cause autism, proponents of neurodiversity particularly devoted to the naturalness of autism and other neurological differences, and researchers seeking cures can develop around or against specific policies. This phenomenon has occurred to a certain degree around the proposed link between the use of the preservative thimerosal in childhood vaccines and the incidence and prevalence of modern autism. This political outcome is not unique to neurological differences. Some have suggested, for example, that the political discourse and, as a result, the research surrounding breast cancer became uniquely focused on cure as a result of a partnership between those believed to be potentially responsible for causing environmental problems that result in breast cancer, and researchers interested in pursuing particular directions in cure research.

Public Policies Relying on Binary Diagnoses

Another source of tension between cure and celebration agenda types derives from the historical tendency to create policy dependent on binary diagnoses. In other words, programs implemented from traditional disability policy often begin with the task of sorting those with disabilities from those without. This practice stems from Victorian Era policy. For example, as Nick Craddock and Michael Owen (2007) point out:

> Emil Capelin would clearly recognize his 19th century dichotomy within current operational classifications of psychosis. However, he might be surprised at its survival, given the extent to which it has been undermined by the weight of currently available empirical evidence. The failure of this evidence to influence diagnostic practice reflects not only the comfortable simplicity of the dichotomous approach, but also the fact that this approach has for many years continued to receive support from some areas of research, particularly genetic epidemiology. (84)

Craddock and Owen emphasize in their conclusion the strength of social infrastructures when it comes to making change. Understanding disability as anything but binary is likely to be especially uncomfortable in the context of cure-oriented agendas based on the conception of disability as disease. Few people want to hear that they "sort of" have a disease, nor are they likely to rally behind expensive efforts to find a cure for others who are "kind of" sick. As Craddock and Owen discuss in their conclusion: "finally, we note that, as a general rule, human beings do not like change and tend to treat proposals for change with suspicion and resistance . . . however, as responsible clinicians, we owe it to our patients to take action urgently" (2007, 90).

Some public policies and programs have attempted spectrum approaches to the identification of individuals with disabilities. For example, in the United States, veterans acquiring functional differences after their military service are routinely rated as having a defined percentage of disability. This percentage of disability is used to determine both program eligibility and benefit levels. Such determinations of percentage of disability are typically associated with care-oriented public agendas, however. When it comes to the development and implementation of cure- and celebration-oriented agendas, diagnosis remains a binary concern despite the fact that, at face value, incorporating spectrum awareness would be relatively simple from the standpoint of these two agenda types.

Creating firm barriers between those counted eligible and those counted ineligible for the provisions of a particular policy is not a challenge unique to disability policy subsystems. For example, eligibility for social welfare programs targeting poverty is generally established through an external definition based on income or, less often, other measures of wealth, which is at best an imperfect measure of potential for deprivation as opposed to poverty itself. Similarly, use of binary diagnosis standards as qualifiers for disability policy is criticized, at least by those who are consumers of such policy, because of inconsistencies in qualification across programs. In other words, individuals with functional differences frequently find themselves qualifying as having a disability under some policies, but not others (Vickers, Basch, and Kattan 2009). Such experiences might be an expected outcome of implementation of policy designed with a constructivist understanding of disability. Certainly the inconsistencies in qualification might be understood in this way. If, for example, infrastructures allowing for employment are systematically less flexible than those governing access to housing, then it could make sense to define disability more broadly for employment than housing policy. In general, however, these programmatic differences are perceived as problematic.

Although the reverse is not necessarily true, neurodiversity cannot exist in the absence of neurological difference. Even though individuals naturally engage personal as well as public aspects of neurodiversity as a matter of course within disability policy subsystems, such involvement becomes complicated when an individual becomes personally motivated to participate in political discourse (or other activities) directed at multiple agenda types. Because of the implications of searches for cures, this can become especially complicated in the case of engagement of both cure- and celebration-oriented agendas. However, developing efforts to simultaneously engage these two agenda types at the individual level becomes easier in the spectrum-based understanding of disability. Employing public and political discourse emphasizing the near universality of spectrums when it comes to disability could ultimately strengthen both celebration- and cure-oriented arguments.

Concluding Thoughts for All Disabilities

Under some circumstances, the strongest, most obvious sources of tension between different agenda orientations in a given policy subsystem also create the best opportunities for broadly desirable social change and effective policy development. The celebration and cure agenda types extant in modern disability policy subsystems hold the strongest tendency to create such opportunities. While seemingly mutually exclusive at first glance (and, truth be told, in day-to-day operation), collective consideration that appreciates and eliminates elements of any functional difference helps to establish the broadest possible understanding of the implications of disability in modern societies.

Dynamics between the discourse and implementation of policy in these two agenda types highlight the question of the degree to which participation in disability policy is voluntary. Considering cure as a question contextualized by the possibility of celebration reinforces the notion of individual choice and, ultimately, the expected variance of disability itself. Pursuing and rejecting cure both become part of truly diverse social and political environments. However, dynamics between celebration and cure agenda types simultaneously bring forth the question of what constitutes social responsibility of both those with functional differences and those without in the context of a society that truly honors diversity.

In part, articulation of this social responsibility involves appreciating the role of circumstances in the experience of disability. It also involves celebrating the gray areas of disability politics, a practice that is arguably easier to create for both celebration- and cure-oriented agenda types. Circumstances are likely to be of particular importance when it comes to individual attitudes toward celebrating disability and receptivity toward cure (or treatment generally). Appreciation for circumstance will naturally require increased flexibility within the disability policy subsystem, which many will (initially at least) reflexively understand as tied only to the potential for increased cost. Whether this expectation proves true or not (reduced cost is also plausible), such an approach turns disability policy discourse toward society's infrastructures and away from exclusively focusing on the individuals with disabilities.

9

Finding
Common Ground

The politics of neurological difference and neurodiversity define vital challenges and opportunities for the twenty-first century. Even though our understanding of neurology left its infancy in recent decades, undoubtedly coming years will bring advances in our understanding of our brains likely to do nothing short of blow our minds. As this understanding grows, so too will the variety (and ideally sophistication) of public and political responses to the diversity of our minds. This variety will in turn increase potential for both cooperation and conflict around public challenges associated with neurological differences. So long as public and political discourse remains vibrant and open, there is reason to believe that both individuals with neurological differences and the rest of the general populations will benefit substantially from consciously neurodiverse societies. Furthermore, the benefits of such discourse to disability policy development would almost certainly extend to all functional differences associated with disability.

These four basic policy agenda types—cause, care, cure, and celebration—are hardly limited to the politics of neurological difference and neurodiversity as they exist in the public and political discourse of disability policy at large. As has been discussed in the concluding sections of Chapters 3–8, lessons drawn from the dynamics of the relationships between agendas can be applied to all disability policies and programs regardless of whether specific functional differences or disabilities at large are under consideration at a given moment in time. While certainly not always the case, quite often the politics of neurological difference and neurodiversity simply highlight or magnify realities extant across the disability policy subsystems in modern democracies.

Bringing Back Essentialism

Conceptions of disability, or any other element of the human experience, depend heavily on context. As Murray Levine explained, "a basic premise is that there is no such thing as a social vacuum . . . all programs are implemented and function in an elaborate social context . . . all programs are social artifacts which are inevitably compromise products of their social surroundings" (2007, 63). For much of human history, the prevailing social context of the politics of neurodiversity and neurological difference has been the unquestioned hegemony of neurotypicality. Minds falling outside the established norm were at best tolerated as charmingly quirky, but were generally identified only as potential threats to sane society and human decency. As the scope and implications of neurological differences became better understood, aspects of the social context also changed. As a result, numerous different policy agendas of four basic types have developed in disability policy subsystems to address public aspects constituting the politics of neurodiversity and neurological difference in modern democracies.

The age of disability as a completely private experience has passed into history. For the most part, this development represents a stunning advancement in human experience and social maturity. A return to traditional conceptions of disability archetypically characterized as blame-based essentialism seems highly unlikely in modern democratic societies given the pace and distance of disability policy development over the past century. Ironically, as part of this advancement, individuals with disabilities (re)gained a right to privacy more in keeping with that enjoyed by the rest of the general population in modern democracies. Without a doubt, there is still room for advancement with regard to the balance between privacy and isolation for individuals with disabilities in modern democracies, but public and political discourse surrounding modern disability policy tends to demonstrate improved understanding of the basic goal of achieving this balance. Disability, it seems, can ultimately be both a public and a private experience at the same time.

Furthermore, as first discussed in Chapter 3, elements of essentialism are being effectively and importantly reincorporated into the most cutting-edge of disability paradigms. Public and political discourse surrounding neurological difference and neurodiversity is contributing much of the political energy and philosophical insights in this ongoing development. Much of the discourse on the politics of neurodiversity highlights ways in which policy stakeholders can work toward simultaneously considering disability "a way of being" and also target elimination of barriers in social and political infrastructures that unnecessarily transform functional differences into disability (or handicap). Adding the politics of neurological difference to this conversation further emphasizes how embracing cure might take place even in the context of a predominantly constructivist understanding of disability.

After all, as described in Chapter 1, public recognition of neurological differences often depends on behavior-based diagnoses. Because of a general lack of diagnostic tools considered more objective in modern societies (such as a blood test), the reality of being differently brained tangibly manifests to both the individual with the functional difference and the rest of the general population only in the context of socially defined rules of behavior. Importantly, this fundamental dynamic exists regardless of the type of functional difference. Even the most stereotypical image of an individual with a disability—an individual in a wheelchair—depends on both a shared understanding of what constitutes a human walking and a common acceptance of medical tests used to discern whether or not individuals at the margin are not capable of doing so for the purpose of public policy implementation. For example, in the United States, Medicare will pay for mobility devices only when prescribed by a physician. Again, the politics of neurological difference simply magnifies for better interpretation that which shapes disability policy at large by explicitly including a notion of widespread dependence upon behavior-based diagnosis.

Ongoing examination of the politics of neurological difference and neurodiversity in the context of the relationships between disability policy agenda types helps in the movement away from reflexive vilification of issue stakeholders connected to somewhat differing understandings of disability. Embracing multiple understandings of disability both facilitates and is facilitated by recognition of distinct yet equally valid and inextricability connected disability policy agenda types. The relationships between these agenda types unavoidably drive both successes and failures in modern disability policy development regardless of whether a specific functional difference or all disabilities are the target of a particular policy innovation.

Democratic Benefits:
Tensions of Attention and the Value of Discontent

Complex disability policy subsystems have evolved in all modern industrialized nations and show little sign of slowed expansion. Cause, care, cure, and celebration agenda politics and policy will each continue to grow for the foreseeable future. Neither the presence of multiple agenda types nor sometimes tense dynamics between proponents of these agenda types are fundamental problems for disability policy subsystems. In fact, to some degree, such tensions strengthen policy subsystems and inspire meaningful progress in the politics of neurological difference and neurodiversity.

Democracy runs on discontent (Baker and Stokes 2006). This discontent manifests most productively in disagreements in agenda types in the discourse of particular policy subsystems. Without such passionate interest (not to mention media attention), issues fall away from both systemic and formal public agendas, and ultimately policy subsystems can wither and die. As a result, policy actors are often more inclined to find areas of disagreement than agreement. Looking beyond this inclination toward the positive potential of such tensions requires patience, understanding, and acceptance of multiple agenda types, and more than a bit of luck.

As a result of this unavoidable reality of democracy, the politics of neurological difference and neurodiversity contribute heavily to the ongoing vitality of disability policy subsystems. This is not to say that interest in disabilities at large has vanished from modern societies. However, the sheer novelty of our understanding of neurological differences and the frequency with which our basic understanding of our brains is transforming raise the baseline level of interest among members of the general population not otherwise engaged in disability policy. Furthermore, the economies of modern democracies increasingly rely on brain-based labor. Diversity of minds is therefore a much more fundamentally important economic issue for modern industrial (or postindustrial) economies than for traditional societies. Like all public and political issues, disability policy must compete for relatively scarce attention on both the formal and systemic policy agendas of modern societies. Strong connections to both novelty and economics provide a comparative advantage for disability policy issues as a result of these elements of neurological difference and neurodiversity.

It is vital for both the politics of neurodiversity and the interests of those with neurological differences that productive disagreement not be allowed to turn into a war of all against all. Tensions of attention and democratic discontent surrounding neurological difference (and disability at large) should be kept deliberately productive in order to maintain positive progress in disability policy development. Because the intentions and goals of stakeholders representing the cause, care, cure and celebration agenda types naturally differ but are often considered in tandem by political systems, productive tensions can dissolve into tendencies to conquer through division. After all, modern societies include not only people and organizations still bent on the exclusion of individuals with disabilities, but also infrastructures built around staunch legacies of discrimination against those with functional differences. Acknowledging and working with tensions between the agenda types are indispensable to the creation of an ever improving context both for neurological difference and neurodiversity and for disability as a general category of diversity.

Ultimate and final resolutions of the more transcendent dynamics between disability policy agenda types are both impossible and, to a large degree, undesirable. It is, however, important to actively pursue successful resolution of the more temporal tensions between agenda types. If for no other reason, such resolutions are crucial due to the very real threat of compassion-fatigue in the general public should the politics of neurodiversity appear permanently intractable. As is the case in much of the democratic political exercise, working with tensions of attention and policy discontent depends on simultaneous recognition of utopian possibilities and the acceptance that arrival at such perfection is not really the goal of productive policy development.

Moving Forward

First and perhaps foremost, recognizing the distinction between beliefs, justification, and policy goals is helpful. As Oliver Woshinsky explains about politics in general, "many of our deepest beliefs are more or less elaborate justifications for, or rationales of, our own interests or the interests of our particular group" (2008, 26). Examining short-term goals to ensure they hold legitimacy beyond personal interest is an important first step for all political activism. All stakeholders engaged in the public and political disability discourse stand to benefit from sustained commitment to this practice. As the old saying goes, the plural of anecdote is not evidence. Remembering this becomes particularly important when it comes to processing personal anecdotes in the context of a well-documented history of oppression.

Second, in public and political discussions surrounding diversity, the issue of mutability of difference often comes up. Debate centers on whether (and the degree to which) a difference perceived as undesirable or inconvenient by the majority results from a choice made by the individual exhibiting the difference. For the most part, there is higher (though certainly not universal) acceptance of public policies and programs that focus on immutable difference, whereas the call for conformity is much more likely to be publicly asserted when the difference is attributed to choice. Of course, like other lines drawn in the sand in public policy context, this position unlikely represents the height of human progress and certainly causes largely unnecessary misery. The conception of choice is, for example, part of the reason individuals across the political spectrum continue to feel comfortable vilifying and opposing policies that might help single parents. Nevertheless, this position on mutability tends to play a role in most policy, even policy considered relatively progressive at this moment in historical time. More sophisticated policy tools designed to mediate between individual and community needs will likely evolve in time.

As a result of this modern dynamic surrounding choice, heated debate has surrounded the question of, for example, whether homosexuality is a chosen lifestyle. Those who are less inclined to include so-called sexual preference in diversity-oriented policies consistently assert that sexuality is chosen, while those who are more inclined to include it are much more likely to insist that some individuals are homosexual more or less from birth. Similarly, popular support for disability policies and programs across the political spectrums in modern democracies tends to begin and end with disability as not associated with choice.

Again, the politics of neurological difference and neurodiversity serve to magnify this dynamic for disability in general. This is because of a common failure on the part of many members of the general population to recognize differences in brains other than those immediately obvious as a result of visual cues or connection to differences in physical functionalities. When encountering an individual with a neurological difference, a substantial proportion of the rest of the general population tends to struggle with, as a matter of great importance, whether or not the individual is choosing to manifest a neurological difference. Simply put, many people fail to understand the existence of differences in brains. This failure of imagination tends to take place less overtly when it comes to the so-called visible disabilities. However, this dynamic of external, often uninformed, and knee-jerk valuation of the responsibilities and efforts of an individual with a disability as compared to a designated typical person shapes how people think about disability policy development and implementation.

Mutability is, to a certain degree, an understandable political concern. Societies are generally expected to have some right to standards and conventions of behaviors and practices. Presumably it is also healthy in the collective sense to maintain some norms, even in the context of a free society. When it comes to the politics of neurodiversity and neurological difference, questions surrounding mutability become especially complex. Especially in the case of mental illness and other neurological differences described as being invisible disabilities, many members of the rest of the general population retain a tendency to think that individuals with neurological difference could stop experiencing and, more importantly, manifesting their neurological differences given enough power of will, a belief that then often becomes a public demand (Corrigan et al. 2007). In addition, despite the high degree of heritability sometimes involved, individuals with neurological differences, like the majority of individuals with disabilities in general, are more often than not members of families in which everyone does not share the same neurological difference. Neurological differences walk a fine line in the mutability versus immutability debate, complicating their expression in diversity-oriented policy. The different agenda types discussed in this book tend to handle questions surrounding this debate using different and at times opposing strategies, but none can afford to ignore it in the long term.

It is important to realize that in political discourse, perceptions of mutability versus immutability of difference are not entirely dominated by biology or scientific discoveries. Substantial precedent exists for jointly managing mutability, diversity, and any perceived inconvenience or discomfort claimed by other members of the general population. Once again, moving policy forward without turning toward unnecessary oppression of the majority or objectification of the minority depends on reasoned understanding of the connection between the characteristic of diversity and identity. For example, because religion is understood as being a fundamentally defining element of personal identity and family connection, at least in the case of the more conventional religious practices in modern industrialized societies, religion is generally perceived as being an immutable characteristic at the individual level despite the absence of any biological reason that would prevent someone from changing their religious practices. So long as no genuine harm is caused to other members of the general population, at least in our ideal perception of modern democracies, diversity of religious practices is supported regardless of how the rest of the general population feels about a particular practice.

Similarly, when an individual sincerely and freely embraces a functional difference as an element of his or her identity, the question of choice has little place in disability policy. Of course, as is paralleled in the example of freedom of religion, this identity cannot legitimately be employed to harm the rest of the general population or society at large, as would be the case if the individual attempted to use the disability as an excuse for breaking other laws or taking advantage of publicly provided care out of pure laziness or greed.

Third, as the field of disability studies expands to include more traditional scientists who do not engage in activism or action-oriented research, the habitual division between proponents of the medical model and those of the social model has become reflexively questioned by some scholars and blindly defended by others. Defining the modern role of scholar and scientist becomes even more complicated for disciplines overtly connected to political activism. As Roger Pielke explained, "the defining characteristic of the honest broker of policy alternatives is an effort to expand (or at least clarify) the scope of choice for decision-making in a way that allows for the decision-maker to reduce choice based on his or her own preferences and values" (2007, 2–3). It helps to remember that science is meant to change over time. As Jonah Lehrer explained, "the genius of the scientific method . . . is that it accepts no permanent solution . . . skepticism is its solvent, for every theory is imperfect . . . scientific facts are meaningful precisely because they are ephemeral, because a new observation, a more honest observation, can always alter them" (2007, 39). Social scientists seeking to play a role in the disability policy subsystem encumber heightened responsibility to understand and clarify dynamics between disability agenda types.

Part of this responsibility involves reasserting the once better-understood concept of the loyal opposition within democratic politics. Once upon a time, at least as we are given to understand it, stakeholders involved in the politics of modern democracies generally understood their political opponents fundamentally as policy opponents rather than as threats to the democratic system itself. In other words, love of country (and usually humanity) was assumed despite political opposition. In recent years this concept of loyal opposition has been all too thoroughly replaced, especially in the United States, with the presumption that political opponents are at best foolish or naive enough to endanger their country and at worst traitors. Healthy public and political discourse depends on reclaiming the concept of the loyal opposition so that policy subsystems can be in a better position to take advantage of potential benefits deriving from multiple agenda types.

Importantly, these advantages include both opportunities for policy development present in symbiosis, and opportunities for improved understandings present in conflicts of understanding. Improved neurodiversity—and disability in general—depends on both inaction and action at their appropriate times. Discerning between a need for change and a need for conservation is easiest when social scientists take on the role of understanding and respecting (and sometimes mediating) the multiple agenda types in a given policy subsystem. Obviously, stronger societies are the outcome of enthusiastic inclusion. However, societies do have a right (and a need) to bound their tolerance of diversity. As has been frequently learned, forgotten, and then relearned over the past several centuries, in successful democracies, these necessary limitations extend only to diversity of action and never to diversity of thought. Vibrant politics of neurodiversity and neurological difference serve to remind us all of this most important of distinctions. Keeping this always in mind is key not only to the development of effective and sophisticated policy directed toward challenges associated with neurological differences, but also to the creation of the best of all possible diversities.

References

Adams, Christopher P., and Van B. Brantner (2006). "Estimating the Cost of New Drug Development: Is It Really $802 Million?" *Health Affairs* 25(2): 420–428.

Anderson, Terry H. (2004). *The Pursuit of Fairness: A History of Affirmative Action.* New York: Oxford University Press.

Ankers, Mary Ann (2009). "The Sleuth: Obama Likens His Bowling Game to Special Olympics." *Washington Post,* March 19, 2009. http://voices.washington post.com/sleuth/2009/03/obama_likens_his_bowling_game.html (accessed May 23, 2009).

Antonetta, Susanne (2005). *A Mind Apart: Travels in a Neurodiverse World.* London: Penguin.

Armstrong, Thomas (2010). *Neurodiversity: Discovering the Extraordinary Gifts of Autism, ADHD, Dyslexia, and Other Brain Differences.* Cambridge, MA: Da Capo Lifelong Books.

Austin, David (2008). "An Epidemiological Analysis of the 'Autism as Mercury Poisoning' Hypothesis." *International Journal of Risk and Safety in Medicine* 20(3): 135–142.

Awbrey, Susan M. (2007). "The Dynamics of Vertical and Horizontal Diversity in Organization and Society." *Human Resource Development Review* 6(1): 7–32.

Bagenstos, Samuel R. (2004). "The Future of Disability Law." *Yale Law Journal* 114(1): 1–84.

Baker, Dana Lee (2006). "Neurodiveristy, Neurological Disability and the Public Sector: Notes on the Autism Spectrum." *Disability & Society* 21(1): 15–29.

Baker, Dana Lee, and Eva Marie Stahl (2004). "Case Study of Interagency Coordinating Councils." *Journal of Disability Policy Studies* 15(3): 168–177.

Baker, Dana Lee, and Shannon Daily Stokes (2006). "Comparative Issue Definition in Public Health: West Nile Virus, Mad Cow Disease in Blood Products, and Stem Cell Research." *Journal of Comparative Policy Analysis* 8(1).

Barnartt, Sharon N., and Richard Scotch (2001). *Disability Protests: Contentious Politics, 1970–1999.* Washington, DC: Gallaudet University Press.

Bassuk, E. L., and H. R. Lamb (1986). "Homelessness and the Implementation of Deinstitutionalization." *New Directions for Mental Health Services* 30(1): 7–14.

BBC News (2006). "Melting Pot America." May 12. http://news.bbc.co.uk/1/hi/world/americas/4931534.stm (accessed May 23, 2009).

Beadle-Brown, J., J. Mansell, and A. Kozma (2007). "Deinstitutionalization in Intellectual Disabilities." *Current Opinion in Psychiatry* 20(5): 437–442.

Berger, Ronald J. (2008). "Disability and the Dedicated Wheelchair Athlete." *Journal of Contemporary Ethnography* 37(6): 647–678.

——— (2009). *Hoop Dreams on Wheels: Disability and the Competitive Wheelchair Athlete*. New York: Routledge.

Berkowitz, Edward D. (1987). *Disabled Policy: America's Programs for the Handicapped*. New York: Cambridge University Press.

Biklen, Douglas, and Richard Attfield (2005). *Autism and the Myth of the Person Alone*. New York: New York University Press.

Biklen, Douglas, and Jamie Burke (2006). "Presuming Competence." *Equity and Excellence in Education* 39(2): 166–175.

Breeden, Lori (2008). Presentation at Neurodiversity: Changing Minds, Changing Worlds class seminar. November 3.

Broderick, Alicia (2009). "Autism, 'Recovery (to Normalcy),' and the Politics of Hope." *Intellectual and Developmental Disabilities* 47(4): 263–281.

Brueggemann, Brenda Jo (2009). *Deaf Subjects: Between Identities and Places*. New York: New York University Press.

Bruner, Darlene Y. (2008). "Aspiring and Practicing Leaders Addressing Issues of Diversity and Social Justice." *Race, Ethnicity, and Education* 11(4): 483–500.

Bumiller, Kristin (2008). "Quirky Citizens: Autism, Gender, and Reimagining Disability." *Journal of Women in Culture and Society* 33(4): 967–991.

——— (2009). "The Geneticization of Autism: From New Reproductive Technologies to the Conception of Genetic Normalcy." *Journal of Women in Culture and Society* 34(4): 875–899.

Burch, Susan, and Ian Sutherland (2006). "Who's Not Yet Here? American Disability History." *Radical History Review* 94: 127–147.

Campbell, Alastair W. (2005). "Mental Health Practice: Can Philosophy Help?" *Australian and New Zealand Journal of Psychiatry* 39(11–12): 1008–1010.

Chambers, Simon (2003). "Deliberative Democratic Theory." *Annual Review of Political Science* 6: 307–326.

Charlton, James I. (2000). *Nothing About Us Without Us: Disability Oppression and Empowerment*. Berkeley: University of California Press.

"A Chronology of the Disability Rights Movement" (n.d.). www.sfsu.edu/~hrdpu/chron.htm (accessed April 3, 2008).

Corrigan, Patrick, et al. (2007). "Will Filmed Presentations of Education and Contact Diminish Mental Illness Stigma?" *Community Mental Health Journal* 43(2): 171–181.

Craddock, Nick, and Michael J. Owen (2007). "Rethinking Psychosis: The Disadvantages of a Dichotomous Classification Now Outweigh the Advantages." *World Psychiatry* 6(2): 84–91.

Cutler, David M., Edward L. Glaeser, and Jacob L. Vigdor (2008). "Is the Melting Pot Still Hot? Explaining the Resurgence of Immigrant Segregation." *Review of Economics and Statistics* 90(3): 478–497.

DeMitchell, Todd A., and Todd Fletcher (2008). "Notes on the Law and Ethics of Do Not Resuscitate Orders in Schools." *Teachers College Record*. www.tcrecord.org (ID number 15164).

Dudas, Jeffrey (2005). "In the Name of Equal Rights: 'Special' Rights and the Politics of Resentment in Post–Civil Rights America." *Law and Society Review* 39(4): 723–757.

Emerson, Eric (2004a). "Cluster Housing for Adults with Intellectual Disabilities." *Journal of Intellectual and Developmental Disability* 29(3): 187–197.

——— (2004b). "Deinstitutionalisation in England." *Journal of Intellectual and Developmental Disability* 29(1): 79–84.

Eom, Kihong, and Donald A. Gross (2007). "Democratization Effects of Campaign Contribution Limits in Gubernatorial Elections." *Party Politics* 13(6): 695–720.

Felce, David (2006). "Both Accurate Interpretation of Deinstitutionalization and a Postinstitutional Research Agenda Are Needed." *Mental Retardation* 44(5): 375–382.

Fenton, Andrew, and Tim Krahn (2007). "Autism, Neurodiversity, and Equality Beyond the 'Normal.'" *Journal of Ethics in Mental Health* 2(2): 1–6.

Figueiredo, Rui J. P., and Geoff A. Edwards (2007). "Does Private Money Buy Public Policy? Campaign Contributions and Regulatory Outcomes in Telecommunications." *Journal of Economics and Management Strategy* 16(3): 547–576.

Fleischer, Doris, and Freida Zames Fleischer (2000). *The Disability Rights Movement: From Charity to Confrontation.* Philadelphia: Temple University Press.

Foucault, Michel (1988). *Madness and Civilization: A History of Insanity in the Age of Reason.* New York: Vintage.

Freeman, Sabrina (2003). *Science for Sale in the Autism Wars: Medically Necessary Autism Treatment, the Court Battle for Health Insurance, and Why Health Technology Academics Are Enemy Number One.* Langley: SKF.

Garber, Ken (2007). "Neuroscience: Autism's Cause May Reside in Abnormalities at the Synapse." *Science* 317(5835): 190–191.

Geller, Jeffrey L. (2000). "The Last Half-Century of Psychiatric Services as Reflected in *Psychiatric Services.*" *Psychiatric Services* 51:41–67.

Genzlinger, Neil (2008). "A Different Sort of 'Hey Kids, Let's Put on a Show!'" *New York Times,* March 25, E6.

Georg, Chris (2008). "*Autism: The Musical* Reveals Effect of the Disorder on Parents." www.efluxmedia.com/news_Autism_The_Musical_Reveals_Effect_of_the_Disorder_on_Parents_15570.html (accessed May 2, 2009).

Gladwell, Malcolm (2008). *Outliers: The Story of Success.* Boston: Little, Brown.

Glannon, Walter (2007). "Neurodiversity." *Journal of Ethics in Mental Health* 2(2): 1–5.

Goddard, Henry Herbert (1912). *The Kallikak Family: A Study in the Heredity of Feeble-Mindedness.* New York: Macmillan.

Gornick, Janet C., Marcia K. Meyers, Erik Olin Wright, and Barbara Bergmann (2009). *Gender Equality: Transforming Family Divisions of Labor.* London: Verso.

Grant, Caroline (2008). "Mama at the Movies: *Autism: The Musical.*" www.literarymama.com/columns/mamaatthemovies/archives/2008/autism_the_musical.html (accessed May 14, 2009).

Gravois, Todd A., and Silva A. Rosenfield (2006). "Impact of Instructional Consultation Teams on Disproportionate Referral and Placement of Minority Studies in Special Education." *Remedial and Special Education* 27(1): 42–52.

Gregory, Tony A. (2006). "An Evolutionary Theory of Diversity: The Contributions of Grounded Theory and Grounded Action to Reconceptualizing and Reframing Diversity as a Complex Phenomenon." *World Futures: The Journal of General Evolution* 62(7): 542–550.

Grinker, Roy Richard (2007). *Unstrange Minds: Remapping the World of Autism.* New York: Basic.

Gros, Gerald N. (2005). "Public Policy and Mental Illnesses: Jimmy Carter's Presidential Commission on Mental Health." *Milbank Quarterly* 83(3): 425–456.

Gross, Bruce H., and Harlan Hahn (2004). "Developing Issues in the Classification of Mental and Physical Disabilities." *Journal of Disability Policy Studies* 15(3): 130–134.

Gruenfeld, D. H., M. E. Inesi, J. C. Magee, and A. D. Galinsky (2008). "Power and the Objectification of Social Targets." *Journal of Personal Social Psychology* 95(1): 111–127.

Haddon, Mark (2003). *The Curious Incident of the Dog in the Night-Time.* New York: Doubleday.

Hall, Elaine (2008). "Emmy for Autism: Miracle Minded Media." www.autism speaks.org/community/ownwords/intheirownwords_emmy.php (accessed May 12, 2009).

Haller, B., B. Dorries, and J. Rahn (2006). "Media Labeling Versus the US Disability Community Identity: A Study of Shifting Cultural Language." *Disability and Society* 14: 709–731.

Hamlin, Alexandra, and Peter Oakes (2008). "Reflections on Deinstitutionalization in the United Kingdom." *Journal of Policy and Practice in Intellectual Disabilities* 5(1): 47–55.

Harmon, Amy (2010). "Nominee to Disability Council Is Lightning Rod for Dispute on Views of Autism." *New York Times,* March 27, A16.

Harvard Law Review (2008). "'Trading Action for Access': The Myth of Meritocracy and the Failure to Recognize Structural Discrimination." *Harvard Law Review* 121:2156–2177.

Haslam, Robert, and Ruth Milner (1992). "The Physician and Down Syndrome: Are Attitudes Changing?" *Journal of Child Neurology* 7(3): 304–310.

Haupt, Riccardo, et al. (2007). "Long-Term Survivors of Childhood Cancer: Cure and Care—The Erice Statement." *European Journal of Cancer* 43(12): 1778–1780.

Hayden, M. F., S. A. Larson, and K. C. Lakin (2002). "Longitudinal Study on the Adaptive and Challenging Behaviors of Deinstitutionalized Adults with Mental Retardation." *American Journal on Mental Retardation* 107(4): 302–320.

Hill, M., and M. Phillips (2006). "Service Provision for Adults with Long-Term Disability: A Review of Services for Adults with Chronic Neuromuscular Conditions in the United Kingdom." *Neuromuscular Disorders* 16(2): 107–112.

Hinckley, David (2008). "A Touching, Tuneful Look at 'Autism.'" *Daily News, Television,* March 25, 62.

Hodgins, Sheilagh, et al. (2007). "A Comparison of General Adult and Forensic Patients with Schizophrenia Living in the Community." *International Journal of Forensic Mental Health* 6(1): 63–75.

Hosp, John L., and Daniel J. Rechsly (2004). "Disproportionate Representation of Minority Students in Special Education Academic, Demographic, and Economic Predictors." *Exceptional Children* 70.

Houser, Daniel, and Thomas Stratmann (2008). "Selling Favors in the Lab: Experiments on Campaign Finance Reform." *Public Choice* 136(1–2): 215–239.

Ishay, Micheline (2008). *The History of Human Rights: From Ancient Times to the Globalization Era.* Berkeley: University of California Press.

Iyer, Anupama (2007). "Depiction of Intellectual Disability in Fiction." *Advances in Psychiatric Treatment* 13: 127–133.

Jacob, R., C. H. Clare, A. Holland, P. C. Watson, C. Maimaris, and M. Gunn (2005). "Self-Harm, Capacity, and Refusal of Treatment: Implications for Emergency Medical Practice—A Prospective Observational Study." *Emergency Medicine Journal* 22: 799–802.

Johnson, Dawn R., Matthew Soldner, Jeannie Brown Leonard, Patty Alvarez, Karen Kurotsuchi Inkelas, Heather T. Rowan-Kenyon, and Susan D. Longerbeam (2007). "Examining Sense of Belonging Among First-Year Undergraduates from Different Racial/Ethnic Groups." *Journal of College Student Development* 48(5): 525–542.

Johnson, Mary (2003). *Make Them Go Away: Clint Eastwood, Christopher Reeve, and the Case Against Disability Rights.* Louisville: Advocado.

Jovanovic, Miodrag A. (2005). "Recognizing Minority Identities Through Collective Rights." *Human Rights Quarterly* 27(2): 625–651.

Kellow, J. Thomas, Georgia C. Frey, and Donna Rosser Sandt (2007). "Perceptions of a Person with Mental Retardation as a Function of Participation in Integrated Versus Segregated Recreation/Sports Activities: An Experimental Analysis." *International Journal of Special Education* 22(2): 1–6.

Kingdon, John W. (2003). *Agendas, Alternatives, and Public Policies.* New York: Longman.

Kirby, David (2005). *Evidence of Harm: Mercury in Vaccines and the Autism Epidemic—A Medical Controversy.* New York: St. Martin's.

——— (2008). "Government Concedes Vaccine-Autism Case in Federal Court—Now What?" *Huffington Post,* February 25. www.huffingtonpost.com/david-kirby/government-concedes-vacci_b_88323.html.

Kitzhaber, John (2002). "Proclamation of Human Rights Day, and Apology for Oregon's Forced Sterilization of Institutionalized Patients." *Statesman Journal,* December 3. www.people1.org/eugenics/eugenics_article_3.htm (accessed May 24, 2009).

Klebanov, Pamela Kato, and Jeanne Brooks-Gunn (2007). "Differential Exposure to Early Childhood Education Services and Mother-Toddler Interaction." *Early Childhood Research Quarterly* 23(2): 213–232.

Kruppers, Petra (2007). "The Wheelchair's Rhetoric: The Performance of Disability." *TDR* 51(4): 80–88.

Lakin, K. Charlie, Robert Prouty, Barbara Polister, and Kathryn Coucouvanis (2004). "States' Initial Response to the President's New Freedom Initiative: Slowest Rates of Deinstitutionalization in 30 Years." *Mental Retardation* 42(3): 241–244.

Lakin, K. Charlie, Robert Prouty, and Kathryn Coucouvanis (2006). "Twenty-Year Retrospective on Proposals to Eliminate the 'Institutional Bias' in Medicaid for Persons with ID/DD." *Mental Retardation* 44(6): 450–454.

Lamb, H. Richard (1984). "Deinstitutionalization and the Homeless Mentally Ill." *Hospital Community Psychiatry* 35: 899–907.

Lamb, H. Richard, and Leona L. Bachrach (2001). "Some Perspectives on Deinstitutionalization." *Psychiatric Services* 52(8): 1039–1045.

Lau, V. M. H., et al. (2007). "The Nursing Gaze: Power Relations in a Study of Nurse-Resident Interactions in Learning Disability." *Journal of Psychiatric and Mental Health Nursing* 14(4): 346–355.

Lehrer, Jonah (2007). *Proust Was a Neuroscientist.* Boston: Houghton Mifflin.

Levine, Deborah, Catarina I. Kiefe, Thomas K. Houston, Jeroan J. Allison, Ellen P. McCarthy, and John Z. Ayanian (2007). "Younger Stroke Survivors Have Reduced Access to Physician Care and Medications." *Archives of Neurology* 64(1): 37–42.

Levine, Murray (2007). "Principles from History: Community Psychology and Developmental Psychology Applied to Community Based Programs for Deinstitutionalized Youth." *Analise Psicologica* 1(25): 63–75.

Lewis, C. F. (2007). "Crazy: A Father's Search Through America's Mental Health Madness." *JAMA* 297: 94–95.

Lewis, Gregory B., and Michael Rushton (2007). "Understanding State Spending on the Arts, 1976–1999." *State and Local Governments Review* 39(2): 107–114.

Linton, Simi (1998). *Claiming Disability: Knowledge and Identity.* New York: New York University Press.

Longmore, Paul (2003). *Why I Burned My Book and Other Essays on Disability.* Philadelphia: Temple University Press.

Lovaas, O. Ivar (1987). "Behavioral Treatment and Normal Educational and Intellectual Functioning in Young Autistic Children." *Journal of Consulting and Clinical Psychology* 53:3–9.

MacIntyre, Gillian (2008). *Learning Disability and Social Inclusion.* Edinburgh: Dunedin.

Mallet, Rebecca (2009). "Choosing 'Stereotypes': Debating the Efficacy of (British) Disability-Criticism." *Journal of Research in Special Education Needs* 9(1): 4–11.

Maslow, Abraham (1943). "A Theory of Human Motivation." *Psychological Review* 50: 370–396.

McCarthy, Jenny, and Jim Carrey (2008). "Jenny McCarthy: My Son's Recovery from Autism." *CNN,* April 4. www.cnn.com/2008/US/04/02/mccarthy.autism treatment/index.html (accessed May 24, 2009).

McCray, Audrey Davis, Gwendolyn Webb-Johnson, and Scott T. Bridgest (2003). "The Effects of African American Movement Styles on Teachers' Perceptions and Reactions." *Journal of Special Education* 37(1): 49–57.

McMahon, Brian T., and Jessica E. Hurley (2008). "Discrimination in Hiring Under the Americans with Disabilities Act: An Overview of the National EEOC ADA Research Project." *Journal of Occupational Rehabilitation* 18(2): 103–105.

McNamara, Mary (2008). "Television Review: A Film That Challenges Stereotypes." *Los Angeles Times,* March 25, E9.

Merin, Jennifer (2009). *Autism: The Musical.* http://documentaries.about.com/od /revie2/gr/autismmusical.htm (accessed May 13, 2009).

Millan, Cesar, and Melissa Jo Peltier (2008). *Be the Pack Leader: Use Cesar's Way to Transform Your Dog . . . and Your Life.* New York: Three Rivers.

Morrow, Marina, and Brenda Jamer (2008). "Making Meaning in a 'Post-Institutional' Age: Reflections on the Experience of (De)institutionalization." *International Journal of Psychological Rehabilitation* 12(2).

Moye, Jennifer, et al. (2007). "Clinical Evidence in Guardianship of Older Adults

Is Inadequate: Findings from a Tri-State Study." *Gerontologist* 47: 604–612.

Nadesan, M. H. (2005). *Constructing Autism*. Milton Park, Oxfordshire: Routledge.

National Council on Disability (2010). "NCD Frequently Asked Questions." www.ncd.gov/faqs.htm (accessed May 18, 2010).

Noll, Steven (2005). "The Public Face of Southern Institutions for the 'Feeble-Minded.'" *Public Historian* 27(2): 25–41.

——— (2009). *Feeble-Minded in Our Midst: Institutions for the Mentally Retarded in the South, 1900–1940*. Chapel Hill: University of North Carolina Press.

Novella, Enric J. (2008). "Theoretical Accounts on Deinstitutionalization and the Reform of Mental Health Services: A Critical Review." *Medicine, Health Care, and Philosophy* 11: 303–314.

O'Brien, Gerald V., and Melinda S. Brown (2009). "Persons with Mental Illness and the Americans with Disabilities Act: Implications for the Social Work Profession." *Social Work in Mental Health* 7(5): 442–457.

Okai, David, et al. (2007). "Mental Capacity in Psychiatric Patients." *British Journal of Psychiatry* 191: 291–297.

Owen, Katherine, Jane Hubert, and Sheila Hollins (2007). "Moving Home: The Experiences of Women with Severe Intellectual Disabilities in Transition from a Locked Ward." *British Journal of Learning Disabilities* 36(4):220–226.

Patson, Philip (2007). "Constructive Functional Diversity: A New Paradigm Beyond Disability and Impairment." *Disability and Rehabilitation* 29(20–21): 1625–1633.

Patterson, Paul H. (2009). "Immune Involvement in Schizophrenia and Autism: Etiology, Pathology, and Animal Models." *Behavioral Brain Research* 204: 313–321.

Pelka, Fred (1997). *The ABC-CLIO Companion to the Disability Rights Movement*. Santa Barbara: ABC-CLIO.

Perry, Joshua E., Larry R. Churchill, and Howard S. Kirshner (2005). "The Terri Schiavo Case: Legal, Ethical, and Medical Perspectives." *Annals of Internal Medicine* 143(10): 744–748.

Pezzin, Liliana E., Robert A. Pollak, and Barbara S. Schone (2007). "Efficiency in Family Bargaining: Living Arrangements and Caregiving Decisions of Adult Children and Disabled Elderly Parents." *Economic Studies* 53(1): 69–96.

Pfeiffer, David (1993). "Overview of the Disability Movement: History, Legislative Record, and Political Implications." *Policy Studies Journal* 21(4): 724–735.

Pielke, Roger A. (2007). *The Honest Broker: Making Sense of Science in Policy and Politics*. Cambridge: Cambridge University Press.

Pitney, John J., Jr. (2010). "Autism Politics: A Research Agenda." Presentation at the Midwest Political Science Association Conference, April.

Pollack, Harold (2007). "Learning to Walk Slow: America's Partial Policy Success in the Arena of Intellectual Disability." *Journal of Policy History* 19(1): 95–112.

Putnam, Robert D. (2001). *Bowling Alone: The Collapse and Revival of American Community*. New York: Simon and Schuster.

Quigley, John M., et al. (2001). "Homeless in America, Homeless in California." *Review of Economics and Statistics* 83(1): 37–51.

Qureshi, H., and A. Alborz (1992). "Epidemiology of Challenging Behavior." *Mental Handicap Research* 5: 120–145.

Reijnders, Stijn L., Gerard Rooijakkers, and Liesbet van Zoonen (2007). "Community Spirit and Competition in Idols." *European Journal of Communication* 22(3): 275–292.

Reynolds, S. L. (2002). "Guardianship Primavera: A First Look at Factors Associated with Having a Legal Guardianship Using a Nationally Representative Sample of Community-Dwelling Adults." *Aging and Mental Health* 6(2): 109–120.

Riccucci, Norma H. (2006). *Public Personnel Administration*. New York: Longman.

Rizza, Robert, David Eddy, and Richard Kahn (2008). "Cure, Care, and Commitment: What Can We Look Forward To?" *Diabetes Care* 31(5): 1051–1059.

Roberts, Andrew (2009). "Mental Health History Timeline." www.mdx.ac.uk /www/study/mhhtim.htm.

Rosen, A. (2006). "The Australian Experience of Deinstitutionalization: Interaction of Australian Culture with the Development and Reform of Its Mental Health Services." *Acta Psychiatrica Scandinavica* 113(429): 81–89.

Roswal, Glenn M., and Mariusz Damentko (2006). "A Review of Completed Research in Sports for Individuals with Intellectual Disability." *Research Yearbook 2006* 12(2): 181–183.

Rothman, David J. (2002). *The Discovery of the Asylum*. Piscataway, NJ: Aldine Transaction.

——— (2003). *Strangers at the Bedside: A History of How Law and Bioethics Transformed Medical Decision Making*. Piscataway, NJ: Aldine Transaction.

Russell, Marta (1998). *Beyond Ramps: Disability at the End of the Social Contract*. Monroe, ME: Common Courage.

Salzer, Mark S., Katy Kaplan, and Joanne Atay (2006). "State Psychiatric Hospital Census After the 1999 Olmstead Decision: Evidence of Decelerating Deinstitutionalization." *Psychiatric Services* 57(10): 1501–1504.

Schechter R., and J. K. Grether (2008). "Continuing Increases in Autism Reported to California's Developmental Services System: Mercury in Retrograde." *Archives of General Psychiatry* 65: 19–24.

Schildrick, Margrit (2008). "Deciding on Death: Conventions and Contestations in the Context of Disability." *Journal of Bioethical Inquiry* 5(2–3): 209–219.

Schweik, Susan (2009). *The Ugly Laws: Disability in Public*. New York: New York University Press.

Scotch, Richard K. (2001). *From Good Will to Civil Rights: Transforming Federal Disability Policy*. 2nd ed. Philadelphia: Temple University Press.

Sealy, Patricia, and Paul C. Whitehead (2004). "Forty Years of Deinstitutionalization of Psychiatric Services in Canada: An Empirical Assessment." *Canadian Journal of Psychiatry* 49(4): 249–257.

Sewell, Edward H. (2008). "Disability and the Media." *Journal of Broadcasting and Electronic Media* 52(3): 506–507.

Shafritz, Jay M., and Albert C. Hyde, eds. (2007). *Classics of Public Administration*. 6th ed. Boston: Thomson Wadsworth.

Shakespeare, Tom (2006). *Disability Rights and Wrongs*. London: Routledge.

Shapiro, Joseph P. (1994). *No Pity: People with Disabilities Forging a New Civil Rights Movement*. New York: Three Rivers.

Smalley, Susan (2008). "Reframing ADHD in the Genomic Era." *Psychiatric Times* 25(7):1–10.

Smukler, David (2005). "Unauthorized Minds: How 'Theory of the Mind' Theory Misrepresents Autism." *Mental Retardation* 43(1): 11–24.

Snow, Kathie (2008). "A Few Words About People First Language." http://ftp .disabilityisnatural.com/documents/PFL-Sh.pdf (accessed April 11, 2009).

Snyder, Sharon L., and David T. Mitchell (2006). *Cultural Locations of Disability.* Chicago: University of Chicago Press.

Spinner-Halev, Jeff, Ann O'M. Bowman, and Lynn M. Sanders (2005). "The Liberal Archipelago: A Theory of Diversity and Freedom." *Journal of Politics* 67(2): 595–597.

Stagliano, Kim (2010). "Ari Ne'eman Nomination to National Council on Disability on Hold." *Age of Autism: Daily Web Newspaper of the Autism Epidemic,* March 29. www.ageofautism.com/2010/03/ari-neeman-nomination-to-national-council-on-disability-on-hold-.html (accessed May 10, 2010).

Talbot, John A. (1979) (reprinted 2004). "Deinstitutionalization: Avoiding the Disasters of the Past." *Psychiatric Services* 55(10): 1112–1115.

Trent, James W. (1994). *Inventing the Feeble Mind: A History of Mental Retardation in the United States.* Berkeley: University of California Press.

Turner, S., et al. (2007). "The Oral Health of People with Intellectual Disability Participating in the UK Special Olympics." *Journal of Intellectual Disability Research* 52(1): 29–36.

Uniacke, Suzanne, and H. J. McCloskey (2008). "Peter Singer and Non-Voluntary 'Euthanasia': Tripping Down the Slippery Slope." *Journal of Applied Philosophy* 9(2): 203–219.

Vickers, Andrew J., Ethan Basch, and Michael Kattan (2009). "Risk Prediction Versus Diagnosis: Preserving Clinical Nuance in a Binary World." *Annals of Internal Medicine* 150(3): 224.

Ward, M. J., and R. N. Meyer (1999). "Self-Determination for People with Disabilities." *Focus on Autism and Other Developmental Disabilities* 14: 133–139.

Ware, Linda (2008). "Worlds Remade: Inclusion Through Engagement of Disability Art." *International Journal of Inclusive Education* 12(5): 563–583.

Weimar, David, and Aidan R. Vining (2005). *Policy Analysis: Concepts and Practice.* 4th ed. Upper Saddle River, NJ: Pearson Prentice Hall.

Wilkinson, Penny, and Peter McGill (2009). "Representation of People with Intellectual Disabilities in a British Newspaper in 1983 and 2001." *Journal of Applied Research in Intellectual Disabilities* 22: 65–76.

Wood, Gordon S. (2005). *The Americanization of Benjamin Franklin.* New York: Penguin.

Woshinsky, Oliver H. (2008). *Explaining Politics: Culture, Institutions, and Political Behavior.* New York: Routledge.

Zeitchick, Neil (2007). "HBO Home to Autism Doc." *Daily Variety News,* June 7, 1.

Index

Pain, 34, 38, 111, 174
Paranormal, 181
Parkinson's disease, 74, 161
Passing, 21, 156, 192–195
Paternalism, 119, 167
Pensions, 43, 104
Person-first language, 41, 53–54
Pink disease, 33
Plato, 56
Political discourse, definition of, 4–5
Politicians, 5, 68, 89, 176, 201–203
Politics, definition of, 4–5
Popper, Karl, 89, 111
Popular culture, 57, 72, 101, 176–183
Positive rights, 29–30, 54
Posttraumatic stress disorder (PTSD), 19, 113
Profit, 150, 153, 188
Protests, 31, 55, 67, 116
Psychiatric disorders, 22, 77
Public discourse, definition of, 4–5
Public expenditures, 65–67, 158
Publicly funded programs, 23, 34, 67, 81, 94, 103, 112, 154, 171, 203

Rainman, 131, 182
"Refrigerator mothers," 151
Rehabilitation, 1, 35–37, 82
Risk, 19, 22, 68, 73, 76, 110–116, 129, 133, 169, 179, 208–209
Roles, 5, 48, 85, 116, 143, 185, 195, 202

Safeminds, 200–201
Schizophrenia, 10–12, 19, 72–79, 102, 105
Scholars, 5, 8, 23–26, 29, 38–42, 53, 88, 116, 168, 197, 222
Science, 37, 88–89, 95, 102, 108–111, 148–150, 201, 222

Separatism, 125–130, 143
Sexuality, 32, 58, 132, 180, 195, 220
Sexual orientation, 3, 20, 195
Slavery, 31, 47–48
Social security, 41, 47, 75, 82, 90
Soldiers, 57, 62–63, 107, 181
Special education, 39, 64, 97–101, 123–124, 132, 135, 140–141, 198–199
Special Olympics, 125–126, 176
Spectrum of care, 77–81
Sterilization, 8, 26, 174
Stewart, Jon, 180
Stigma, 36, 107, 121, 159, 202
Suffering, 25, 34, 67–72, 106–121, 159, 172, 191–196
Supercrip phenomena, 168
Survivor, 74, 159
Symbolic policy, 29, 40, 55, 204, 208–209

Talent, 34, 143, 169, 173, 183, 196
Television, 179–180
Tolerance, 20, 39–40, 61, 74–78, 192, 223
Tourette's syndrome, 17, 74

Ugly laws, 32
Unemployment, 119, 153
United Nations, 74, 106, 204

Vaccines, 200–202, 208–211
Veterans, 19, 90, 107, 212
Victim, 8, 35, 93, 138, 201
Voting, 29, 49, 181, 201–203, 211

World Health Organization (WHO), 10
World War I, 35
World War II, 62, 66

About the Book

How can society best respond to people with atypical neurological development? Should we concentrate on providing medical care, or on ensuring civil rights? Addressing these questions, Dana Lee Baker offers a provocative analysis of the ways that intersecting agendas—prevention, civil rights, providing specialized care, and celebrating disability culture—compete to make disability rights policy. The result is a thoughtful and timely consideration of the tensions shaping all quarters of disability advocacy.

Dana Lee Baker is an assistant professor of political science and criminal justice at Washington State University, Vancouver.